Dorian Unbound

DORIAN UNBOUND

Transnational Decadence and the Wilde Archive

Sean O'Toole

Johns Hopkins University Press
Baltimore

© 2023 Johns Hopkins University Press
All rights reserved. Published 2023
Printed in the United States of America on acid-free paper
2 4 6 8 9 7 5 3 1

Johns Hopkins University Press
2715 North Charles Street
Baltimore, Maryland 21218
www.press.jhu.edu

Library of Congress Cataloging-in-Publication Data is available.

ISBN 978-1-4214-4652-3 (hardcover)
ISBN 978-1-4214-4653-0 (paperback)
ISBN 978-1-4214-4654-7 (ebook)

A catalog record for this book is available from the British Library.

Special discounts are available for bulk purchases of this book. For more information, please contact Special Sales at specialsales@jh.edu.

CONTENTS

Preface *vii*

INTRODUCTION 1

PART ONE DECADENT HYBRIDITY

1

"Fantastic Shadows": Wilde's Queer Form 15

PART TWO INHERITED WORLDS

2

Gothic Legacies: *Melmoth*, Ireland, and the
Specter of Imperial History 41

3

Aesthetic Antecedents: Lady Wilde and the
Pre-Raphaelite Cult of *Sidonia* 61

PART THREE NETWORKED FORMS

4

Transatlantic Forebears: Painted Betrayals in
Hawthorne, Poe, and James 89

5

Epigrammatic Inheritance: Peacock, Meredith, and the
Forgotten English Lineage 107

CODA 129

Notes *135*
Bibliography *151*
Index *165*

PREFACE

As I was finishing this book, events unfolding across the academy and the globe made its focus seem newly relevant and its reach potentially far more extensive than I could have anticipated at the outset. The concurrence crystallized in a single image, as unambiguously surreal as the moment. Arriving in the midst of the first COVID-19 lockdown, the Spring 2020 special issue of *Victorian Studies* featured on its cover an arresting black-and-white photograph of the Crystal Palace on fire in 1936.

"A blazing arch of lucid glass / Leaps like a fountain from the grass / To meet the sun," William Makepeace Thackeray had presciently written on the occasion of the Palace's opening in London's Hyde Park in 1851.[1] Thackeray's lines capture both the human-scale wonder and Icarus-like ambition of the glass, iron, and wood construction, the centerpiece of the Great Exhibition of that year and a symbol of the Victorian age ever since. The image's power in 2020—the otherworldly glow of the iconic glass arched roof lit up against a smoke-filled night sky—derived in part from a widespread sense that the present world was also on fire. Protests against police killings of Black people filled streets otherwise emptied by pandemic. Fascism and authoritarianism were resurgent worldwide. And signs of an accelerating climate catastrophe materialized everywhere. The journal's contents soon added another, more auspicious layer of meaning to the resonant image. Titled "Undisciplining Victorian Studies," the special issue offers an unflinching and radically generous scholarly intervention by guest editors Ronjaunee Chatterjee, Alicia Mireles Christoff, and Amy R. Wong. As their introduction explains, the editors were inspired by the call of Christina Sharpe's *In the Wake: On Blackness and Being* (2016) to become "undisciplined," to reject the entrenched partitioning of knowledge and instead "to invent 'new modes' of research and teaching that offer a 'method of encountering' what Sharpe evocatively names

Crystal Palace Fire, 1936, photographer unknown. Wikimedia Commons

'a past that is not past' "—in her formulation, the long historical wake of the transatlantic slave ship.[2]

While careful to recognize that Sharpe is not addressing Victorian scholars directly, Chatterjee, Mireles Christoff, and Wong see the opportunity that her call creates for the field. More pointedly, since "scholars of Victorian literature and culture are, in fact, scholars of Atlantic slavery," they mark the silence and evasion that has generally characterized that study and the "multiple rigidities, cultural and conceptual, that have kept Victorian studies isolated from other fields."[3] Becoming undisciplined, by contrast, is fundamentally to rethink field-formation and even to unmake scholarly fields themselves. Of particular interest to the present study, the work of undisciplining is critical in that it involves "exploding the field's limited geographic imaginary," but its project is ultimately constructive and capacious: "The work for which we are advocating, then, extends *across field boundaries* with respect to *their limiting views of both geography and period*."[4] As Nasser Mufti puts it in his contribution to the issue, "Hating Victorian Studies Properly," this kind of unbounded

Preface ix

thinking "should not be understood as doing away with Victorian studies, nor as the seamless integration of outside discourses into those of the Victorian"; rather, it "might be understood as the task of making it impossible to speak of something as merely 'Victorian.'"[5]

At the same moment of this radical revision of the field, the stirrings of a newly discrete area of study were also making themselves known. Decadence studies, or the "new Decadence" as it has been called, has undergone profound methodological shifts and a field formation of its own in recent years.[6] Long situated awkwardly between Victorian and modernist studies but belonging to neither—or perhaps, as Mufti might have it, hating both properly—literary and artistic Decadence of the late nineteenth century is now the subject of active reconsideration. Scholars have begun to find in its energies and circulations a more pervasive network of correspondences across geography, time periods, and artistic media than the usual framing of it as a liminal movement in a select few European capitals has typically allowed.[7] This work has quickly gained the markings of a legitimate field of its own even as it continues to evolve, the prefix of its key terms "transnational" and "transhistorical" indicating not linear progress but a tendency toward moving in multiple directions *across, beyond, to the other side of* seemingly solid definitional and disciplinary borders.[8] Matthew Potolsky, for example, has charted the creation of a new "cosmopolitan community" in Decadence's reach "beyond the frame of any localized national coterie to new and radically international frameworks."[9] Regenia Gagnier has pointed to the global effects of modernization in arguing that literary Decadence did not merely spread as a European cultural movement but "arose repeatedly and distinctly in response to changes or crises *within* various nations and cultures" all across the world.[10] Stefano Evangelista has in turn articulated a convincing historical and theoretical case for the transnational orientation of Decadence, locating in some of its earliest definitions and practices of translation a firm rejection of "any exclusively national affiliation."[11] Decadence denotes, for Evangelista, "a process rather than an act of completion: it is a mode of becoming that opens up ideas and texts to transformative possibilities not only by stretching them in time but also by pushing them beyond the national contexts of their original formulations."[12] At stake is recovering "specific links that are difficult to see when working within a sealed national tradition" as well as a broader theoretical understanding of Decadence's "radical logic of entanglement."[13]

In some important and revealing ways, this shift marks a return to the transnational perspective of the Decadents themselves, in effect seeing around the historical obstacles of modernists' embarrassment or uneasiness with them in the homophobic and nationalistic aftermath of Oscar Wilde's 1895 imprisonment for "gross indecency with other male persons." Elisa Bizzotto and Stefano Evangelista's edited collection *Arthur Symons: Poet, Critic, Vagabond* (2018) provides a useful model and a case in point. Symons, a self-styled vagabond and travel writer who introduced Decadence to English readers and engaged with authors and artists of many nations, seems ready-made for the study of an interdisciplinary, transhistorical, and transnational Decadence. Yet he has been sorely overlooked and is only now beginning to receive his due. The key role that Symons played in defining and then distancing himself from the notoriously vague term "Decadence" is especially telling here. Far along on the road to British high modernism post-Wilde, in *The Symbolist Movement in Literature* (1899) Symons calls Decadence a "straying aside from the main road of literature" and an "interlude, half a mock-interlude" that "diverted the attention of the critics while something more serious was in preparation."[14] In his earlier essay "The Decadent Movement in Literature" (1893), however, Symons had defined Decadence quite differently, as a reflection of a much more consequential cultural mood—a "disease of form," another aspect of the *maladie fin de siècle*: "It has all the qualities that mark the end of great periods, the qualities that we find in the Greek, the Latin, decadence: an intense self-consciousness, a restless curiosity in research, an oversubtilizing refinement upon refinement, a spiritual and moral perversity. If what we call the classic is indeed the supreme art—those qualities of perfect simplicity, perfect sanity, perfect proportion, the supreme qualities—then this representative literature of today, interesting, beautiful as it is, is really a new and beautiful and interesting disease."[15] The strain of transhistoricism and transnationalism in Symons's 1893 definition became by 1899 in need of what he called "something more serious" and, it would seem, less overtly queer.[16] What would it mean to return to this earlier moment, before the need for something more respectable was felt (or projected) as necessary for a skeptical new generation of modernist writers, to take Decadence's unruly currents seriously? What methods and disciplinary structures enable it to be known—or need to be transcended?

Dorian Unbound joins these two burgeoning and vitalizing critical streams—the expansion of the geographic imaginary of Victorian studies and the emergence of a new Decadence studies—with a feel for the archives, both as they currently exist and as they might be reconceived. The title refers both to the releasing of one important Decadent archive from the bounds of the national, metropolitan, and temporal paradigms that have tended to define it and, in a double sense, to so many loose papers that make up Wilde's novel *The Picture of Dorian Gray* (1890/1891) as an archival record, not just a book. The study's motivating idea is that the attention Anglophone critics have rightly paid to Wilde's contexts in Victorian Aestheticism and French Decadence has had the unintended effect of obscuring a much broader network of transnational contexts that Wilde had been accumulating since he was a young boy and drawing creative inspiration from since the early 1880s. This book thus sets out to make two scholarly interventions. The first is a critical and methodological intervention, making visible the powerful, pervasive, and subtle ways in which transnational contexts shaped Wilde's imagination. Second, the book begins to redress a profound disciplinary imbalance in how we have come to understand Wilde as a Decadent writer, expanding the archive beyond that established by scholars working mainly within a Victorianist English-studies framework by reading for Wilde's transhistorical and transnational contexts. We know, for instance, all about Wilde's meteoric rise to the pinnacle of London society, but what about Wilde rereading works by his own family or studying outmoded and eccentric writers from Dublin, Pomerania, Baltimore, and Box Hill?

The idea for the book made itself known during a fellowship at the William Andrews Clark Memorial Library at the University of California, Los Angeles. I was there to research my long-standing interests in Wilde's relation to the Irish Gothic, the long reach of Poe's legacy, and Wilde's complicated stance toward Victorian predecessors like George Meredith. The decisive moment came when I saw William Morris's astonishingly beautiful edition of Lady Wilde's 1849 translation of Wilhelm Meinhold's *Sidonia the Sorceress* (*Sidonia von Bork, die Klosterhexe*, in the original German). The edition was reissued for the Kelmscott Press in 1893, just a few years after the appearance of *Dorian Gray*—not a coincidence, I suspected. Printed in black and red ink on handmade paper, the text is produced in the style of an illuminated manuscript, with an intricate border of intertwining vines and leaves, similarly ornate dropped capitals, and an elegant cream binding. The effect was irresistible, not least because of the novel's unlikely passage through the nineteenth century, from humble Pomeranian beginnings to an association with some of the most celebrated names and movements of the age: an English translation that achieved cult-like status among the Pre-Raphaelite Brotherhood, helped inspire Wilde's *Dorian Gray*, and led Morris to reissue his

Kelmscott edition in its aftermath, the layers of history and cultural meaning accruing like a palimpsest. As I detail in chapter 3, this artifact provides a useful example of how the archives often tell stories different from, or revealingly aslant, the received narratives. In this case, the notion that *Dorian Gray* is primarily to be read in relation to its well-known immediate contexts had to make room for an occult German novel about a seventeenth-century sex panic and an entire tradition of artistic production that it inspired in England in the 1850s and beyond.

Archive building, like literary influence, is a notoriously slippery game, but as I found in the research for this book, in Wilde's case it is a necessary one. His highly allusive writing demands careful and nuanced reading—including the reading of "influence" itself—and it is our failure if we shrink from its challenge. The rewards, fortunately, are proportionally large. In addition to a more complex understanding of Wilde and his work, fresh literary histories, conceptual tools, and theoretical frameworks emerge.[17] The readings in the chapters that follow all begin from glancing affinities—call it a weak method, in the strongest sense—but they ultimately bring together bodies of literature that have been all but lost to a highly disciplined scholarly view or that were not previously thought to be connected at all. (Has no one really written of the "male stunner" in relation to *Dorian*?, I asked. An interdisciplinary dissertation on Goya and the 1890s, anyone?) The result is a networked Wilde whose most volatile and lasting transgression is not the homoeroticism that he dared to make so palpable, although that is the one he ultimately paid so dearly for in his time, but the unruly affiliations across geography and period—including especially savvy negotiations of literary form—that condition that very feeling of solidness and perceptibility, of seeing and being seen.

The idea that Wilde's highly original novel is also extremely allusive is not, then, as paradoxical as it might initially seem. In the way that it draws on and remakes literary history, *Dorian* was inventive precisely because of, not despite, its allusiveness. Joseph Bristow and Rebecca N. Mitchell's luminous work on the significance of Wilde's "Chatterton" notebook in *Oscar Wilde's Chatterton: Literary History, Romanticism, and the Art of Forgery* (2015) provides a beacon here. This notebook features copious clippings of passages from other sources on the early Romantic poet Thomas Chatterton, sometimes with annotation and emendation in Wilde's hand, but without attribution. Often understood as evidence of Wilde's plagiarism—consistent with the accusations of several of Wilde's contemporaries, most famously the American artist James McNeil Whistler, and with a strain of criticism since—the

Chatterton notebook is simply, for Bristow and Mitchell, what it is: "a well-researched notebook."[18] They elaborate: "The critical focus on Wilde's apparent plagiarism has distracted attention from what truly matters about this important document, which throws extensive light on a pivotal moment when Wilde's creative output and intellectual life underwent several astounding shifts"—the moment in the 1880s, that is, when he was "reshaping his career as a successful journalist and authoritative writer who would soon excel in many different literary genres."[19] I will return to this point in more detail—it is one of the through lines of the book—but for the purposes of this preface, Wilde's reuse and reassembling of the literary past is to be best understood as fundamentally creative and immensely generative. It performs its own theory of influence. A consummate student of literary history, Wilde enacts the kind of novelty that T. S. Eliot would later posit—the "historical sense" that "not only the best, but the most individual parts of [the poet's] work may be those in which the dead poets, his ancestors, assert their immortality most vigorously."[20] Importantly, I will argue, Wilde's originality also derives from a keenly self-conscious sense of working in a transnational field. This began at quite an early age for Wilde, given his upbringing poised between cultures in a prominent, hyperliterate Anglo-Irish household, and his Irish and English education, first at Trinity College and then at Oxford, where he read widely, lost his Irish accent, and earned a rare "double first" (first-class honors in the British undergraduate degree classification) in Classical Moderations and Literae Humaniores. The persistence of his childhood love of Irish and German romances, two of which were by literal ancestors—his granduncle and his mother—well into the mature creative phases of adulthood also bears this narrative out, as we will see in chapters 2 and 3.

This study, too, is indebted to the insights and provocations of past accounts even as it responds differently to the need for broader historical and theoretical understanding. Instead of pursuing Decadence's contemporaneous affiliations and afterlives or the causes of its many manifestations across the globe, as scholars have done, I look to Wilde's artistic conception of transnationality as a fundamentally imaginative, retrospective, and archive-building process of transmission—a mode of becoming based on whom you read and borrow from and expand.[21] In this important sense, this book both is and is not a tightly focused study: it finds in the *Dorian* archive, specifically, an extraordinarily rich site of exchange between British, European, and North American traditions across several centuries but also a situated, nuanced, and empirically enriching framework for a transnational Decadence.

Limited in part by what Wilde read, this study urges a more expansive transnational perspective on an archive that self-consciously defines itself as beyond national affiliations yet remains largely—stubbornly, disappointingly—Northern and white.[22] Chapter 2 makes a great deal of Wilde's seemingly casual references to the histories of colonial Ireland, imperial Spain, US slavery, and the Belgian exploitation of the Congo, and a coda explores the implications of an important contemporary global resonance in the work of British-Nigerian artist Yinka Shonibare. But if this book reveals a pervasive whiteness in Wilde's transnational sources, it aims, at least, to make it impossible to speak of *Dorian Gray* or of Wilde as "merely Victorian," or even as properly British or Irish. Other limits are no doubt owing to the fact that, as Chatterjee, Mireles Christoff, and Wong remind us, "there is no way for any of us to stand entirely outside the pernicious ideologies that shape modernity, the modern university, and contemporary subjecthood."[23] I have been the beneficiary of many of those ideologies, often unwittingly—or, in the way that privilege has, having to think only that I earned it—even as I have been subject to others. I strive to think and act differently and, crucially, more collaboratively. Most of all, what I take from "Undisciplining Victorian Studies" is that it is "necessarily an ongoing and unfinished project."[24] It is my hope that this book's archival and transnational impulses will bring other studies forward—at the very least, yield more attention to the opportunities and the fires in our midst—even if, unavoidably, it does not tell the whole story. Perhaps we can only do that together, anyway.

This book could not have been written without the unstinting love and support of many people. One of the joys of its completion is that I can publicly thank them and hopefully now have the time to begin to repay the debt.

Everyone at Johns Hopkins University Press has been an absolute pleasure to work with, in particular my editor Catherine Goldstead, who believed in the book and whose intelligence, good humor, and unfailing calm have guided it at every stage to publication. The Press's faculty board and two peer reviewers offered invaluable feedback and encouragement and helped me make this work everything that it could be. I also owe a huge thanks to my discerning and sharp-sighted copyeditor, David Goehring, and to Sergey Lobachev, who produced the index.

Institutional support provided the necessary time and funds to complete this research. I gratefully acknowledge the generous help of my union the Professional Staff Congress of the City University of New York's research award program, the Weissman School of Arts and Sciences dean's fund, and the University Seminars of Columbia University's Aaron Warner fund, all which helped me over the finish line. A 2012 National Endowment of the Humanities summer seminar at the William Andrews Clark Memorial Library at UCLA provided the opportunity and intellectual community that forged and sustained this work over the years. The seminar was led by Joseph Bristow, who helped me see the path to this project (any imperfections are my own), and I will forever be indebted to his knowledge of Wilde and his incredibly generous mentorship and interest in my work. Many thanks to the colleagues and friends I met there, especially Pearl Brilmyer, Ronjaunee Chatterjee, Michael Davis, Petra Dierkes-Thrun, Betsy Dougherty, Ryan Fong, Abigail Joseph, Rebecca Mitchell, Benjamin Morgan, and Jamil Mustafa, and to the entire library staff, especially Scott Jacobs and Shannon Supple. I am also grateful for the support and encouragement of my department chairs in recent years: Timothy Aubry, Eva Chou, and Jessica Lang.

I have been unbelievably lucky in mentors, colleagues, and friends. Those who have been frequent, in some cases daily, supports and interlocutors during the writing of this book include my brilliant colleagues at Baruch, especially Allison Deutermann, Stephanie Insley Hershinow, and Mary McGlynn, and my friends, William Berger, Gloria Fisk, Grecia Haigwood, John Lucas, Bill May, Matthew McNamara, Michael Miller, Rebecca Mitchell, Patrick Mullen, Alex Ross, Kim Shipley, and Craig Sloane, who nourish and motivate me in all the important ways. To everyone else who has buoyed me through this process with kindnesses large and small and whom I do not have space enough here to name individually: a heartfelt thank you.

Earlier versions of parts of this book have been published in article form in the Modern Humanities Research Association's *Yearbook of English Studies* (2019), edited by Rebecca N. Mitchell, and the collection *Wilde's Other Worlds*, edited by Michael F. Davis and Petra Dierkes-Thrun. In addition to the fine editors of these publications, I owe a debt of gratitude to Richard Kaye, who helped to bring nuance and clarity to an early version of chapter 1, which is slated to appear in his forthcoming volume from Oxford University Press, *The Picture of Dorian Gray in the Twenty-First Century*. I am grateful for permission to reprint this material in revised and expanded form.

I have also presented pieces of this work at various conferences, including meetings of the Modern Language Association, the North American Victorian Studies Association, the American Conference for Irish Studies, the International Society for the Study of Narrative, the CUNY C19 Conference, the first international conference on George Meredith in Lincoln, England, and the Société Oscar Wilde at the Centre Culturel Irlandais in Paris. In addition, I was invited to speak in the very early stages of the project at the Columbia University Irish Studies Seminar. My work has benefited greatly from the generous reception and helpful questions and comments that I received at these events, and I express my deep gratitude to my fellow panelists and to the conveners, especially Tanya Agathocleous, Claudia Capancioni, Alice Crossley, Mary McGlynn, and David Rose. For their encouragement, questions, advice, and collegiality at these and other venues, I am grateful to Carolyn Betensky, Eleanor Courtemanche, Jonathan Farina, Rae Greiner, Margaret Harris, Anne Humpherys, Maha Jafri, Melissa Shields Jenkins, Anna Kornbluh, David Kurnick, Vincent Lankewish, Michael Lewis, Deborah Lutz, Anne McCarthy, Amy Martin, Mary Mullen, Adrienne Munich, Cara Murray, Patrick O'Malley, Sarah Parker, Simon Reader, Caroline Reitz, Jason Rudy, Talia Schaffer, Sally Shuttleworth, Jonah Siegal, Simon Stern, Ann Stiles, Megan Ward, and Nancy Yousef.

I was drawn to Wilde and to Victorian studies, in part, because they seemed to hold the answers to what has formed much of the present world and what still needs (un)doing. The presence of Eve Kosofsky Sedgwick, whose writing brought me into the academy and with whom I was fortunate to work as a graduate student, is on every page (the foibles, again, are mine alone). Formative experiences studying with John Brenkman, Rachel Brownstein, John Glavin, Lynda Hart, Wayne Koestenbaum, Steven Kruger, Rebecca Pope, Amy Robinson, and Martha Nell Smith have left their mark and continue to shape my thinking to this day.

I wish to thank my own students, as well, especially members of the seminars on Oscar Wilde that I have been fortunate enough to teach at Princeton and at CUNY, for their intellectual courage and for showing me and each other what future worlds are possible.

In November 2019, in the midst of a thankfully brief health scare, I promised not to take the life on the other side of the hospital window for granted. Little did I know how much that life was about to change, but I thank Rich Devine, Gloria Fisk, and Michael Miller for seeing me to the other side with good coffee and characteristic cheer.

My sister, Erin O'Toole-DeHoyos, has been a pillar of support and always brings laughter, love, and light. My parents, Thomas O'Toole and Noreen Seaphoenix, were the first to encourage me to read widely and to make my own home in the world. This book is dedicated to them.

Dorian Unbound

Introduction

Notorious since its first publication in 1890, Oscar Wilde's novel *The Picture of Dorian Gray* has entered the global cultural imagination as only the rarest works of art do. Translated into countless languages and adapted across numerous genres and media—films, plays, musicals, ballets, an opera, a telenovela, a graphic novel, a manga set in Edo-era Japan, a David Bowie video, and a rendition in photography by the British-Nigerian artist Yinka Shonibare— the book is now synonymous with ageless beauty achieved at the expense of a terrible bargain.[1] At the same time, the infamous 1895 trial for "gross indecency" has cast a long shadow over Wilde's earlier life, and the view of him as the "apogee of gay experience and expression," in Alan Sinfield's words, now shapes readers' encounters with his work.[2] This is especially true of *Dorian Gray*, Wilde's only novel and his most daringly homoerotic text, which was read aloud and entered as evidence against him at the Old Bailey. As a result, it can be easy to forget that *Dorian Gray* had creative and intellectual beginnings and not just an afterlife—that the imaginative genesis for the novel has a story of its own. This book aims, in part, to recover that story.

Dorian Unbound reveals that Wilde's novel was transnational and multi-genre from the very start, taking its cue from a central impulse of Decadent culture: the desire to upend traditional models of literary influence by embracing hybridity, importation, and cross-border contamination. The familiar and well-documented contexts of Victorian Aestheticism and French Decadence have long been crucial to understanding Wilde's novel, but their centrality can be as obscuring as it has been illuminating. This book argues that the focus on these contexts has eclipsed an intellectual landscape of equal importance: the transnational archive of imaginative materials that Wilde had begun collecting in his youth and gave full expression to in his most mature work. In this archive, the book discovers an intellectually itinerant Wilde, unbounded by the categories that would come to define him. It also adds to the growing body of work that identifies a more dynamic idea of Decadence—not as a fleeting vogue of the fin de siècle but as a pervasive network of connections between place, period, and art forms. Focusing on a canonical text and its lesser-known contexts to rethink Decadence, the study contributes to the broader reappraisal of literary periodicity, transnationalism, and aesthetic forms actively underway in literary studies. We know Wilde as a critic of Victorian culture ahead of his time, but this book reveals the intimate relation of a surprisingly backward-looking and un-Victorian set of sources to this critique. "A man who can dominate a London dinner-table can dominate the world," Wilde quipped in *A Woman of No Importance* (1893).[3] But the way to dominate the London dinner-table, it turns out, was to embrace the world—Decadence's ethos of transnationalism.

Wilde, of course, was expert in both spheres. Given the preponderance of seemingly casual references to world literature and history, opera and theatre, newspapers, the telegraph, and other forms of media, including the yellow-backed novel that supposedly corrupts Dorian, and all manner of worldly arts, we are repeatedly, even ostentatiously invited to read the novel in terms of border crossings. Wilde's ability to hold court is also well known. For instance, the conversation at the table where Wilde, Arthur Conan Doyle, and the American publisher J. M. Stoddart dined in London in the autumn of 1889 was a characteristically memorable one. According to Conan Doyle's account, it was a "golden evening" for him:

> [Wilde's] conversation left an indelible impression on my mind. He towered above us all, and yet had the art of seeming to be interested in all that we could say. He had delicacy of feeling and tact, for the monologue man, however clever, can never be a gentleman at heart. He took as well as gave, but what he gave was unique. He had a curious precision of statement, a delicate flavour of humour, and a trick of small gestures to illustrate his meaning, which were peculiar to himself. The effect cannot be reproduced.[4]

By the end of the evening, Stoddart had commissioned both authors to write for his Philadelphia-based *Lippincott's Monthly Magazine*. Conan Doyle wrote *The Sign of Four*, the second of his Sherlock Holmes novellas, and Wilde quickly penned *The Picture of Dorian Gray*, a story of a beautiful young man and his aging portrait—a story he must have been turning over in his mind for some time.

Throughout his life, Wilde especially liked reading stories about portraits, as we will see in several of this book's chapters, and he had just recently published one himself: "The Portrait of Mr. W. H." (1889). The story is a dazzling display of bravura concerning the dedicatee of Shakespeare's *Sonnets*, Mr. W. H., and the theory that he was the beautiful young actor Willie Hughes. On the fickleness of desire, the allure of influence, and the contagion of belief, the story verges on theory itself. It also represents one of the first attempts to bring homoerotic desire into mainstream English fiction as self-evident, taking it for granted that the figure of Shakespeare (no less) was attracted to men. Homoerotic love would feature prominently in his new work of fiction as well, a fact that Stoddart would try to tone down in his edits to the typescript where he did not censor it outright, an aspect of the composition history which I closely examine in chapter 1. Both Conan Doyle's and Wilde's novellas were eventually published in the February and July 1890 issues of *Lippincott's*—how beguiling it must have been to read them one after the other for the first time—and the story might have ended there.

The novel had one dedicated fan from the very start, at least. Wilde's mother wrote to him to say that she nearly fainted at the final scene, praising it as "the most wonderful piece of writing in all the fiction of the day."[5] In general, however, the backlash against *Dorian Gray* was extensive, sharp, and swift. The repudiation came first in the form of outraged unsigned reviews. To cite one example that may stand in for the rest in both content and tone, the reviewer for the *Scots Observer* wrote, with a notable reference to "The Portrait of Mr. W. H." also:

> Why go grubbing in muck heaps? The world is fair and the proportion of healthy-minded men and honest women to those that are foul, fallen, and unnatural is great. Mr. Oscar Wilde has again been writing stuff that were better unwritten. [...] The story—which deals with matters only fitted for the Criminal Investigation Department or a hearing in camera—is discreditable alike to author and editor. Mr. Wilde has brains, and art, and style, but if he can write for none but outlawed noblemen and perverted telegraph-boys, the sooner he takes to tailoring (or some other decent trade) the better for his own reputation and the public morals.[6]

The mentions of "outlawed noblemen" and "perverted telegraph-boys" refer to the Cleveland Street scandal of 1889, the highly publicized affair that implicated Lord Arthur Somerset, equerry to the Prince of Wales, Henry James Fitzroy, Earl of Euston, Prince Albert Victor, the Prince of Wales's son and heir, and numerous young men employed by the Post Office in a male brothel scheme operating in Cleveland Street, Fitzrovia, in central London.[7] While it is amusing to imagine Wilde as a tailor—"do you dress to the left or to the right, sir?"—it is difficult not to see in this attack a foreboding glimpse of his eventual exposure under the 1885 Criminal Law Amendment Act, a law that made it easier to corroborate even the suggestion of same-sex activity, now codified as "gross indecency," than the prior laws criminalizing "buggery" or sodomy.[8] It was not by chance that *Dorian Gray* would play a star turn in Wilde's prosecution as evidence of a corrupting influence.[9] In the interim, after the initial uproar and his attempts to defend his work in the press, Wilde would add a defiant preface and six additional, more conventionally Victorian chapters in creating a longer version of the novel, which Ward, Lock & Co. brought out in a single volume in April 1891. After the novel's publication, in biographer Richard Ellmann's words, "Victorian literature had a different look."[10]

Ellmann's pronouncement is revealing in more ways than one. *Dorian Gray* changed the course of Victorian literature in its remaining decade, but it also compelled a revised account of the traditions that preceded it and helped compose it. Before providing an overview of this book's structure and line of argument, it will be helpful first to define the critical backgrounds with and against which I read Wilde's contribution to a *longue durée* transnational Decadence. Perhaps unsurprisingly, the extensive critical heritage has focused heavily on Wilde's contemporary and proximate contexts in Victorian Aestheticism and French Decadence, and to beneficial effect. In particular, the writings and teachings of Walter Pater, with whom Wilde studied for a time at Oxford (and who had had his own share of scandal several years earlier), have rightly been understood as a key source of inspiration.[11] Most critical readings of the novel mention Pater's name, and some of the best critical accounts center squarely on this connection; several of these readings usefully chart its limits, in turn. I am thinking in particular of John Paul Riquelme's insightful essay on the "aesthetic Gothic," Joseph Bristow's prodigious oeuvre on both Pater and Wilde, and most recently, Dustin Friedman's revealing study, *Before Queer Theory*.[12] For Riquelme, Wilde's novel "proceeds against the background of Pater's writings," often resonating with the best-known passages from the conclusion to his *Studies in the History of the Renaissance* (1873, hereafter *The Renaissance*) and from his chapter on the Mona Lisa in an essay on Leonardo da Vinci in that same volume.[13] But the novel also "provides in narrative form a dark, revealing double for Pater's aestheticism, that emerges from a potential for dark doubling and reversal within aestheticism itself."[14] Importantly, Riquelme frames the "dark enlightenment" of Wilde's aesthetic Gothic not as a mere repetition of Pater's more anodyne version but as a generative and fundamentally creative critique: "The duplication produces not a repetition of Pater but a new version of his views that says what he cannot or will not articulate, including a recognition of the dark dynamics of doubling and reversal that inhabit those views."[15] Riquelme concludes: "Wilde neither imitates nor follows Pater in his aesthetic Gothic narrative. Instead, he echoes him as a way to evoke, refuse, and transform what he finds in the earlier writer."[16]

Bristow usefully reframes the question of sources as a central interpretive challenge of the novel. He finds in its slippery method of acknowledging and at times seeming merely to copy those who came before a message about the perils of citation itself—of distorting the original by merely imitating or uncritically reiterating it. The characters of Dorian Gray and Lord Henry do this, for instance, in misappropriating Pater by evacuating his call for bodily sensation of any critical thought. According to Bristow, Wilde's novel "draws on its literary antecedents somewhat differently from the ways in which Lord Henry rehearses them and Dorian Gray tries to realize them," and readers are invited to notice the difference.[17] Part of what and how the novel comes to mean, then, is "to suggest that Pater's concepts—transmitted through Lord Henry's quotable adaptations—might run afoul in the wrong hands."[18] Similarly, Lord Henry's gift of a Decadent yellow book "can only perpetuate in Dorian Gray a cycle of serial boredom, in which he discovers that his cultural preferences and behavioral performances have already been inscribed in a long recapitulative line of racial ancestors, historical predecessors, and literary precursors. Mimesis, it seems, is Dorian Gray's fundamental mode, one that reaches down into his very bones, and it is a debilitating and uninspiring form of imitation that proves deathly."[19] As a result, the novel's chapters show that those who would merely copy the Aesthetic creed that Wilde advocates in his defiant preface are ultimately anathema to it, Bristow concludes: "The story of Dorian Gray very much looks as if it undermines the aesthetic precepts that Wilde promulgates in 'The Preface.' But, then, perhaps his point is to dramatize through fiction a critique of what might happen to those individuals who simply reflect—rather than reflect on—the belief that art exists for its own sake."[20] This argument has some congruence with Riquelme's in contending that Wilde is commenting on and not simply imitating Pater, but

Bristow reads the novel as not so much a productive critique of the earlier writer's work as it is a demonstration of how easily his Aesthetic philosophy can be misapprehended by others. "What we have to do," urges Pater after all, "is to be for ever curiously testing new opinions and courting new impressions, never acquiescing in a facile orthodoxy"—including an orthodoxy of *The Renaissance* itself.[21]

Delving into the archival record, Friedman finds convincing additional evidence that Wilde's admiration for Pater clearly marked his earliest forays into intellectual and creative life as well as included major disagreements, even if those disagreements were largely kept from public view. (Bristow believes, rightly I think, that Wilde and Pater "were respectfully open in making fair-minded comments about each other's writings."[22]) After becoming acquainted at Oxford in 1878, the two men would write favorable reviews of each other's work and maintain a lifelong correspondence. Wilde continually praised *The Renaissance* to others, calling it "my golden book," and to W. B. Yeats he said, "I never travel anywhere without it."[23] However, in a commonplace book that he kept as a student at Oxford in the 1870s, Friedman notes, Wilde copied out a passage from Pater's essay "Winckelmann," on the pioneering eighteenth-century German Hellenist, but then added an astute reply of his own. To Pater's insistence that we "renounce metaphysics in order to mould our lives to artistic perfection," Wilde skeptically responded: "Yet surely he who sees in colour no mere delightful quality of natural things but a spirit indwelling in things is in a way a metaphysician."[24] As in the case of the Chatterton notebook, here again is proof of Wilde's practice of a studious, reflective engagement with a predecessor whom he greatly admired—one might say, admired enough to criticize.

The other powerful influence that continually reappears in the critical heritage is the context of French Decadence (or *Décadence*), specifically the experimental 1884 novel by Joris-Karl Huysmans, a Frenchman of Dutch descent, titled *A Rebours* (literally *Against the Grain* but more often translated as *Against Nature*).[25] The prevalence of this context in the criticism reflects the unambiguous role that *Against Nature* plays within Wilde's plot. The yellow-covered French fiction that Lord Henry gives Dorian recounts the aesthetic experiences and pursuits of a "wonderful young Parisian," a neurasthenic invalid who is clearly recognizable as Huysmans's reclusive protagonist, Duc Jean Floressas des Esseintes.[26] Wilde's narrator recounts that this "novel without a plot" is written in a "curiously jeweled style, vivid and obscure at once," with metaphors "as monstrous as orchids, and as subtle in colour," and a "heavy odour of incense" pervades it pages—all details redolent of Huysmans's original work (107). The influence of this "poisonous" book on Dorian is described exhaustively in the central chapter 11 of Wilde's novel, in which Dorian finds in his young hero "a kind of prefiguring type of himself" (107, 108). Yet, as Bristow notes, Dorian imitates only Des Esseintes's "fetishistic collecting and yearning for sexual gratification," not his meditative attempts to "explain his habitual ennui."[27] Once again, Dorian's mere copying of a precursor without a critical engagement with ideas is shown to be the real poison.

To what extent are the critical moves that have productively situated Wilde in relation to—and against—his antecedents useful beyond the customary orbits of Victorian London and fin de siècle Paris? How has the robust focus on contexts both contemporary and proximate, to which this study is indebted for its very possibility, obscured less evident contexts past and distant? Why and how did Wilde's transnational contexts for *Dorian* generate significant imaginative opportunities, and what is to be gained from taking these contexts seriously, attending to them closely, and recovering a clearer sense of this archive? These are some of the central questions that I take up in the chapters that follow.

Part One, "Decadent Hybridity," begins by reading *Dorian* for what haunts it: a canny, creative use of literary history. It establishes how Wilde took up and redeployed a complex hybrid of literary forms in an attempt to avoid censorship in Victorian England. Deftly mixing elements of the Bildungsroman, Gothic horror, romance, melodrama, and satire, Wilde was able to reroute and partially cover the queer energies that the novel initially mobilizes before transforming into something much darker. This formal strategy reveals a queer artistic resilience in the face of Victorian prohibition but also, more fundamentally, a novelist aware of inhabiting a transnational field and self-consciously engaging in a *longue durée* project, reworking past ideas and cultural forms in highly inventive new fashion.

The book then broadens out to examine distinct transnational strands of this inheritance. Part Two, "Inherited Worlds," traces lines of influence from Wilde's mother's literary background as the niece of the Irish Gothic writer Charles Maturin (*Melmoth the Wanderer*, 1820) and as the English translator of a German historical romance by Wilhelm Meinhold (*Sidonia the Sorceress*, 1847), which became a craze among the Pre-Raphaelite artists in Victorian London. As Lady Wilde, she also convened an important Dublin salon that

Wilde attended as a boy. From a dawning literary consciousness to his final years in exile when he took the name of Maturin's famous wanderer, Melmoth, to avoid snubs, these early influences shed new light on Wilde's narrative interests and his development as a writer. Part Three, "Networked Forms," then examines Wilde's discovery of genealogies of his own choosing—flashpoints in the making of his only novel: popular US magic-picture narratives (the artist tales of Hawthorne, Poe, and James) and a countertradition of English experiments in dialogue form (the epigrammatic writings of Thomas Love Peacock and George Meredith). Wilde's creative engagement with these traditions has been eclipsed by the focus on Victorian Aestheticism and French Decadence, but each yields a fascinating instance of the "backward turn" that Heather Love has argued marks "even the most forward-looking modernist literature" and that I suggest entailed a crucial turning outward, across national borders, at the fin de siècle.[28]

Rather than offer an encyclopedic account of Wilde's sources for *Dorian*, many of which are already well documented, this study brings the novel into surprising new focus through the lens of its fugitive transnational contexts. As noted in the preface, these contexts are broadly transatlantic. I emphasize the transnational, however, because a close reading of the novel reveals that the act of crossing—of evoking, combining, and transforming seemingly distant sources and disparate genres—is at least as important as the particulars of place. Thus, this reading also points to something quite different from the global or even the cosmopolitan in Wilde—a more jagged and queer hybrid form that keeps the borders crossed insistently, self-consciously present. (Interestingly, this cagey formal logic tends to go unremarked in discussions of the novel's transatlanticism, as well as its more overt Orientalism and oft-touted cosmopolitanism.) With the exception of a link to Goya's etchings that I reveal in chapter 2, these contexts have all been known to critics for some time, in some cases in Wilde's own day. But they have not previously been brought together in a sustained argument or exploited to the full. In *Dorian*, Wilde harnessed literary history and drew crucial resources and strategies from seemingly distant forms in staging his defiant confrontation with late-Victorian England. This lineage has been difficult to see, however, given the predominance of the novel's more contemporary and proximate contexts in England and France. A more expansive look reveals how a transnational archive gave shape to—indeed, enabled—Wilde's challenge to Victorian culture. In turn, enlarging the geographic scope of literary Decadence by way of the

Wilde archive enriches the evidential base for broader theories of the transnational.

Chapter 1 prepares the ground for the book's central argument by examining *Dorian*'s extravagant mix of genres and styles. Cutting against the well-rehearsed arguments about Wilde's direct borrowings from Pater, Huysmans, and others, I suggest that the novel's hybrid form provides evidence of a more complicated transnational inheritance, which Wilde drew on and strategically reassembled in an attempt to evade censorship. In particular, the Gothic mode made possible for Wilde a legally necessary redirection of the energies of the queer Bildungsroman that the early chapters of *Dorian* set in motion. At stake in this rereading is the capacity to see what has remained largely hidden despite a profusion of illuminating readings of the novel's undercurrent of queer expression in recent decades: the transnational forms of its very articulation.

Chapter 2 examines the interpolated story of Dorian's ancestry and its conspicuous allusions to Anglo-Irish history, alongside a key Romantic source for Wilde's novel, Maturin's *Melmoth the Wanderer*. Building on Patrick R. O'Malley's persuasive reading of *Melmoth* and a tradition of Anglo-Irish writing that attempted to revise and to forget the violent colonial past, I demonstrate how Wilde put the Gothic mode that he inherited to very different use: to frame the very question of what to do with the past as a haunted and haunting problem. In addition to rerouting the novel's constitutive queer energies, I suggest, the Gothic prompts a broader meditation on the freighted legacy and persistence of imperial memory. In this, Wilde brings Gothic horror to the service of his own brand of realism, showing the contemporary world of compulsory heterosexuality and colonial history to be a waking nightmare.

The focus of the third chapter is *Sidonia the Sorceress* (1847), Meinhold's historical romance featuring a haunted portrait, sexual transgression, and a terrible transformation, which was translated by Wilde's mother, then Jane Francesca Elgee, in 1849. The story of Sidonia, a real-life Pomeranian noblewoman who was tried for witchcraft and decapitated in 1620 for casting a spell of sterility on the House of Pomerania, achieved cult status in Victorian England. Dante Gabriel Rossetti made a habit of quoting from now Lady Wilde's translation, and Edward Burne-Jones produced a remarkable 1860 painting of the uncanny double portrait described in Meinhold's novel, clearly a model for Dorian's more famous magically aging portrait. This chapter makes visible the continuities between Wilde's novel and this seemingly distant literary form. *Dorian*'s doppelgänger portrait and the sterility of the romance at its heart can be traced, I suggest, to Meinhold's novel by way of Lady Wilde's popular English translation and Burne-Jones's haunting visual depiction. Together with the previous chapter's focus, this nexus reveals a pattern of influence that predates Wilde's experiments in Aestheticism and moves in unaffiliated fashion across national literatures, periods, and art forms.

Chapter 4 focuses on the American contexts for *Dorian*: the commissioning and editing of the story for *Lippincott's Magazine* and a US tradition of magic-picture narratives that would have assured an audience primed for Wilde's story on both sides of the Atlantic even without his well-publicized 1882 North American lecture tour. These narratives include Nathaniel Hawthorne's "The Prophetic Pictures" (1837) and "Edward Randolph's Portrait" (1838), Edgar Allan Poe's "William Wilson" (1839) and "The Oval Portrait" (1842), and Henry James's artist tales, "The Story of a Masterpiece" (1868) and "The Liar" (1888). I contend that this tradition informs Wilde's narrative interests and formal choices in *Dorian*, especially in the way that the stories problematize and undercut the moralizing logic by which they seem to work. In addition to assimilating his audience's tastes and predispositions, Wilde learned from his American precursors how to operate within and against a censorship-prone dominant culture—and to do so by canny negotiations of literary form. For example, Wilde's novel invites us to question the beliefs and actions of its main character through a careful use of free indirect discourse, an insight that affords a reading of the novel's seemingly moralizing conclusion as, ironically, a cautionary tale about looking for morality in art. Wilde's formal interventions are subtler than the reliance by these American authors on more conspicuous techniques of narrative framing and unreliable first-person narration, but they completely transform the well-worn magic-picture tradition in the process—an annexation by which Wilde can be seen both to borrow from and to transcend his sources.

The final chapter considers the profound impact of now largely forgotten English epigrammatic writing on Wilde's work and thought. By way of conclusion, it offers an exception that proves the rule by suggesting that the focus on Victorian Aestheticism has obscured numerous sources even within the English context. A transnational lens also reveals, I contend, the limitations of the supposed "home" context itself. Specifically, while most studies trace influence from Pater and Victorian Aestheticism to Wilde, this chapter offers an alternative literary history, largely from the peripheries. It traces

Wilde's use of the epigram form to confront an enervated Victorian social conservatism to the experimental "conversation novels" of Thomas Love Peacock, of Lower Halliford, Shepperton, and George Meredith, of Box Hill, a history that the Liverpudlian poet Richard Le Gallienne captured in his little-known book *George Meredith: Some Characteristics* (1890) but that has since all but disappeared. This alternative English lineage (or Celtic-English, in the case of Meredith, who described himself as "half Irish and half Welsh"[29]) underscores the generative quality of these influential formal experiments, as well as Wilde's feel for literary history in his creative attempts to reinvent the social world. At stake in this rereading are the broader implications of understanding *Dorian* as a social satire, an experiment in the form and use of dialogue, and a gateway to Wilde's society comedies of the 1890s—all very different concerns than the Aestheticism lens alone yields. Even as Wilde reworked his transnational sources to create something original, he looked back to another English tradition, largely superseded by Aestheticism, to invent a way forward. A brief coda considers how contemporary artists like Yinka Shonibare continue this tradition by commenting on and remaking *Dorian* for a truly global twenty-first century.

This book thus offers a new account of the importance of transnational contexts in the forging of Wilde's imagination and in the genealogy of literary Decadence. To the important question of the value of the archival detail in an age of Digital Humanities computational analysis and in the wake of the V21 manifesto's call for Victorian studies to shed its infatuation with "an endless accumulation of mere information," this study suggests that Wilde's transnational archive is particularly well positioned to blow the dust off of a "positivist historicism"—that is, to think reflexively about both the objects of study and their historical frames.[30] A reevaluation of Decadence's persistent and peripatetic tendencies, this book aims to show, illuminates a wider field of study as well as the methods and (un)disciplinary structures that enable it to become known.

PART ONE

DECADENT HYBRIDITY

CHAPTER ONE

"Fantastic Shadows"

Wilde's Queer Form

The studio was filled with the rich odour of roses, and when the light summer wind stirred amidst the trees of the garden, there came through the open door the heavy scent of the lilac, or the more delicate perfume of the pink-flowering thorn.

From the corner of the divan of Persian saddle-bags on which he was lying, smoking, as was his custom, innumerable cigarettes, Lord Henry Wotton could just catch the gleam of the honey-sweet and honey-coloured blossoms of a laburnum, whose tremulous branches seemed hardly able to bear the burden of a beauty so flamelike as theirs; and now and then the fantastic shadows of birds in flight flitted across the long tussore-silk curtains that were stretched in front of the huge window, producing a kind of momentary Japanese effect, and making him think of those pallid, jade-faced painters of Tokyo who, through the medium of an art that is necessarily immobile, seek to convey the sense of swiftness and motion. The sullen murmur of the bees shouldering their way through the long unmown grass, or circling with monotonous insistence round the dusty gilt horns of the straggling woodbine, seemed to make the stillness more oppressive. The dim roar of London was like the bourdon note of a distant organ. (5)

In these opening paragraphs of *The Picture of Dorian Gray*, Wilde's narrator takes us inside the artist Basil Hallward's studio as he works on the full-length portrait of the novel's title. The scene, one of the work's most conspicuously emblematic descriptions, offers a crux for articulating a number of formally as well as thematically important issues in the novel. With the metropolitan location and urban environment—the "dim roar of London"—pushed to the background and transposed into the modality of an organ, hints of the Edenic garden enter through the open doors of the artist's studio. Focalized through the dandy Lord Henry, who lies smoking on "a divan of Persian saddle-bags" (smoking and flinging oneself on a divan being two of the favorite activities of the novel's men), the third-person narrator lures us in first by the nose. The hyperbolic sensuousness, the thick fragrances and overburdened branches, as well as the overextended syntax—the tortuous subordinate clauses and laborious definite articles (*the* trees, *the* blossoms, *the* woodbine)—make this modern Eden seem a queer one, indeed. The atmosphere in the all-male space is charged, perfumed, and weirdly saturated, the eccentricity punctuated by the decidedly un-English furnishings (the Turkish divan, Persian saddle-bags, Indian silk curtains) and the inert, un-masculine pose of the aesthete, Lord Henry. Yet, as Wilde presents it, nothing could be more natural. The agent is rendered unclear: the queerness seems to occur spontaneously, from without, as a matter of course, unmotivated—"*there came through the open door* the heavy scent of the lilac"—a simple predicate, neither affirmed nor denied. Here, effects—smells, gleams, murmurs, even stillness—seem to take on the sense of causes, and to be formidably active.[1]

The conspicuous description of heavy scents, tremulous branches, and a general excess of beauty that will soon characterize the artist's sitting subject, Dorian Gray himself, is, however, then abruptly broken off: "fantastic shadows of birds in flight" flit across the long silk curtains, producing "a kind of momentary Japanese effect"—the stark, flat, immobile quality of Japanese screen painting. The sudden introduction of a foreign artistic idiom thus redirects, or at least holds in suspension, the accumulation of sensual images and male gazes—Lord Henry looking at Basil looking at Dorian.[2] This interruption suggests both an image (the Japanese *byōbu* or folding screen) and an operation (the interpolation of distinct artistic genres) for registering an eroticism that is as palpable as it is restrained—indeed, screened—throughout the novel.

Critics have been quick to note the novel's transgressive quality, first in contemporary reviews that called it "vulgar," "unclean," "poisonous," "discreditable," "effeminate," "perverted," and "unnatural" and in recent decades in forceful queer reevaluations.[3] Eve Kosofsky Sedgwick's influential work situated the novel within the late nineteenth-century definitional crisis of homo/heterosexuality, finding in its apparent tensions and contradictions (Greek/Christian, art/kitsch, homo/hetero) a foundational articulation of the very terms for a modern homosexual identity.[4] A profusion of queer readings followed, and *The Picture of Dorian Gray*'s pivotal role in the history of sexuality is a now-familiar comprehension of the novel.[5] Surprisingly little attention, however, has been paid to the extent to which sexuality inheres in the novel's formal components, or to the key role that a transnational Decadent hybridity plays in the novel's formal achievement. In this chapter, I propose that *Dorian Gray*'s subtly complex opening scene offers crucial information about how to read the work as a whole, establishing first in imagery a tension and rhythm that will later be repeated by the form of the novel itself: an initiation and early promise of revelation, excitement, and pleasure, followed by an apparent flattening, closing off, and refusal or redistribution of desire. The foundational role of the novel's transnational sources, as signaled in miniature here by the Japanese *byōbu*, will then be taken up by the book's remaining chapters.

When critics do raise the question of form in discussions of *Dorian Gray*, it is usually in reference to the novel's perceived disorderliness—its seemingly chaotic mix of narrative modes, styles, and temporalities. Nils Clausson, for instance, has persuasively argued that the novel comprises two competing genres, one literary and one popular: the "Paterian self-development" plot and the "Gothic degeneration" plot.[6] According to Clausson's reading, the opening chapters are dominated by Dorian's self-discovery and development, thus initiating a Bildungsroman-like story of what Isobel Murray has called "the growth, education, and development of an exceptional youth, who through personalities, a book, a picture, is moulded or moulds himself, discovering what he believes in."[7] As what is being "developed" and "discovered" becomes increasingly transgressive, however, the novel is suddenly taken over by a discourse of moral degeneration. The pivotal chapter 11, in which Dorian disappears into a sensual decadence over the course of eighteen years, marks the shift. Yet Clausson, like many critics over the years, finds that the generic duality of the novel is evidence of artistic failure—an excessive or "flawed work, riven by generic dissonances."[8] He concludes: "The incompatibility of the novel's double genre undermines Wilde's attempt to tell a subversive story of dissidence and transgression leading to self-development and liberation."[9]

By contrast, in this chapter I put Clausson's useful terms in the service of a different argument, one that sees the novel's generic hybridity not as arbitrary or unwise but as constitutive, revealing the specific historical conditions of the novel's composition and publication, and ultimately key to its mysterious power—namely, the lasting feeling that, despite the seeming clarity of the strongly moralizing ending, the novel "has not been fully understood," in Joyce Carol Oates's memorable phrase.[10] Specifically, I argue that the blending of these seemingly contrary generic strands is evidence of a queer representational strategy by which Wilde is able to register both the felt experience of homoerotic desire and the need to secrete that desire in late nineteenth-century England. By arguing this, I also seek to build on and extend Ed Cohen's reading of the way that *Dorian Gray* "moves both with and athwart late Victorian ideological practices that naturalized male heterosexuality" to the form of the novel itself.[11] Importantly, as this book suggests, Wilde's formal solution to a thematic problem ultimately looked to transnational sources and to a Decadent strategy of generic hybridity to get his novel past the Victorian-era censors.

Viewed from this perspective, the novel's generic dissonance is, in fact, the point. The hybrid form of *The Picture of Dorian Gray* contains a record of both historical limitations and their circumvention: Wilde was able to publish his scandalous story in *Lippincott's Monthly Magazine* in 1890—eventually, with significant emendations—and yet still let readers in on the secret at its core. Although the censored and heavily revised manuscripts show that Wilde backed away from some of the more controversial language of the original text, he can also be seen to have doubled down on his hybrid formal strategy when he transformed the magazine story into a freestanding novel in 1891. Responding to the scandal that the *Lippincott's* text nonetheless produced, Wilde made even further use of genre shifting and mixing in adding significant elements of (heterosexual) romance, melodrama, and satire. By harnessing multiple formal approaches and genres that overlap, compete, and yet never quite resolve themselves, Wilde was ultimately able to articulate his dissident message by hiding it in plain sight.

At stake here is a view of what I am calling *queer form*, the embedding of meaning at particular moments in the history of sexuality not only in individual characters and themes but also in the very structures and modes of representation itself. Much of the work in this area has focused on *style* and on more obliquely queer contemporaries such as Henry James.[12] Perhaps because Wilde was more obviously and unashamedly queer in subject matter and theme (and in the not-synonymous but now tyrannically associated matter of his biography), he has not been read as closely for his formal innovations. He was, it is true, considerably more conventional in terms of fictional style. *Dorian Gray*'s biggest secret might just be how Victorian a book it is, with its third-person omniscient narrator, stock characters, and stereotyped nineteenth-century settings—Sibyl Vane and family, the "hideous Jew" hawking in front of the squalid theater, the opium den, "this grey, monstrous London of ours" (43)—and its seemingly neat, moralizing, cautionary-tale conclusion. But in 1890 and 1891 Wilde made bold and perceptive uses of available generic and formal plot devices—namely, the erotic triangle of the coming-of-age story of the Bildungsroman tradition and the popular portrait-as-mirror motif of Gothic narratives dating back at least to the 1840s.[13] The result was a hybrid form so original and canny that it has gone largely unremarked upon, or, in the exceptional case, underestimated, for over a century.

"Some Secret Cord": Generic Dissonance as Dissident Form

The Picture of Dorian Gray thus begins with both a hyperbolic sense of sensuousness and a shadow theater: "[T]here came through the open door the heavy scent of the lilac," on the one hand, and "fantastic shadows of birds in flight" darting across a concealing curtain, on the other. Once this double movement of the crucial opening scene intimates the novel's formal strategy for registering a queer presence all the while seeming not to—suggesting but then screening it by interposing a foreign, highly stylized artistic genre at the very moment it verges on appearing—Dorian's education begins. As a close reading of the novel's odd blending of genres reveals, the Gothic elements that would seem to take over the Bildungsroman narrative operate much like the silk curtains in the opening scene: they shroud Dorian's initiation to self-knowledge as the object of homoerotic desire and yet register, in shadow form, something concealed. Reminding Lord Henry of Japanese screen painting, the curtains interpose a foreign artistic medium into the London scene, just as the Gothic story of the uncanny portrait's transformation will work to recuperate the story of an English aristocrat's transgressions back into a conventional morality tale, all the while registering lingering traces.

First, however, the opening chapters of the novel follow a trajectory of Aesthetic self-discovery and liberation of the senses famously exalted by Walter Pater in his conclusion to *The Renaissance*, as Dorian pursues Lord Henry's advice to discover his own truth through experience:

> The aim of life is self-development. To realize one's nature perfectly—that is what each of us is here for. People are afraid of themselves, nowadays. [. . .] And yet [. . .] I believe that if one man were to live out his life fully and completely, were to give form to every feeling, expression to every thought, reality

to every dream—I believe that the world would gain such a fresh impulse of joy that we would forget all the maladies of medievalism, and return to the Hellenic ideal—to something finer, richer, than the Hellenic ideal, it may be. [. . .] We are punished for our refusals. (18–19)

Lord Henry's advice most clearly echoes the aesthetic philosophy set forth in Pater's "Conclusion":

Not the fruit of experience, but experience itself, is the end. A counted number of pulses only is given to us of a variegated, dramatic life. How may we see in them all that is to be seen in them by the finest senses? How shall we pass most swiftly from point to point, and be present always at the focus where the greatest number of vital forces unite in their purest energy?

To burn always with this hard, gemlike flame, to maintain this ecstasy, is success in life.[14]

Under the influence of Basil's adoring picture and Lord Henry's aesthetic philosophy, urging him to "give form to every feeling, expression to every thought, and reality to every dream" because "the only way to get rid of a temptation is to yield to it" (20), Dorian begins to experience a new permissiveness and curious sensations, or, echoing Pater, "pulses":

He was dimly conscious that entirely fresh influences were at work within him. Yet they seemed to him to have come really from himself. The few words that Basil's friend had said to him—words spoken by chance, no doubt, and with willful paradox in them—had touched some secret cord that had never been touched before, but that he felt was now vibrating and throbbing to curious pulses. (19)

The erotic nature of these "curious pulses" and of Dorian's "secret cord" becomes clear precisely because it goes unnamed and thus becomes *the* open secret.[15] (The word "secret" appears fifty times in the novel, twenty-nine times in the first ten chapters alone. At the level of the novel then, too, queerness registers by the very refusal to say what is nonetheless communicated through repetition, connotative accrual, and associative signification.[16]) The result is at once an extravagant atmosphere of interpretive possibility and yet a strong sense of the likelihood of a single, displaced referent: *the* secret of homosexuality.

The secret of the painting is, of course, at first Basil's secret. Thus, the erotic content of the secret emerges, as well, in the context of the artist's not wanting to exhibit the painting because he has "put too much of [himself] into it," that it "told too much" (98)—"the secret of [his] own soul" (8). And it becomes clear in the context of Basil's story of meeting Dorian at a party, an originary scene in which he uses some of the same loaded language of "curiosity," tinged perhaps by the fear of a recurrence of past experience:

> I suddenly became conscious that some one was looking at me. I turned
> half-way round, and saw Dorian Gray for the first time. When our eyes met,
> I felt that I was growing pale. A curious sensation of terror came over me. I
> knew that I had come face to face with someone whose mere personality was
> so fascinating that, if I allowed it to do so, it would absorb my whole nature, my
> whole soul, my very art itself. (9)

Initiated by Dorian's gaze in this account, although without any clear sense of intention or agency (the phrases "I suddenly became conscious" and "when our eyes met" both echo the agentless construction of "there came through the open door" in the novel's opening line), the seduction is at least partially successful. Dorian does agree to sit for Basil, although the artist's "curious sensation of terror" portends trouble; indeed, this moment exemplifies the merging of the language of Aesthetic transformation and Gothic horror that will soon mark the novel as a whole. But Dorian, for the moment, is simply awakened to new sensations and new possibilities. His education in himself—his self-discovery and development—puts the novel's beginning chapters squarely, if somewhat ironically, in the Bildungsroman tradition.

To realize that particular self, however, Dorian must lead an increasingly double life. After he is unable to sustain his infatuation for the young actress Sibyl Vane—or at least for the heterosexual fantasy of the roles she plays on stage—Dorian cruelly rejects her when the mask cracks. In a parody of the stereotyped romance plot, she only knows him as "Prince Charming." She kills herself, leading him to notice for the first time a distortion in his image in the portrait, which Dorian now learns "held the secret of his life, and told his story" (79). Thus begins the shift in the narrative from a highly saturated, intersubjective world of homoerotic rivalries to a paranoid, prescriptive, zero-sum game of mirroring, a movement that the encroaching Gothic story of the picture will bring about and, in seeming to resolve itself, bring the novel to an end. A sign of the coming foreclosure of the desire awakened in the novel's opening scene is also present, and it too involves a transposition into a different artistic genre and a screen—literally, this time. To hide the newly discovered mark, Dorian draws an old gilt Spanish screen in front of the altered picture, which was to "bear the burden of his shame" and to become to him "the most magical of mirrors" (90, 91). Wilde writes: "As it had revealed to him his own body, so it would reveal to him his own soul" (91).

Here we enter the shadow theater of the Gothic. The fact that Dorian's screen is Spanish and not Japanese is significant in that it signals a formal distance between Dorian and Wilde's narrator. The operation that the reference to the Japanese screen performs at the level of the narrative—to suspend and redirect the flamboyant display of the opening scene just before the introduction of Dorian's "extraordinary personal beauty" in the all-male space of the studio (5)—is similar to that of the Spanish screen for Dorian within the plot: to screen the illicit. But Wilde's choice of the Japanese screen is much more self-conscious and knowing (not to mention in vogue stylistically, in queer artistic circles, in 1890), whereas Dorian's Spanish screen is old and, in invoking the Continent, Catholicism, and the Gothic tradition instead of the latest fashion, suggests a critical distance between the story of Dorian's degeneration and the larger narrative's more complicated multiform construction. That is, Dorian is completely invested in the overdetermined Gothic degeneration story, but Wilde signals here that the novel is not, nor should we be as readers. Just as the description of a queer Eden in London is flattened, abstracted, and rendered opaque by the metaphor of the Japanese screen in the novel's opening scene, the Aesthetic self-development narrative of the book's first half is similarly interrupted and transformed by a screen of a different artistic order. This time the screen is not a metaphor but rather makes up a somewhat clichéd part of the diegetic plot—the old Spanish screen that a panicked Dorian pulls in front of his portrait to hide the first sign of his shame and the picture's magical properties. A crucial meta-critical awareness can be seen to issue from this subtle distinction, namely, that Dorian's model of moral panic is not equal to Wilde's more strategic manipulations of genres and narrative point of view. For Dorian tries to hide the signs of his transgression completely, but Wilde makes his palpable and at least intermittently visible. Whereas the queer project inspired by Sedgwick and others has largely been to situate *The Picture of Dorian Gray* within "a cross-section of inaugural discourses of homo/heterosexuality" present in 1890 and to explore the tensions and contradictions that "have set the terms for modern homosexual identity," in what follows I focus on Wilde's blending and careful manipulation of available and seemingly opposed genres, on which the novel crucially depends for its meanings and effects, and how this shapes Wilde's strategic queer dissidence—at the level of the storytelling in addition to the story told.[17] That Wilde's earliest thinking about these genres was firmly rooted in transnational sources and developed into a full-fledged transnational Decadence is the subject of the individual chapters that follow.

"The Hiding Must Be Seen": Form's Ghost Effects

Chapter 11 of *Dorian Gray*, an extensive catalogue of Dorian's increasingly decadent obsessions that divides the novel into two halves, marks the decisive shift from queer Bildungsroman to Gothic degeneration plot, from what must be screened to the screen. There are elements of both throughout, of course, but in the early chapters the Gothic remains as faint as London's "dim roar," "the bourdon note of a distant organ" (5); and, in the later chapters, the self-development narrative would seem to give over completely to that of the paranoid Gothic. Yet, unlike Dorian's panicked and more conventional form of total concealment, Wilde's multiform screen of hybrid genres registers "fantastic shadows" of what goes on in this murky background. Indeed, at the level of the novel chapter 11 works much like the tussore-silk curtains of the novel's opening set piece; it too redirects the reader's gaze away from a palpable and increasingly conspicuous contemporary queerness and toward the relative safety of a backward-looking Aestheticism, all the while registering the ghost effects that overlay it and that appear nonetheless.

The chapter is long and temporally disorienting—eighteen years are compressed into roughly as many pages—further designating a shift out of the modes of realism and coming-of-age and into melodrama, horror, and the supernatural. Dorian, supposedly "poisoned" (124) by the yellow book Lord Henry gives him, now devotes himself to the study of beautiful things, in search of nourishment and comfort: "He had mad hungers that grew more ravenous as he fed them" (109). Meanwhile, he makes something of a spectacle of himself: "Curious stories became current about him"; "men would whisper to each other in corners, or pass him with a sneer, or look at him with cold searching eyes, as though they were determined to discover his secret" (120). Perfumes, musical instruments, jewels, embroideries, and ecclesiastical vestments: all become for Dorian a means of escape. The following description elucidates my argument by recasting the novel's opening scene and bears quotation in full:

> For these treasures, and everything that he collected in his lovely house, were to be to him means of forgetfulness, modes by which he could escape, for a season, from the fear that seemed to him at times to be almost too great to be

borne. Upon the walls of the lonely locked room where he had spent so much of his boyhood, he had hung with his own hands the terrible portrait whose changing features showed him the real degradation of his life, and in front of it had draped the purple-and-gold pall as a *curtain*. For weeks he would not go there, would forget the hideous painted thing, and get back his light heart, his wonderful joyousness, his passionate absorption in mere existence. Then, suddenly, some night he would creep out of the house, go down to dreadful places near Blue Gate Fields, and stay there, day after day, until he was driven away. On his return he would sit in front of the picture, sometimes loathing it and himself, but filled, at other times, with that pride of individualism that is half the fascination of sin, and smiling with secret pleasure at the misshapen *shadow* that had to bear the burden that should have been his own. (119; emphasis added)

Here the "misshapen shadow" of the "hideous painted thing" beneath the concealing shroud recalls the terms and the operation of the novel's opening scene. Like the tussore-silk curtain screening the "birds in flight" in Basil's studio, the pall that Dorian drapes over the artist's adoring portrait both hides and designates—there, as here, in shadow form—what verges on but cannot fully appear. (And like the old Spanish screen's difference from the Japanese *byōbu*, the vaguely ecclesiastical pall that Dorian uses to cover the picture contrasts sharply with the more modern, translucent, and cosmopolitan Indian silk of the narrative's opening description, driving an additional wedge between Dorian's and the narrator's perspectives.) Similarly, at the formal level, the generic shift to the Gothic story of the painting's magical transformation both hides and registers the queer self-development narrative, a canny use of uncanny generic devices. As if to call attention to this, the operative phrase from the novel's emblematic opening scene—"fantastic shadows"—returns to mark the end of the relationship between Dorian and Basil. As the two men ascend the stairs to view the disfigured portrait in the climactic scene in which Dorian stabs Basil to death, "the lamp cast fantastic shadows on the wall and staircase" (130). This repetition marks the distance from the opening scene's intersubjective cosmopolitan-pagan-queer Eden, which, in having been rendered a shameful secret, is shown to have led via its repression to a kind of monomaniacal Inferno instead.

Dorian's degeneration in the Gothic half of the novel thus recuperates the transgressive Paterian half back into the moralizing late-Victorian norms that naturalized male heterosexuality. The blending of genres, then, was no mere accident or failed experiment but rather a highly self-conscious (and still rather risky) response to contemporary publication practices and laws the likes of which had just sent Zola's English translator to jail for three months, in 1889, for obscenity. (Ironically, it was the pages of the *Lippincott's* version of *Dorian Gray* that Edward Carson would use to cross-examine Wilde in 1895, making much of the revisions Wilde made to the book version in response to the public outrage that the *Lippincott's* edition caused; little did Carson know that the purging and revision of the novel's most salacious passages had begun earlier, in the manuscript, as we will see.) Indeed, for very practical reasons, Wilde's attempt to articulate the experience of homoerotic desire in *Dorian Gray* was forced to seem *not* to be what it was, or at least "Paterian" Wilde had to appear to be eclipsed by the more Continental "Gothic" Wilde. And yet that experience is communicated nonetheless—as is, importantly, in the novel's formal components, the *strategy*—to Wilde himself and to others. Contrary to the sense that the Gothic paranoia completely overtakes the queerness of the book's opening chapters, the novel never quite surrenders or resolves its various formal approaches; rather, it uses them, artfully and strategically.

The complicated operation *The Picture Dorian Gray* performs—to make visible the shadow desires it also screens—is something like what Roland Barthes writes about the complexities of hiding *tout court*:

> Yet to hide a passion totally (or even to hide, more simply, its excess) is inconceivable: not because the human subject is too weak, but because passion is in essence made to be seen: the hiding must be seen: *I want you to know that I am hiding something from you*, that is the active paradox I must resolve: *at one and the same time* it must be known and not known: I want you to know that I don't want to show my feelings: that is the message I address to the other. *Larvatus prodeo*: I advance pointing to my mask: I set a mask upon my passion, but with a discreet (and wily) finger I designate this mask.[18]

Human subject, passion, active paradox, mask: it is still true, as Richard Ellmann claimed in 1968, that Wilde "laid the basis for many critical positions which are still debated in much the same terms, and which we like to attribute to more ponderous names."[19] Before Sedgwick, Thomas Mann and André Gide compared Wilde with Nietzsche, and Ellmann added Barthes's name to the list. As a multiform work, *Dorian Gray* is not simply an anticipatory or postmodernist text, however; reading its formal innovations in terms of the artistic and philosophical movements that followed it is tempting but makes too little of its experimental edge. Taking up Ellmann's cue, Jonathan Dollimore has argued convincingly that Wilde "prefigures" elements of modernism and postmodernism while "remaining importantly different from—and not just obviously prior to—both."[20] Wilde's critique is characterized, in contrast with modernism, not by angst but by "something reminiscent of Barthes's *jouissance*," and, unlike some versions of postmodernism, it "includes an acute political awareness and often an uncompromising political commitment."[21] Indeed, part of what counts as political in Wilde's only novel is to be found in the experimental form that it takes. With a discreet and wily finger, Wilde designates his mask—the hiding of the passion that cannot but must be seen—by way of *Dorian Gray*'s conspicuous mixing of genres. In its formal construction—its meaningful combination of literary conventions from a wide variety of traditions—the novel points to a presence without an image, only shadows.

Thus, the opening scene of *The Picture of Dorian Gray* can be seen to provide important cues for reading the novel as a whole and for developing new perspectives on Wilde's queer formalism. An excitement and a recognition of queer desire, interrupted by a screening of the illicit, followed by a strategic redirection that both succeeds in closing down desire and yet registers its shadow traces: for the novel as a whole, the hybrid generic construction achieves what in the opening set piece the introduction of the medium of the Japanese screen achieves for Wilde's narrator. By contrast, Dorian's archaic and rather un-Aesthetic Spanish screen and purple-and-gold pall signal a difference between his own investment in the Gothic degeneration story and the narrative's more complicated operation. This view of Wilde's blending of available literary genres across diverse traditions indeed demonstrates that formalism need not be beholden to "the humanistic, moral imperatives of the New Criticism," as Eric Savoy, Caroline Levine, and others have rightly argued.[22] Instead, it can usefully be seen to entail historical forces such as those that Regenia Gagnier's work on Wilde has explored, including the social institutions "in which art forms are developed and distributed," as well as Wilde's "manipulations" of the Victorian public through the use of ostensibly divergent formal components: melodrama and satire in the social comedies, as Gagnier suggests, as well as the Bildungsroman and the Gothic in the novel.[23] It is to the marketplace of Victorian publishing and to queer political critique that such formalism ultimately takes us.

"~~There Was Love in Every Line~~": Revision and the Politics of Form
Dorian Gray's publication history offers crucial additional evidence for the novel's tricky manipulations of both contemporary ideology and conventional novel form. Building on Donald Lawler's work on the novel's multiple versions beginning in the 1970's, several recent editions of the novel have made its history of extensive revision more legible and accessible than ever, namely Joseph Bristow's comprehensive variorum edition for Oxford University Press (2005) and Nicholas Frankel's annotated, "uncensored" edition for Harvard University Press (2011). The revision history on display in these editions makes clear two additional and related points about Wilde's queer formalism. First, the strategic use of genres that was part of the work's original design was not initially enough to get the novel published in its original form in 1890; importantly, numerous local deletions and changes were also necessary. Second, in responding to public outrage over the already censored *Lippincott's* version, Wilde quietly deepened his commitment to a strategy of formal hybridity, adding more genre bending, not less, in remaking his magazine story into a stand-alone work of art that would be recognizable and marketable to a contemporary audience in 1891. Working in the opposite direction of the deletions and censorings, this form of revision involved the insertion of new chapters providing more depth of background to Dorian's character, heterosexual family melodrama, and social satire, thus rounding out the queer edges of the original work's more sharply binary hybrid form pitting Bildungsroman self-development against Gothic degeneration. Not only did Wilde use a strategy of multiform construction, then, he also actively deployed an iterative series of constrained, pragmatic formal choices in relation to the contemporary expectations and responses of novel readers, adding an element of textual instability and shape-shifting on the tortuous path to publication that characterized much queer writing of the mid- to late nineteenth century on both sides of the Atlantic.[24]

Wilde indeed had a difficult time getting his only novel published. That the initial strategy of using the Gothic to cover and to seem to condemn the queerer aspects of Dorian's aesthetic education had to be supplemented by a cascading series of editorial concessions and by the novelization of what had essentially been a short story or novella lends further support to the view of the novel as a formal achievement. Indeed, the historical contingencies related to Victorian sexual norms shaped the novel's publication at every level.

This Number Contains a Complete Novel,

THE PICTURE OF DORIAN GRAY.

By OSCAR WILDE.

JULY, 1890.

LIPPINCOTT'S

MONTHLY MAGAZINE.

CONTENTS.

		PAGE
THE PICTURE OF DORIAN GRAY	Oscar Wilde	1-100
A UNIT (Poem)	Elizabeth Stoddard	101
THE CHEIROMANCY OF TO-DAY	Ed. Heron-Allen	102
ECHOES (Poem)	Curtis Hall	110
KEELY'S CONTRIBUTIONS TO SCIENCE	C. J. Bloomfield-Moore	111
ROUND-ROBIN TALKS, II.	J. M. Stoddart	124
CONTEMPORARY BIOGRAPHY: SENATOR INGALLS	J. M. Stoddart	141
WAIT BUT A DAY (Poem)	Rose Hawthorne Lathrop	149
A DEAD MAN'S DIARY, xii., xiii.		150
NIGHT (Sonnet)	William C. Newsam	153
THE INDISSOLUBILITY OF MARRIAGE { I.—Elizabeth R. Chapman		154
{ II.—George T. Bettany		155
A PRIMROSE (Poem)	Emily Hickey	157
THE SICK SETTLER, I.	John Lawson	159

PRICE ONE SHILLING.

London: WARD, LOCK AND CO., Salisbury Square, E.C.
Philadelphia: J. B. LIPPINCOTT Co.

All rights reserved.]

Front cover of the July 1890 issue of *Lippincott's Monthly Magazine.* © The British Library Board, Eccles 396

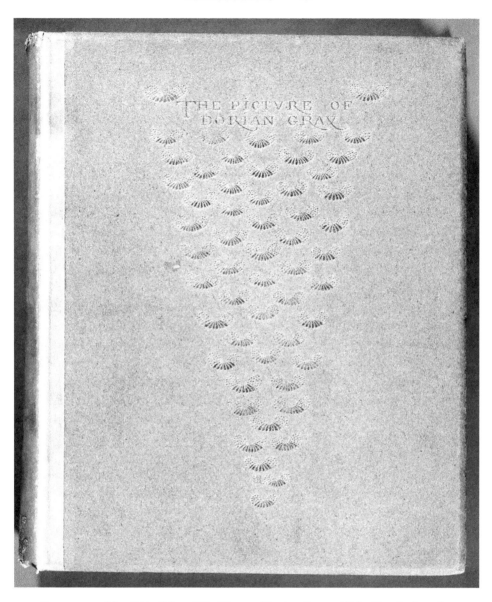

Front cover of the 1891 edition of *The Picture of Dorian Gray*, published by Ward, Lock & Co. HEW 12.10.15, Houghton Library, Harvard University

To review, briefly, what we call *The Picture of Dorian Gray* actually has five different textual versions or "faces": (1) a presumably lost first draft; (2) the 1890 fair-copy holograph manuscript, currently located at the Morgan Library; (3) the 1890 typescript, which was copied from the holograph manuscript—

at Miss Dickens's Typewriting Office in the Strand (run by none other than Charles Dickens's granddaughter Ethel)—currently at the Clark Library, UCLA; (4) the *Lippincott's* publication, produced from the typescript; and (5) the expanded and revised 1891 book publication with six new chapters and the famous "marigold" cover and design by Charles Ricketts.[25] The stark contrast between the popular magazine cover and the elegant Ricketts design further suggests the extent of the transformation Wilde undertook in response to the earlier story's scandalous publication.

Less well known but extremely significant is that, according to late-Victorian publishing practices, both the holograph manuscript and the typescript became the possession of *Lippincott's,* and so Wilde produced the revised book version from offprints of the heavily censored magazine copy, suggesting that he did not so much approve of the alterations to the *Lippincott's* text in incorporating them into the 1891 book as he did not have access to the originals.[26]

As even a cursory comparison makes clear, in the earlier versions of the novel Wilde originally aimed for a surprisingly more daring homoerotic text. Yet before Wilde's editor at *Lippincott's,* J. M. Stoddart, excised the most scandalous passages from the original typescript, Wilde appears to have wanted to dial back the homoeroticism to a degree, as evidenced by the changes he made in his own hand in the Morgan manuscript. These changes are by now well documented, but they bear a quick examination in the context of Wilde's formal circumventions: the novel's censorship has justly garnered much attention, but when it is seen in connection with the further genre mixing brought about by the addition of six new chapters in 1891, a clearer picture emerges of both the extent of the opposition Wilde faced and the formal ingenuity of his response. Early references to Dorian's "beauty," for instance, are toned down to the somewhat less enthusiastic "good looks," and Basil no longer grasps Lord Henry's hand as originally planned, a gesture that perhaps suggests a prior relationship between the two.[27] Basil's "passion" is tempered accordingly, now merely "feeling," and "pain" becomes the more abstract "perplexity" (*CW* 7). Wilde excises more physical touching between the men in the account Basil gives to Lord Henry of Dorian brushing against him while he paints, having first changed "cheek" to "hand" before scratching out the whole thing:

> "It is one of the best things I have ever done. And why is it so? Because, while I was painting it, Dorian Gray sat beside me, and, as he leaned across to look at

"*Fantastic Shadows*"   31

it, his <cheek?> /hand?\ just <brushed my cheek> /touched my hand\. The world becomes young to me when I hold his hand, and when I see him, the centuries yield all up their secrets!" (*CW* 13)

Indeed, Basil's love of Dorian receives the most attention in Wilde's early self-censorings, as it will later with Stoddart's changes to the *Lippincott's* typescript. Consider these choice passages, each of which required additional changes for the novel-length 1891 version:

"Then why won't you exhibit his portrait?" [Lord Henry asks] "Because I have put into it all the extraordinary romance of which, of course, I have never dared to speak to him. /He will never know anything about it.\ But the world would <might> guess it<.> /, and\ where there is really love, they would see something evil, where there is spiritual passion they would suggest something vile. I will not bare my soul to their shallow, prying eyes." [In the 1891 text, "all the extraordinary romance" becomes "some expression of artistic idolatry."] (*CW* 13–14, 177)

"As a rule, he is charming to me, and we walk home together from the club arm in arm, or sit in the studio and talk of a thousand things. Now and then, however, he is horribly thoughtless, and seems to take a real delight in giving me pain. I can quite understand it. I can imagine myself doing it. But not to him, not that I did it. Once or twice we have been away together. Then I have /had\ him all to myself. I am horribly jealous of him of course. I never let him talk to me of the people he knows. I like to isolate him from the rest of life, and to think that he absolutely belongs to me. He does not, I know. But it gives me pleasure to think [?] that he does. Harry! I have given this <boy> /young man\ my whole soul <?>. /seems to take a real delight in giving me pain. Then I feel, Harry, that I have given away my whole soul to someone\ /who\ treats it as if it were a flower to put in his coat [. . .]." [In the 1891 text, ", and we walk home together from the club arm in arm, or" is also deleted.] (*CW* 14, 178)

After these self-censorings in Wilde's own hand, more serious cuts were made by Stoddart in the typescript used to prepare the text for publication. The following examples are representative of the kind of purging that Stoddart undertook, including the deletion of a sentence that describes what Alex Ross has aptly called "the ancient ritual of cruising":[28]

Where he went to, he hardly knew. He remembered wandering through dimly-lit streets with gaunt black-shadowed archways and evil-looking houses. Women with hoarse voices and harsh laughter had called after him. Drunkards had reeled by cursing, and chattering to themselves like monstrous apes. ~~A man with curious eyes had suddenly peered into his face, and then dogged him with stealthy footsteps, passing and repassing him many times.~~ (*CW* 65)

Sometimes the changes were minor but the alteration of meaning quite profound:

"It is quite true that I have worshipped you with far more romance of feeling than a man ~~should ever give~~ usually gives to a friend. Somehow, I have never loved a woman. I suppose I never had time." [In the 1891 text, these lines are deleted.] (*CW* 90, 264)

"It is my masterpiece. But, as I worked at it, every flake and film of color seemed to me to reveal my secret. ~~There was love in every line, and in every touch there was passion.~~ I grew afraid that the world would know of my idolatry. I felt, Dorian, that I had told too much." [In the 1891 text, "told too much" is followed by "that I had put too much of myself into it."] (*CW* 91, 265)

"There was something ~~infinitely tragic in a romance that was at once so passionate and so sterile~~ tragic in a friendship so colored by romance." (*CW* 93)

Thus, by removing or rewriting any reference to any late-night encounters with "curious eyes" or "stealthy footsteps" or to a "romance" that was as "passionate" as it was "sterile," Stoddart obscured and made less physical the relationships between the novel's men, presumably in order to avoid the threat of scandal.[29] As these and the many other examples made widely available by the excellent recent editions of the novel show, the multiple versions of *Dorian Gray* tell a much broader story about the Victorian social norms that shaped the novel's composition and publication at every stage. Wilde's formal maneuvers—screening queer desire yet rendering it still discernable in shadow form—nonetheless required numerous further local censorings, a fact that speaks to just how far and how boldly the novel's formal innovations initially dared to go.

Beyond these local edits to the *Lippincott's* story, the revisions for the 1891 book-length version entailed even larger-scale formal interventions and restructurings. These changes have received far less attention—in part, because they are harder to see—but they underscore the extent to which Wilde relied on genre mixing as a formal strategy. Indeed, Wilde responded to criticism of the original hybrid story with further hybridization and genre shifting: the failure of the original formal strategy was that its deployment was insufficiently robust. In novelizing the *Lippincott's* story, Wilde had to meet contemporary readers' expectations of novel form as well as preempt any further scandal. The original strategy of blending formal approaches can be seen here to have expanded exponentially, across the entire span of the narrative. The added six chapters—chapters 3, 5, and 15 through 18 (the original chapter 13 became two chapters, 19 and 20, in the 1891 revision)—flesh out the somewhat schematic binary hybrid of the Bildungsroman and the Gothic in the *Lippincott's* story. These chapters not only lengthen the narrative but greatly expand Wilde's use of the additional genres of romance, melodrama, and satire, thus diluting the far starker, binary power of the original story and frequently shifting it into a more obviously heterosexual register. As the rest of this study demonstrates, to achieve this effect Wilde drew on a transnational archive that has been obscured by a critical tendency to focus on the novel's more immediate and proximate contexts of Victorian Aestheticism and French Decadence. Less blatant than the local edits and censorings of the earlier versions of the novel, these formal-generic changes were ultimately successful in providing additional cover and have tended to go largely unremarked precisely because they are so canny.

For instance, in the 1891 revision Wilde added the romantic story of Dorian's origins, which as we will see in chapter 2 draws heavily on a version of the early nineteenth-century Gothic in Ireland. He now becomes the son of the extraordinarily beautiful Margaret Devereux (a surname that recalls the plantation of Ireland by Walter Devereux in 1573 with the support of Elizabeth I) and a "penniless young fellow," who was killed a few months after the marriage in a duel orchestrated, according to rumor, by Dorian's angry grandfather. His mother returned, we are told, but she never spoke to her father again. She gave birth to Dorian before dying within a year, leaving him an inheritance that includes the country estate Selby that figures in the later intercalated chapters. The story of Dorian's parentage stirs in Lord Henry the sense of "a strange, almost modern romance":

> A beautiful woman risking everything for a mad passion. A few wild weeks
> of happiness cut short by a hideous, treacherous crime. Months of voiceless
> agony, and then a child is born in pain. The mother snatched away by death,
> the boy left to solitude and the tyranny of an old and loveless man. Yes; it was
> an interesting background. It posed the lad, made him more perfect as it were.
> Behind every exquisite thing that existed, there was something tragic. (33)

This background provides Dorian with a past and the glimpse of the kind of deeper psychological portrait that was conventional in longer-form realist fiction of the time but completely lacking in the original 1890 story. In a particularly revealing moment, underscored by Wilde's use of free indirect discourse to merge the narration with Lord Henry's consciousness at "Yes; it was an interesting background" in the above passage, we are told that the romantic story "posed the lad." It makes him "more perfect" for Lord Henry, who is thinking in terms of depth rather than of surfaces now (*"Behind* every exquisite thing, there was something tragic") and already of the mixing of genres, romance and tragedy. But it also makes Dorian a more perfect novel character, now complete with a profile and a romantic past of his own.

Wilde further expanded the original magazine story by providing more background and prominence to Sibyl Vane's working-class family, closely linking the main plot of the queer-rivalry-turned-Gothic-mirroring story to the more conventional heterosexual melodrama of the Vane family subplot. " 'Mother, mother, I am so happy!' whispered the girl, burying her face in the lap of the faded, tired looking woman, who with back turned to the shrill intrusive light, was sitting in the one-arm chair that their dingy sitting-room contained," begins the new chapter 5, after Dorian, or, as she knows him, "Prince Charming," has proposed (53). The stark contrast of economic backgrounds depicted in this new chapter is compounded by the disparity between Sibyl's romantic fantasies ("what does money matter? Love is more than money") and Mrs. Vane's cynical realism ("Foolish child! foolish child!"), and the narrative descriptions become decidedly melodramatic: "The waving of crooked, false-jewelled fingers gave grotesqueness to the words" (53). When Sibyl's coarse brother James, who is about to leave for Australia, senses the danger of her position, we get this description: "This young dandy who was making love to her could mean her no good. He was a gentleman, and he hated him for that, hated him through some curious race-instinct for which he could not account, and which for that reason was all the more dominant within him" (58). The desperation of Mrs. Vane's urgency to marry her daughter to someone whose name is yet unknown and the heightened emotion of James Vane's "curious race-instinct" and sense of impending doom shifts this added chapter into the register of melodrama. The chapter crescendos and the link between the main plot and James Vane's revenge plot is cemented when he swears: "If he ever does you any wrong I shall kill him" (60). He repeats the spiteful words ("They cut the air like a dagger. The people round began to gape") and then once again, in front of their mother, who has just confessed to being unwed to his father, also a highly connected gentleman: "If this man wrongs my sister, I will find out who he is, track him down, and kill him like a dog. I swear it" (62). The genre shifting of the added Vane family melodrama and the implausible coincidences of James Vane's revenge plot (a late-night chance meeting in the East End, a deus-ex-machina hunting accident) lengthen the narrative but also work to blend with and soften the comparatively stark generic hybrid of the original magazine story, a formal strategy that evidently required further obfuscation of the illicit sexuality at its center.

Perhaps most notably, however, Wilde greatly expanded the element of social satire in revising the magazine story into a novel. This too works to deescalate and redirect attention from the formal evasions underway in the intertwining self-development and Gothic plots and further elaborates the novel's multiform construction. In addition to the expansions of the romantic story of Dorian's origins and the gritty, working-class Vane family melodrama, the "great aristocratic art of doing absolutely nothing" is repeatedly lampooned with the introduction of Lord Henry's bachelor uncle, Lord Fermor, and his aunt, Lady Agatha. These new characters and their dinner party guests provide a predictably earnest ground for Lord Henry's praise of folly and philosophy of pleasure, including newly added lines such as these:

"Humanity takes itself too seriously. It is the world's original sin." (37)

"To get back one's youth, one has merely to repeat one's follies." (37)

"Nowadays most people die of a sort of creeping common sense, and discover when it is too late that the only things one never regrets are one's mistakes." (38)

The startling compression, relentless pace, and rapier wit of the dialogue that will soon mark Wilde's West End comedies, and that derives, in part, from a countertradition of English epigrammatic writing to be explored in chapter 5, can be seen in many of the sections added to the 1891 novel. Consider, for example, this exchange, which appears in sharp contrast to both the language of aesthetic self-development and the sense of Gothic horror:

"We are talking about poor Dartmoor, Lord Henry," cried the Duchess, nodding pleasantly to him across the table. "Do you think he will really marry this fascinating young person?"

"I believe she has made up her mind to propose to him, Duchess."

"How dreadful!" exclaimed Lady Agatha. "Really someone should interfere."

"I am told, on excellent authority, that her father keeps an American dry-goods store," said Sir Thomas Burdon, looking supercilious.

"My uncle has already suggested pork-packing, Sir Thomas."

"Dry-goods! What are American dry-goods?" asked the Duchess, raising her large hands in wonder, and accentuating the verb.

"American novels," answered Lord Henry, helping himself to some quail. (35)

The intercalated chapters thus create the impression of a wider social milieu and a more stinging social commentary. Lighter, humorous touches like these also round out the novel's otherwise quite dark social vision and provide some comic relief within the now-longer narrative arc.

Most importantly, however, the addition of satirical scenes like this one works to appease conventional middle-class novel readers by exploiting their class and national biases, and, in doing so, further trains attention away from the illicit sexuality at the original story's center. Satire is a particularly seductive form in this regard in that it offers a position of perceived superiority from which to laugh, which readers then become loath to relinquish. In the 1891 text, the new satirical scenes help cast the potentially offensive original material in the context of a larger social comedy, a winking irreverence that invites middle-class readers to feel "in" on the laugh and therefore less likely to question—or even remark—any inconvenient particulars. Wilde's inclusion of a joke about American novels performs a similar operation and underscores the point: he especially had ground to make up with the British public, who had been much less tolerant of the transgressions of one of its own than the American public had been of an eccentric foreigner. The joke at American culture's expense can be seen here to purchase a certain measure of British tolerance at a particularly critical moment in the book's history—or at least offer the reassurance that aspersions will be cast all around—precisely by exploiting the self-interest involved in not seeing what else is plainly there.

This function of the added satire as formal screen is also apparent late in the novel when we are returned to an aristocratic setting in the midst of the novel's gruesome climax. At the end of chapter 14, Alan Campbell, under threat of blackmail for an unnamed crime, is forced to decompose Basil's dead body. Chapter 15, the first of the chapters added to the end of the book, then suddenly opens in Lady Narborough's drawing room, returning us to a satirical comedy of manners and, for Dorian, "the terrible pleasure of a double life"—another of the novel's phrases that perfectly combines the language of Aesthetic feeling and a Gothic sense of dread, now blended with bitingly satirical wit (147). At Lady Narborough's, French phrases fly, as do jokes about rumor-mongering ("'It is perfectly monstrous,' [Lord Henry] said, 'the way people go about nowadays saying things against one behind one's back that are absolutely and entirely true'"), marriages of convenience ("A man can be happy with any woman as long as he does not love her"), and limiting oneself in one's pleasures ("Moderation is a fatal thing. Enough is as bad as a meal. More than enough is as good as a feast") (150–2). Dorian leaves the party, which has operated for readers as a perhaps welcome distraction from a particularly lurid moment in the plot, and goes home to burn Basil's coat and bag in the fire. Thus, even at the level of the plot the added satire momentarily redirects attention away from, and thus prevents complete immersion in, the climax of the Gothic plot.

The next two chapters, also added to the 1891 novel version, repeat this pattern. The seedy opium den, where Dorian meets a former acquaintance-turned-drug-addict whose reputation Dorian has mysteriously ruined, and where he narrowly escapes James Vane, bent on revenge (chapter 16), leads to repartee between Lord Henry and the Duchess of Monmouth at Dorian's country estate, Selby Royal, before a skulking James Vane is accidentally killed (chapters 17–18), thus preparing the way for the novel's famous conclusion in which Dorian tries to destroy the "one bit of evidence against him," the picture, but in stabbing it only kills himself (chapters 19–20). Wilde's addition of social satire to the book-length version therefore not only provides comic relief; it also plays an important role in the longer narrative's structuring, and particularly in the displacing of some of the homoerotic energies of the magazine version's more starkly binary structure onto the more class-based tensions and critiques of British imperialism and national character brought about by the new chapters. Those chapters' dilation of Dorian's aristocratic background and social milieu and of the working-class Vane family subplot draw more strongly on the genres of romance, melodrama, and satire to create something more like a full-fledged novel than a sharply drawn but somewhat schematic and two-dimensional horror story. Indeed, the more substantive formal revisions of the *Lippincott's* text show that the novelization of Wilde's earlier, more archetypal magazine story was an extension and an elaboration of the original strategy to create a new hybrid form that could both hold the story he wanted to tell and, crucially, still be published. Importantly, the later inclusion of elements of romance, melodrama, and satire to rework the starker, queerer opposition of Aesthetic transformation and Gothic degeneration in the original story is a difference of degree, not of kind.

By expanding the current understanding of sexuality in *The Picture of Dorian Gray* to include the sexuality *of* the novel—both its fundamental multiform construction and its history of strategic revisions—I hope to have shown the importance of the novel's formal relations with contemporary ideology and publishing practices to a full appreciation of its dissident message and of its place within the histories of sexuality and the novel. The 1890 *Lippincott's* version might be the more cohesive, better work artistically (and, pedagogically, it is essential that students explore it), but the expanded 1891 book version ultimately tells the fullest story about what could and could not be published in late-Victorian Britain and America, and how to circumvent dominant ideology. As we will see in the chapters that follow, a crucial and underappreciated aspect of this story is the extent to which this formal achievement drew on sources and traditions beyond the usual orbits of Victorian Aestheticism and French Decadence.

PART TWO

INHERITED WORLDS

CHAPTER TWO

Gothic Legacies

Melmoth, Ireland, and the Specter of Imperial History

There was something fascinating in this son of Love and Death.
Oscar Wilde, *The Picture of Dorian Gray* (34)

One version of the story that this book tells begins with the romantic tale of Dorian's parents and the suggestion of an Anglo-Irish heritage: his father was killed in a duel by a mercenary hired by his beautiful mother's aristocratic father, whose historically resonant surname, Devereux, is that of one of the first colonial settlers in Ireland. The conspicuous background of "this son of Love and Death," a sobriquet for Dorian that echoes the title of a 1799 Francisco de Goya caprice of the same subject, would seem to point to important contexts in the history of colonial Ireland and, perhaps more unexpectedly, imperial Spain.[1]

Wilde admired Goya and saw himself in the tradition of the great outsider artists of the past, as we know from *De Profundis* (1897), where he defended his notorious practice of "feasting with panthers" and entertaining "the brightest of gilded snakes," blackmailers and felons: "To entertain them was an astounding adventure; Dumas *père*, Cellini, Goya, Edgar Allan Poe, or Baudelaire would have done just the same."[2] The reference is oblique but reflects a growing interest in Goya in the 1890s: the National Gallery in London acquired its first three pieces by the Spanish artist in 1896.[3] The belatedness of the interest in Goya at the National Gallery was undoubtedly a result of the English critic John Ruskin's burning of a copy of *Los Caprichos* (*The Caprices*) out of disgust at their "immorality" in 1872.[4] Yet the links between English and Spanish satire were already well established. Published as an album in 1799, *Los Caprichos* was immediately associated with the genre of eighteenth-century English satirical prints made famous by William Hogarth

Plate 10 from *Los Caprichos*, "El amor y la muerte (Love and death)," 1799 (etching, burnished aquatint, burin), Francisco de Goya (1746–1828). Metropolitan Museum of Art, New York. Gift of M. Knoedler & Co., 1918

and Thomas Rowlandson; like the English prints that they echo, Goya's sardonic etchings were also intended for export.[5] We know, for instance, that there were early English admirers: the antiquarian Francis Douce bequeathed the *Caprichos* to the Bodleian Library in 1834, well before Ruskin's fiery repudiation and Wilde's attendance at Oxford, where he might have first seen them, in the 1870s.[6] The influential artist and poet Dante Gabriel Rossetti, an early London acquaintance of Wilde's who will figure prominently in chapter 3, owned a first edition until his death in 1882.[7] And the hero of Huysmans's influential French novel *Against Nature* (1884) whiles away "the interminable hours" and immerses himself in the artist's "vertiginous scenes," attesting to the "universal admiration" for Goya's etchings among European aesthetes and collectors.[8] The points of possible contact are as various as they are compelling.

As with any origin story, however, this starting point forms only part of a more complicated picture. In the case of Wilde's allusions to empire in the romantic story of Dorian Gray's parentage, that picture comes into sharper focus by way of an intermediary text, a Gothic novel by an Irish Protestant clergyman that reimagines Anglo-Irish history through imaginary contact with Catholic Spain. That clergyman was Wilde's granduncle, Charles Robert Maturin (1780–1824) and the novel, his fifth, *Melmoth the Wanderer* (1820), a text that is routinely associated with Goya's macabre vision and is often illustrated by publishers with his art.[9] Cited by biographers and critics, the links between *Melmoth the Wanderer* and *The Picture of Dorian Gray* nonetheless remain little understood.[10] As this chapter demonstrates, a closer look at Maturin's influence on Wilde affords a critical reappraisal of both authors in light of the imperial history that haunts their texts. Imported and transformed by Wilde, the Gothic of early nineteenth-century Ireland, channeling late eighteenth-century Spain, became newly resonant at the fin de siècle as a highly productive transnational Decadent archive.

Ireland and the British Question: Remembering Imperial History

For many years, critics located *Dorian*'s critique of imperialism in its unmistakable anti-Englishness and anti-Britishness. The quest to recover "the Irish Wilde" in the 1990s promised to bring greater attention to the specifically Irish dimensions of Wilde's writing and of his only novel in particular.[11] This effort, however, took on serious criticism in the following decade, largely on methodological grounds. In his 2000 survey of recent trends in the field, for instance, Ian Small cautioned against "paradigms" that "rely upon highly selective details of the life which in turn are used to instruct us in how to read the works."[12] Bruce Bashford took issue with the strategy of what he called "reasoning by analogy," by which critics "extracted" Irish historical contexts from Wilde's literary texts by a logic of similitude. For example, Mary King's claim that Wilde depicts the East End opium den that Dorian visits as an Irish "shebeen," or unlicensed bar, in order to broaden the novel's interrogation of empire, requires, in Bashford's view, the "tactic" of transposing Orientalism into Celticism.[13] In King's defense, the opium bar is called "Daly's," and it is described as featuring "a tattered green curtain" and looking "as if it had once been a third-rate dancing-saloon," details which seem to invite a layered historical reading rather than a simple analogy (162, 157).[14] Of course, there is a real risk of creating what Richard Haslam, following Small and Bashford, has called "thematic pigeonholes," and of finding all-determining causes in mere contexts.[15] As Henry James once observed to a friend: "Everything Oscar does is a deliberate trap for the literalist."[16]

The work of taking the Irish dimension of Wilde's writing seriously has continued nonetheless, at its best answering Neil Sammells's call not to seek some mythic Irish or Celtic "core" but rather to recognize "alternative identities simultaneously maintained" and to confront the "shifting complexities that define Wilde's work."[17] At a minimum, the relevance of this work can be seen in its having produced yet another line of critique: Éibhear Walshe has persuasively shown that in the past century Irish nationalist discourses and the postcolonial lens have also, inadvertently, distorted perceptions of Wilde's sexuality.[18]

I revisit these past debates to suggest that the colonial contexts by which Wilde introduces the romantic story of Dorian's parentage in chapter 3 of the novel offer a different approach. These contexts work, I argue, not by analogy but by association and accretion—that is, not to reveal what Wilde *is really* talking about when he references Daly's bar or the London docks but rather to keep Ireland and the British question present *as a question*, ever reminding readers that the past that Dorian inherits and seeks to forget is also freighted with generational, national, and imperial history. This strategy becomes especially significant when we consider Wilde's retrospective engagement with the Irish Gothic in light of more recent criticism: in particular, *Dorian Gray*'s echoes of *Melmoth the Wanderer*, a book that Patrick R. O'Malley has convincingly read as part of a tradition of Anglo-Irish writing that attempted to forget the violent colonial past and that I read as a major source for Wilde's novel. This source not only helps explain where some of Wilde's thinking about Irish history and its literary representation came from; it also sets up an interpretation of the novel as staging a canny intervention. In *Dorian*, Wilde put the Gothic mode that he inherited to very different use: not to revise the violent history of Anglo-Irish conquest and Ascendancy but rather to frame the question of what to do with the past as a haunted and haunting problem.

"It Posed the Lad": The Story of Dorian's Parentage

In chapter 3 of *The Picture of Dorian Gray*, Wilde's narrator recounts the mysterious story of Dorian's origins. The narration is conspicuous, in no small part, for its seemingly casual allusions to numerous historical contexts: imperial Spain, US slavery, Irish plantation and famine, and the Belgian exploitation of the Congo. The first of six chapters added to the expanded book version of the novel in 1891, chapter 3 is often understood as part of Wilde's attempt to novelize the story that he had presented in far starker, and arguably more effective, form in *Lippincott's Monthly Magazine* the year before. This new chapter provides Dorian a backstory and so, the conventional thinking goes, a deeper psychological portrait of his character and social background. While this reading is, in a practical sense, no doubt true, the interpolated chapters also allowed Wilde to answer his severest critics; as Haslam has effectively demonstrated, they display "the intensity and the national feeling" of his response to the expressions of anti-Irish sentiments in the press debates about the first edition of the story, references to Swiftian "mental rottenness," for example.[19] While the focus has tended to fall on the scenes of social satire that Wilde added to the novel in order to augment and harshen his critiques of English and British national character, a process that conveniently also served to lower the temperature somewhat on the original story's overt homoeroticism, the romantic tale of Dorian's origins can be understood to work in tandem with Wilde's nationalist counter-critique. And because Dorian's family backstory adds layers of historical meaning to his wish to secrete the past in his portrait, it also bears directly on how we read the novel's central image and theme.

The narration of Dorian's story begins obliquely, with a search for someone who might remember the distant past firsthand. It is a notable moment in a novel seemingly so preoccupied with the desire to forget the deeds of the past and the signs of time's passing:

> At half-past twelve next day Lord Henry Wotton strolled from Curzon Street over to the Albany to call on his uncle, Lord Fermor, a genial if somewhat

> rough-mannered old bachelor, whom the outside world called selfish because it derived no particular benefit from him, but who was considered generous by Society as he fed the people who amused him. His father had been our ambassador at Madrid when Isabella was young and Prim unthought of, but had retired from the diplomatic service in a capricious moment of annoyance on not being offered the Embassy at Paris, a post to which he considered that he was fully entitled by reason of his birth, his indolence, the good English of his dispatches, and his inordinate passion for pleasure. The son, who had been his father's secretary, had resigned along with his chief, somewhat foolishly as was thought at the time, and on succeeding some months later to the title, had set himself to the serious study of the great aristocratic art of doing absolutely nothing. (29)

The satire of aristocratic lassitude and self-satisfaction adds a familiar Wildean irony to the conclusion of this passage; however, this familiarity also risks overshadowing the allusion to Isabella II (1830–1904), the Bourbon queen of Spain from 1833 to 1868, and a less pronounced but more radical suggestion of a political instability at the heart of imperial monarchy: "Prim" refers to Juan Prim (1814–70), a Catalan officer and Spanish military leader who played an important role in Isabella's overthrow in the revolution of 1868. Intensifying the sense of instability in this historical reference is the fact that Isabella's king-consort, Francisco de Asís, was rumored to be gay and not the father of most, if any, of her children. He was also her double-first cousin, meaning both parents of each spouse were also the uncle and the aunt of the other. Tales of the avunculate, indeed: as Eve Sedgwick has memorably argued, aunts and uncles function as important alternative topoi in Wilde's writing, as the "presiding representative[s] of the previous generation," yet a step to the side of what she called the "totemic force of the Oedipal father-son imperative."[20]

Against this backdrop of Lord Henry's uncle's connection with the British diplomatic service, the romantic story of Dorian's parentage unfolds:

> "Mr. Dorian Gray? Who is he?" asked Lord Fermor, knitting his bushy white eyebrows.
>
> "That is what I have come to learn, Uncle George. Or rather, I know who he is. He is the last Lord Kelso's grandson. His mother was a Devereux, Lady Margaret Devereux. I want you to tell me about his mother. What was she like? Whom did she marry? You have known nearly everybody in your time, so you

might have known her. I am very much interested in Mr. Gray at present. I have only just met him."

"Kelso's grandson!" echoed the old gentleman. "Kelso's grandson! . . . Of course. . . . I knew his mother intimately. I believe I was at her christening. She was an extraordinarily beautiful girl, Margaret Devereux, and made all the men frantic by running away with a penniless young fellow—a mere nobody, sir, a subaltern in a foot regiment, or something of that kind. Certainly. *I remember the whole thing* as if it happened yesterday. The poor chap was killed in a duel at Spa a few months after the marriage. There was an ugly story about it. They said Kelso got some rascally adventurer, some Belgian brute, to insult his son-in-law in public—paid him, sir, to do it, paid him—and that the fellow spitted his man as if he had been a pigeon. The thing was hushed up, but, egad, Kelso ate his chop alone at the club for some time afterwards. He brought his daughter back with him, I was told, and she never spoke to him again. Oh, yes; it was a bad business. The girl died, too, died within a year. So she left a son, did she? *I had forgotten that.*" (30–31; emphasis added)

The tension between remembering and forgetting the past is already on view in this remarkable passage, well before Dorian's portrait takes up the burden in chapter 7. Lord Fermor "remember[s] the whole thing as if it happened yesterday," but forgets the key fact that Dorian's mother had a son. Not coincidentally, the passage also resonates with oblique references to colonial history. These allusions, each referring to a type as much as to an individual—"*a* Devereux," "*some* rascally adventurer, *some* Belgian brute," "a mere nobody, sir, a subaltern in a foot regiment, or *something of that kind*"—comprise a constant reminder of the imperial past.

Wilde's choice of the surname "Devereux," for instance, places the story of Dorian's background squarely within colonial context. Walter Devereux, first Earl of Essex (1541–76), established one of the first plantations in Ulster in 1573, with the support of Elizabeth I. His son Robert Devereux served as Chief Secretary for Ireland during the Nine Years' War and had a personal secretary who chronicled his courtly life during the Tudor conquest of Ireland. That personal secretary's name was Sir Henry Wotton (1568–1639), as in Lord Henry Wotton, Dorian's newfound mentor and source of aesthetic inspiration. As Esther Rashkin has shown, Dorian's mother's name yields even more to close reading, and the references to it reverberate throughout the novel, not just in this brief episode in which her tragic story is recounted. For instance, Margaret is from the Latin *margarita* or "pearl," a jewel to which there are sixteen references in the novel, not the least of which is the description of Dorian's appearance at a costume ball as Anne de Joyeuse, Admiral of France, "in a dress covered with five hundred and sixty pearls" (115).[21] He also adorns his ecclesiastical cloak (euphemistically?) with "seed-pearls" (118).[22] The Norman surname "Devereux" also contains the French word *véreux*, meaning "decayed, vile, rotten, corrupt, shameful, debased, defiled"— or, literally, "worm-eaten"—the very terms in which Dorian describes his disfigured portrait throughout the novel.[23] He covers the painting with his grandfather's purple shroud in the old schoolroom that his grandfather built for him, as if it were his birthright to "hide something that had a corruption of its own, worse than the corruption of death itself—something that would breed horrors and yet would never die. What the worm was to the corpse, his sins would be to the painted image on the canvas. They would mar its beauty and eat away its grace. They would defile it and make it shameful" (101).[24] The thematic centrality of the details of the interpolated story of Dorian's background as read by Rashkin and others suggests a more pervasive importance for the seemingly casual references to imperial history. As Mary King has suggestively argued: "The Devereux connection haunts *Dorian Gray*."[25]

We hear much less about Dorian's nameless "subaltern" father, by contrast, but the significance of his role in the story of Dorian's background is just as profound, if not more so. In British military terms dating back to the seventeenth century, a subaltern is a junior officer, literally a subordinate, below the rank of captain and generally among the various grades of lieutenant. Wilde, of course, did not have access to the Marxist and postcolonial meanings that would accrue to this term in the twentieth century via the work of Antonio Gramsci, Gayatri Spivak, and others.[26] But his use of the military sense of a junior officer, "a mere nobody, sir" in the words of the British aristocrat, immediately following an allusion to the Catalan officer who brought about the Spanish queen's deposition, suggests that those later meanings were available, if still inchoate, in figurative associations between rank, class, and nation. The *OED* would seem to confirm this in offering as an early example Horace Walpole's use of "subalterns" for servants in his 1764 *Castle of Otranto*.[27] This usage suggests that the word's portability as a metaphor for all manner of social hierarchies began much earlier and, indeed, in the Gothic mode, not to mention in the underexplored queer antiquarianism that further links Walpole and Wilde. In the romantic story of Dorian's parentage, an acutely Gothic awareness of internecine class relations is, at the very least, surrounded and inflected by references to empire. In addition to the conspicuous choice of the family name Devereux, the details of Spa, a resort town in Belgium, and of the "Belgian brute" who is paid by Dorian's grandfather to kill his father in a duel, would certainly have produced further colonial associations in late nineteenth-century readers, this time to Leopold II's use of mercenaries during Belgium's brutal occupation of the Congo.

Other passing references to empire, and to Ireland and Britain in particular, accumulate elsewhere in this same chapter. At the society lunch that Lord Henry attends at his Aunt Agatha's after leaving his uncle, the discussion turns to the problem of poverty in London's East End, where many Irish fled to escape famine. The novel's association of American and Irish plantations comes into view momentarily right after an extended discussion of the United States, when Lord Henry says that the problem of the East End is "the problem of slavery," as Rashkin and others have noted (37).[28] I would add that another key figure in these satirical society scenes, Mr. Erskine, who bears a Scottish rather than an English surname, is shown to be on familiar terms on this and other topics with the novel's English aristocrats, recalling perhaps that Scottish interests often joined with English interests in the new ruling planter class in Ireland.[29] At the end of chapter 3, Erskine and Lord Henry are shown to be on equal social footing, unlike Dorian's "subaltern" father, when Erskine places his hand on Lord Henry's arm and invites him to drink wine and to expound on his "philosophy of pleasure" on a visit to his country house. Erskine then agrees with Lord Henry's line: "Of all people in the world the English have the least sense of the beauty of literature" (39). An attentive Dorian makes the same gesture of touching Lord Henry's arm before departing with him at the very end of the chapter, and it should be noted that national alliances are never far away in the novel's erotic and class dynamics.

In an ironic and somewhat mysterious twist, the chief historian of Dorian's past, Lord Fermor (a variant of "farmer"?), uses the Irish term "jarvies" for "cabmen" in recounting Dorian's grandfather's mistreatment of the working class, even though the narrator uses "cabman" elsewhere. As Joseph Bristow offers in an explanatory note to the World's Classics Edition, Wilde went out of his way to delete "cabmen" in the manuscript in favor of the Irish expression here (199). Ambiguity remains, however. The narrator states: "Only England could have produced him," suggesting that Lord Fermor is not an Irishman (30). Yet the suggestive substitution was clearly intentional, as the manuscript indicates. Would an Anglo-Irish subject at the time not also be "produced by England," given the asymmetrical colonial relationship? And might that subject have been even more inclined to perform (or to parody?) Englishness in order to compensate for a perceived otherness and/or to display a steadfast loyalty? The Welsh journalist Gareth Jones would remark several decades later in an interview with the Irish unionist politician and first Prime Minister of Northern Ireland, Lord Craigavon, "that Ulster characteristic which makes Ulster-men more British than the British."[30] The second part of Wilde's narrator's assessment seems as important as the first: "Only England could have produced him, and he always said that the country was going to the dogs. His principles were out of date, but there was a good deal to be said for his prejudices" (30). Whether or not Lord Fermor has an Anglo-Irish connection, his use of "jarvies" is a curious detail and adds yet another ambiguity about social background to a novel that is full of them. Precisely because this curious substitution does not provide a clear explanation and so remains oblique, it continues the pattern of raising the specter of imperial history in the narration of Dorian's family lineage while remaining safely under the cover of seemingly incidental—yet flamboyantly conspicuous—allusions.

As a result, an alternative portrait of Dorian posed against a background of the past begins to emerge. Wilde's narrator ends the scene in chapter 3 with Lord Henry and his uncle, as it was begun, with a stroll through London's West End:

> Lord Henry passed up the low arcade into Burlington Street and turned his steps in the direction of Berkeley Square.
>
> So that was the story of Dorian Gray's parentage. Crudely as it had been told to him, it had yet stirred him by its suggestion of a strange, almost modern romance. A beautiful woman risking everything for a mad passion. A few wild weeks of happiness cut short by a hideous, treacherous crime. Months of voiceless agony, and then a child born in pain. The mother snatched away by death, the boy left to solitude and the tyranny of an old and loveless man. Yes; it was an interesting background. It posed the lad, made him more perfect, as it were. Behind every exquisite thing that existed, there was something tragic. (33)

The story's suggestion of a "strange, almost modern romance" leads to a grammar of fragmented thought and a rare use of free indirect discourse in the novel, twice in the same paragraph—"So that was the story of Dorian Gray's parentage"; "Yes; it was an interesting background"—as if to emphasize the canny operation that the passage achieves. At the very moment of slipping into Lord Henry's consciousness, the narrative adopts the language of portraiture, asserting that the bachelor uncle's story "posed the lad" against the "interesting background" of the past. This alternative portrait rivals Basil Hallward's three-dimensional painting, onto which Dorian projects his wish to remain forever young, not subject to past deeds, and thus radically detached from history. By contrast, the imaginary portrait that forms in Lord Henry's mind counters Dorian's attempts to dispense with the past and to subsume history into pure aestheticism. To be sure, Lord Henry continues to fetishize Dorian in this moment; his personal stake has little to do with Dorian's melodramatic family history beyond an appreciation of it as an ennobling tragedy, a term that remains squarely within the aesthetic realm, if perhaps a downward shift from the ineffable aestheticism of the "exquisite." However, the narration of this moment as it forms in Lord Henry's mind nonetheless creates a radically different portrayal, one that readers, if not individual characters, are asked to keep in tension with the dominant portrait of Dorian's paranoid projection. This rival portrait excavates the recesses of history and ensures that the background remains stubbornly present, not as some master key but as a persistent problem.

As if to underscore this tension, the novel surfaces historical memory for the reader an additional time, recalling the imperial context of the surname Devereux and having Dorian consciously turn away from that legacy, an operation that again directs the reader's attention to persistence of historical memory at the level of narration even as it is secreted at the level of the plot. The pivotal chapter in which Dorian's obsessive collection and decadent pursuits are catalogued in detail, chapter 11, literalizes and redoubles Dorian's turn from the past in representing other portraits that do not have magical properties but only refer to the generational, national, and imperial past: the Devereux family picture-gallery. The individual parent's romantic story now emerges as part of a larger history and a collective guilt. Dorian wanders through the "gaunt cold picture-gallery" of his ancestral country house looking at the portraits of family members "whose blood flowed in his veins" (121). These canvases recall the past as literal lineage to Dorian, who ponders whether he had something of his aristocratic ancestor's "temperament" and whether it was "some dim sense of that ruined grace" that caused him to make the "mad prayer that had so changed his life" in Basil Hallward's studio (121). In his reading of the significance of heredity in the novel, James Eli Adams links this strain of thought to Wilde's engagement with Victorian evolutionary theory as a "form of memory that transcends the individual life."[31]

Adams writes: "No influence is more despotic than heredity, Wilde insists, and yet declaring its power, and pronouncing oneself abjectly determined and mastered by it, nonetheless offers an arena in which one can experience at least a sense of freedom, a feeling of having chosen one's experience, embraced one's own desires."[32]

The novel's fascination with heredity suggests it as a kind of destiny, a barely perceptible biological force, throughout; for example, both Dorian and James Vane, although each has just one aristocratic parent, betray a certain "race-instinct" (58). In the family picture-gallery, however, the narrator tellingly captures only Dorian's opinion: "*To him*, man was a being with myriad lives and myriad sensations, a complex multiform creature that bore within itself strange legacies of thought and passion, and whose very flesh was tainted with the monstrous maladies of the dead" (121; emphasis added). As Adams notes, Dorian's opinion is at odds with what Jeff Nunokawa has called the novel's "trajectory of de-essentialism" by which Dorian's "erotic passions appear less and less an expression of inherent attributes, and more and more a function of external influence."[33] I would add that Wilde's narrator formally emphasizes both the subjectivity of Dorian's "dim sense" (in the twin sense of indistinct and stupid) and the departure it represents from the rest of the novel's thinking about the importance of external influence. In the line right before naming the opinion as belonging to Dorian, the narrator first voices it in the first person before displacing it, at once distancing the narrative from the view and calling attention to that operation, the only time in the novel that the narrator speaks as "I": "Is insincerity such a terrible thing? I think not. It is merely a method by which we can multiply our personalities. Such, at any rate, was Dorian Gray's opinion" (121).

For Dorian, the external turns out to be already possibly internal, contagious, inherited: "Had some strange poisonous germ crept from body to body till it had reached his own?" (121). With these scattered musings, the austere picture-gallery becomes for him a hall of mirrors: he "knew what he had got" from each ancestor (122). To the extent that it seems to produce the "poisonous germ" that it seeks there, his thinking about heredity is performative rather than merely descriptive. Instead of a sincere meditation in this instance—the thinking is already stolen from the opening pages of *A Rebours*—Wilde offers a highly ironic idea of heredity as an imaginative act, a kind of creative misreading (appropriation?) that expands to include all collective history: "There were times that it appeared to Dorian Gray that the whole of history was merely the record of his own life, not as he had lived it in act and circumstance, but as his imagination had created it for him, as it had been in his brain and in his passions" (122).

Importantly, this performative turn of the imagination coincides with a turning away from the biological family organism and toward the sensing body of aesthetic experience, an "inheritance" that paradoxically (queerly?) can only occur retroactively, after initiation to awareness of it, through a receptive act of aesthetic perception: "Yet one had ancestors in literature, as well as in one's own race, nearer perhaps in type and temperament, many of them, and certainly with an influence of which one was more absolutely conscious" (122). The ultimate "poisonous germ" for Dorian turns out to be the fateful book that Lord Henry gives him, which in turn becomes a "means of forgetfulness, modes by which he could escape" for the eighteen-year span that chapter 11 compresses as Dorian descends further and further into an aesthetic (and presumably sexual) decadence. Safely returned to the "more absolutely conscious" realm of external influence from Dorian's ideas about an inherited "ruined grace," we read at the chapter's conclusion: "Dorian had been poisoned by a book" (124). The Devereux family portraits, steeped in imperial and aristocratic history, become the ground for Dorian's extravagant journey of aesthetic forgetting. For the reader, however, the ground of this forgetting yields a heightened and continued awareness of that history and the operations by which it is erased, now amplified as collective—the ancient Devereux line—and not just the story of a disobliging individual parent. "Those were the ancestors," as *A Rebours* would famously begin.[34]

Thus, the addition of the story about Dorian's parentage and family background is complementary to, and not just contemporaneous with, the expansion and sharpening of the novel's satire of English national character that Wilde inserted into his novel at the same time. The allusions to imperial history in the story of Dorian's lineage are too many and too conspicuous to write off as merely coincidental or ornamental; yet they remain cryptic, and attending to them individually can, it is true, feel like falling into a trap. Taken cumulatively, however, as I have been suggesting, they comprise a kind of enduring memory at the level of narration that cuts against Dorian's project of forgetting at the level of the plot. In the following section, I conclude that the novel's own origin story sheds some additional light on the significance of this tension. Wilde's reworking of aspects of a romantic tale told by his own granduncle, Charles Maturin, makes it clear that colonial memory is central to the novel's thinking about the dangers of transfiguring history into art so as to forget the past.

"Terror Has No Diary": The Irish Gothic as Decadent Archive

Charles Robert Maturin, Irish Protestant clergyman and writer of Gothic novels, is perhaps best known for his 1820 novel *Melmoth the Wanderer*, an extravagantly dark narrative structured by a dizzying sequence of stories within stories. The novel is evidence that Maturin consciously tried to outstrip the late eighteenth-century Gothic fictions of Matthew Lewis and Ann Radcliffe. Critics, on the whole, did not much appreciate it. The words most frequently used by Maturin's contemporaries to describe *Melmoth* were "wildness" (code for "Irish" at the time), "nonsense," "grotesqueness," "want of veracity," "blasphemy," "brutality," and, as the *Quarterly Review* critic put it, "dark, cold-blooded, pedantic obscenity."[35] Across the Channel, Honoré de Balzac wrote an ironic sequel, the parody *Melmoth Reconcilié* (1835). Charles Baudelaire, however, saw something radically modern in the demonic iconoclasm, writing in "Reflections on Some of my Contemporaries" (1861) that "Maturin [has] projected splendid and shimmering beams on to that latent Lucifer who is installed in every human heart."[36] Alternately read as a sign of the last throes of an exhausted genre and the early stirrings of modern art, *Melmoth* finds itself at several major crossroads in the literary history of the long nineteenth century. Maturin was also part of Wilde's family history through marriage; his mother, Jane Elgee Wilde (1821–96), was the daughter of Maturin's wife's sister. In exile after his release from prison in 1897, Wilde renamed himself "Sebastian Melmoth," after Saint Sebastian, heavenly protector of homoeroticism in the nineteenth century, and the title character of Maturin's novel, as a well-worn calling card with Wilde's handwriting on the back attests.

The name Melmoth itself has a curious legacy, appearing in a large number and range of literary references, perhaps the strangest of which is Nabokov's *Lolita*, in which Humbert Humbert's car is named "Melmoth." Other notable literary allusions include characters in Nathaniel Hawthorne's *Fanshawe* (1828) and in Anthony Trollope's *The Way We Live Now* (1875).

Maturin's more enduring and significant legacy, however, was his transmission of a variety of early nineteenth-century Irish Gothic that informed Wilde's narrative interests in the late 1880s. Reading *Dorian Gray* alongside *Melmoth the Wanderer* makes clear the extent to which Wilde both self-consciously summoned and sought to rework aspects of his ancestor's novel in his own fiction. The result was mutually beneficial. After having fallen into almost total neglect following Maturin's death in 1824, *Melmoth* was reprinted

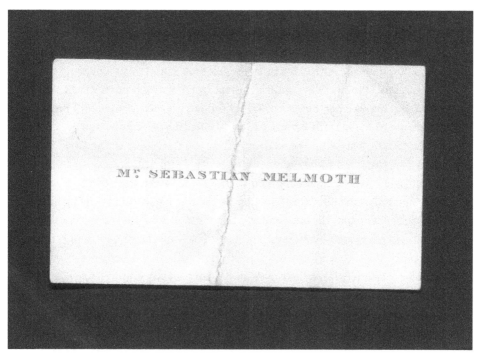

Calling card in the name of "Mr. Sebastian Melmoth" (pseudonym) with address in Oscar Wilde's handwriting scribbled on verso, 1900. The William Andrews Clark Memorial Library, University of California, Los Angeles

by Richard Bentley in 1892, just after the publication scandal of *Dorian*, with a memoir of the author as reported by Wilde and his mother.

Despite the formal extravagances of *Melmoth the Wanderer*—at one point, there are seven layers of nested narratives—the novel centers on a simple premise. A truncated summary of the intricate plot will benefit the reading that follows. Long ago, a young man named Melmoth sold his soul in a pact with the devil to have his life extended for 150 years, and then traveled the world in search of someone who would agree to take over the pact for him. Many years later, a young Dublin student, John Melmoth, learns of this story from his uncle, who has secreted away an old portrait and a decaying manuscript involving their mysterious ancestor named "Melmoth." The manuscript is narrated, in fragments, by a stranger named Stanton, who was wrongly imprisoned in a madhouse after several encounters involving Melmoth. He refuses Melmoth's bargain and narrowly escapes, later depositing the manuscript with the Melmoth family. Sufficiently frightened, John destroys the portrait in accordance with his uncle's dying wishes. Haunted by his ancestor in his dreams, John later sees Melmoth laughing at the site of a shipwreck. He tries to approach but falls into the sea, only to be saved from drowning by a Spaniard named Alonzo Monçada, the sole survivor of the wreck, who proceeds to tell John his tale of imprisonment in a monastery during the Inquisition, and his own narrow escape. What follows is a *mise-en-abîme* of nested narratives: Monçada tells the story of transcribing an old scholar's story about a young Spanish girl shipwrecked on an island in the Indian Ocean (the "Tale of the Indians"); her father hears the story of a disinheritance due to a missing will (the "Tale of Guzman's family"), followed by the story of a Yorkshire woman jilted at the altar (the "Tale of the Lovers"), now told to the Spanish girl's father, who tells the old scholar, who tells Monçada, who tells John, who tells us via a narrator, by Melmoth himself. The important point here is that each narrative ends with the main character's refusal or escape before Melmoth can close the deal to take over his hellish pact. Six hundred pages later, at the novel's conclusion John and Monçada are suddenly interrupted by Melmoth, who confesses: "I have traversed the world in the search, and no one to gain that world, would lose his own soul!"[37] Envisioning the salvation of his near-victims and approaching the end of his unnaturally extended life, he asks John and Monçada to leave him alone for his last few mortal hours. They hear terrible sounds from the room, but when they enter, the room is empty. They follow Melmoth's tracks to the top of a cliff, and see his handkerchief on a crag below. "Exchanging looks of silent and unutterable horror," they return "home," both literally and metaphorically (606–7).

By comparison with this baroque plot, *Dorian*'s story of a magically transforming portrait seems remarkably straightforward, even conventional by 1891. Wilde did not escape Melmoth's clutches as easily as Maturin's Gothic heroes, however; his novel bears several noticeable imprints of Maturin's dark vision. Like Dorian's magic picture—which "held the secret of his life, and told his story [. . .] it was watching him with its beautiful marred face and its cruel smile" (89)—the portrait that John Melmoth finds in his uncle's closet also has a strange compulsory agency over the living—"he raised himself with an involuntary start, and saw the picture gazing at him from its canvas" (67). It, too, is hidden away, evidence of a deeply held secret whose destruction an act of violence to the canvas is meant to bring about. Glimmers of the climactic moment of Wilde's novel—in which Dorian struggles to reverse the bargain he has made by stabbing the hidden portrait—can be found in the description of John Melmoth's destruction of his ancestor's picture. Here is Maturin:

> He seized it;—his hand shook at first, but the mouldering canvas appeared to assist him in the effort. He tore it from the frame with a cry half terrific, half triumphant;—it fell at his feet, and he shuddered as it fell. He expected to hear some fearful sounds, some unimaginable breathings of prophetic horror, follow this act of sacrilege, for such he felt it, to tear the portrait of his ancestor from his native walls. He paused and listened [. . .] but as the wrinkled and torn canvas fell to the floor, its undulations gave the portrait the appearance of smiling. Melmoth felt horror indescribable at this transient and imaginary resuscitation of the figure. He caught it up, rushed into the next room, tore, cut, and hacked it in every direction, and eagerly watched the fragments that burned like tinder in the turf-fire which had been lit in his room. (67)

The horror reaches a climax later that same night, when Melmoth makes a ghostly appearance that leaves a physical mark:

> The wind was high that night, and as the creaking door swung on its hinges, every noise seemed like the sound of a hand struggling with the lock, or of a foot pausing on the threshold. But (for Melmoth never could decide) was it in a dream or not, that he saw the figure of his ancestor appear at the door?— hesitatingly as he saw him at first on the night of his uncle's death,—saw him enter the room, approach his bed, and heard him whisper, "You have burned me, then; but those are flames I can survive.—I am alive,—I am beside you." Melmoth started, sprung from his bed,—it was broad day-light. He looked round,—there was no human being in the room but himself. He felt a slight pain in the wrist of his right arm. He looked at it, it was black and blue, as from the recent gripe of a strong hand. (67–68)

The description of the violence to Dorian's portrait shares some striking similarities with these passages. Here is Wilde:

> [Dorian] looked round and saw the knife that had stabbed Basil Hallward. [. . .] As it had killed the painter, so it would kill the painter's work, and all that that meant. It would kill the past, and when that was dead, he would be free. It would kill this monstrous soul-life, and without its hideous warnings, he would be at peace. He seized the thing, and stabbed the picture with it.
>
> There was a cry heard, and a crash. The cry was so horrible in its agony that the frightened servants woke and crept out of their rooms. [. . .]

> When they entered, they found hanging upon the wall a splendid portrait of
> their master as they had last seen him, in all the wonder of his exquisite youth
> and beauty. Lying on the floor was a dead man, in evening dress, with a knife in
> his heart. He was withered, wrinkled, and loathsome of visage. It was not till
> they had examined the rings that they recognized who it was. (187–88)

Both John and Dorian "seize" the portraits they are about to destroy, which
are rendered inanimate first by the text—"he seized *it*"; "he seized *the thing*."
The "wrinkled" canvas in Maturin is transmuted into Dorian's suddenly
"wrinkled" skin in Wilde, the smile a mark of conscious cruelty in both. Each
novel also makes use of material evidence left behind at the scene to confirm
the real presence of the supernatural, on which the thrill of Gothic horror
relies: in Maturin, the bruise on John's arm and the footprints and handkerchief on the crag below the cliff from which the ghost of his ancestor eventually disappears; in Wilde, the dagger Dorian uses to destroy the painting but
also the painting itself, now restored to its former glory, and Dorian's dead
body, recognizable only by the rings on his hand. In both works, these tokens
of the factuality of the Gothic tales also stand in for bloody violence, which
is elided in the text. In Wilde, the description of the stabbing of the portrait
itself seems to perform a kind of self-reflexive violence, the narration abruptly
shifting from an interiorized free indirect discourse—"It would kill this monstrous soul-life"—to a more objective outside point of view—"There was a cry
heard." This sudden reversal also finds a precedent in Maturin in the abrupt
shift back to the outer frame story, which ruptures the ever-receding interiority of the novel's seemingly endless story-within-story structure.[38]

These lexical, thematic, and formal echoes suggest that *Melmoth* had a
profound effect on Wilde.[39] Recent criticism that places Maturin's Gothic in
a specifically Anglo-Irish context has been particularly useful in considering
not only discrete, local influences on Wilde's novel but also Wilde's retrospective engagement with the Irish Gothic and with the crisis of history that
was the Decadent 1890s. Christina Morin, for example, has argued that the
novel's paratextual footnotes recalling the Irish setting of the outer frame narrative "attest to Maturin's continued preoccupation with Ireland as he wrote
and the spectral overlap of Ireland with the imagined worlds of his text. The
effect of this overlap is to translate the fictional tales of cultural alienation
into a very real one close to Maturin's heart," that is, an Anglo-Irish one.[40]
Formally, although for different reasons, Wilde's dispersal throughout *Dorian
Gray* of oblique allusions to Ireland and to empire more broadly operate in

much the same way as Maturin's quirky footnotes: to create a "spectral overlap" between the imperial past and present, between the proximate and seemingly distant. Morin's conclusion about Maturin's novel could just as easily apply to Wilde's: "Breaking down the borders between geographical and temporal zones, *Melmoth* encourages its reader to do the same."[41]

Particularly illuminating in this regard is Patrick O'Malley's subsequent reading of *Melmoth* as a working-through of a set of dueling histories about Ireland's bloody history, a "tension between a politics of historical remembrance and one of strategic forgetting," terms that I have been using to think about *Dorian*'s strategic allusions.[42] Like Morin, O'Malley argues for a metahistory that is more than simply allegorical, but his analysis goes a step further in locating allusions to Irish history within the narrative itself; the progression of dates across *Melmoth*'s various tales—1646, 1649, 1676, 1677, 1683—creates, for example, an "inexorable drumbeat through the second half of the seventeenth century" that abruptly stops as it approaches 1690, the consequential year of the Battle of the Boyne and the triumph of Williamite Protestantism that followed, as if the novel "is drawn irresistibly toward a site of historical fascination and at the last moment insists upon looking away."[43] Maturin's novel displays, variously, in O'Malley's words, a "telling impulse to *narrate* the violent past in order to exorcise it more fully," to "articulate the bloody tragedies of the past precisely in order to forget them, to overwrite them" or "defang" them by turning them into Gothic chills, and ultimately to make Ireland's bloody past "more amenable to a vision of a Protestant-dominated future," a "strategic amnesia that deliberately *forgets* rather than stanches those wounds."[44] In this connection, O'Malley focuses on Wilde's 1889 story "The Portrait of Mr. W. H.," an important precursor to *Dorian*, and he does so with good reason, as that story deals explicitly with historical recovery. As I have been suggesting, the archiving of the past in Dorian's portrait as well as in the narrative's strategic use of allusions also summons the question of imperial history to powerful effect. In echoing his predecessors Goya and Maturin, Wilde points backward to a lineage of artistic and literary influences that both exemplifies and illuminates the crisis of historicism at the novel's center: the question of what to do with a past that remains hauntingly present.

Despite the profusion of colonial contexts in the romantic story of Dorian's origins, skeptics like Haslam are technically correct that "[Wilde's] fictional works contain no explicitly Irish characters or settings."[45] But Dorian's desire to kill the past takes on wider significance when these references are taken together to signify historical memory itself. The impulse to remember persists in the narrative of Dorian's origins despite Dorian's own compulsion to forget. The horror of the Gothic mode seems to privilege forgetting, but Wilde carefully maintains a tension throughout, with an accretive strategy of seemingly passing references, ever reminding readers of the historical memory moving counter to the plot of forgetting. Dorian's relation to the past via the portrait is not the same as the novel's relation to the past via the narrator. The constant reminders of colonial history in Wilde's narrative stand in marked contrast with Maturin's attempt to revise history away in the interests of a more peaceful Protestant future. The terms are Wilde's now, however—not the specific cultural and religious contexts that O'Malley reads Maturin as exorcizing in *Melmoth*, but the larger question of thinking historically itself. Rather than choosing one version of history over another, Wilde cannily re-presents the very problem. The romantic past becomes a Decadent archive.

One last insight brings this point home, so to speak. In *Dorian*, the destruction of the portrait happens at the novel's conclusion whereas in *Melmoth* it instigates the storytelling. For Wilde, the violence is not that which triggers the narrative and must ultimately be erased in favor of one version of history—the narrative of Protestant Ascendancy, in Maturin's telling; rather, it is that which concludes ironically by reanimating the very crisis of historicism that Maturin's novel tried to solve. Ravaged by time, Dorian's dead body doesn't conveniently disappear from the narrative as Melmoth's does; instead, it remains stubbornly on the scene as evidence—not in favor of one historical narrative over another but as a persistent riddle. As O'Malley has persuasively shown, Maturin's brand of Gothic and an entire tradition of Anglo-Irish writing attempted to forget the violent past by transmuting history into art. *The Picture of Dorian Gray* literalizes that process in the figure of Dorian's magically transforming portrait. But it also develops a competing picture in the narrated story of Dorian's origins, the "strange almost modern romance" that "posed the lad" against the background of family, national, and imperial history. In the tension between these two models, the novel foregrounds and refuses the choice between remembering and forgetting that structures the very debate; instead, it conjures the historical archive that, although torn, cut, and hacked in every direction, remains hauntingly present.

CHAPTER THREE

Aesthetic Antecedents

Lady Wilde and the Pre-Raphaelite Cult of *Sidonia*

In 1820, Charles Maturin wrote to his friend the novelist Walter Scott to say that in *Melmoth the Wanderer* he had "determined to display all by *diabolical* resources, [to] out-Herod all the Herods of the German school"—to exceed in violence and extravagance, that is, the German authors Friedrich Schiller, E. T. A. Hoffmann, and Johann Wolfgang von Goethe, who were enjoying great popularity at the time.[1] The macabre results of this competition, Maturin's transposition of the Gothic into a specifically Anglo-Irish historical context and its lasting effects on Wilde's imagination, were on full view in chapter 2. In this chapter, I consider the far-ranging influence of the 1849 translation from the German by Wilde's mother, then Jane Francesca Elgee, of the Gothic historical romance by another Protestant priest, the Pomeranian Wilhelm Meinhold, *Sidonia von Bork, die Klosterhexe* (1847–48), or *Sidonia the Sorceress*, as it is more popularly known in English. In an 1889 review in *Woman's World*, Wilde credited this translation, along with Lady Duff Gordon's translation of Meinhold's earlier novel *Maria Schweidler, die Bernsteinhexe* (1838), or *The Amber Witch* (1843), as "my favourite romantic reading when a boy."[2] Surprisingly, whether it is because of the sheer weirdness of Meinhold's novels or because they only became widely known in ladies' translations or otherwise tend to be written off as a slight or merely juvenile interest, this earlier tradition has not generally received the close scholarly attention that it deserves.[3] While *Sidonia the Sorceress* is not the only or even the primary origin for Dorian's diabolical qualities, Meinhold's novel provides a richly illuminating context for the idea of fatal beauty in Victorian Decadent writing.

Like *Dorian*, Meinhold's *Sidonia the Sorceress* features a haunted portrait,

Sidonia von Bork 1560, 1860 (watercolor and gouache on paper), Edward Burne-Jones (1833–98). Tate Gallery, London. Bequeathed by W. Graham Robertson, 1948. Photo: Tate

sexual transgression, and a terrible transformation. The story of Sidonia, a real-life Pomeranian noblewoman who was tried for witchcraft and decapitated in 1620 for casting a spell of sterility on the House of Pomerania, achieved cult status in Victorian England, especially among the artists of the Pre-Raphaelite Brotherhood. In the 1850s, Dante Gabriel Rossetti made a habit of quoting from now Lady Wilde's translation, and Edward Burne-Jones produced a remarkable 1860 painting of the uncanny double portrait described in Meinhold's novel, clearly a model for Dorian's more famous magically aging portrait.

As Meinhold describes it, Sidonia stands in all her youthful glory in the picture's foreground while her later incarnation as a wizened sorceress in execution robes lurks forebodingly in the background. Additionally, William Morris reissued an astonishingly beautiful edition of this translation for his Kelmscott Press in 1893, on the coattails of Dorian's publication just a few years earlier. The connection has also been recognized in the archives: Morris's ornately decorated Kelmscott edition is now part of the world-renowned Oscar Wilde collection at UCLA's Clark Library.[4] The Clark copy includes a tipped-in receipt for payment of £25 to Lady Wilde for the reissue of her translation, an early form of residual, now largely forgotten. The translator's name was not mentioned until this edition appeared.[5] According to biographer Karen Tipper, Elgee considered the work "simply an exercise, the first serious challenge to her translating ability and certainly not a novel for which she felt any affinity."[6]

But Wilde is known to have owned a beloved copy of his mother's translation as a child and to have returned to it at various times as an adult.[7] This chapter explores the strong affinities between Wilde's novel and this seemingly distant text. Dorian's doppelgänger portrait and the sterility of the romance at its heart can be traced, I suggest, to Meinhold's novel by way of Lady Wilde's popular English translation and Burne-Jones's haunting visual depiction. Together with chapter 2's focus, this nexus reveals a pattern of influence that predates Wilde's experiments in Aestheticism and moves in unaffiliated fashion across national literatures, periods, and art forms. Beyond the usual contexts of nationalist politics, poetry, and salon culture that tend to garner attention when it comes to Lady Wilde's life and legacy, her translations—and translation itself as a way of being and of knowing—had an arguably greater impact on her son's imagination and, by extension, on Decadence's transnational reach. In addition to offering a more complex view of Wilde, retraining attention on Meinhold's spectral haunting of nineteenth-century literature and art reveals several key aspects of a wider transnational Decadence: the late-century reinvention of essentially mid-century figures like the femme fatale and the erotic "stunner," the significance of translation as a Decadent principle and practice, and the challenge to the modern sense of imperial-national "tradition" itself.

Lady Wilde, "Soul of a Nation" and Cross-Cultural Translator

No longer neglected in scholarly discussions as she once was, Jane Francesca Elgee, who became Lady Wilde when her husband of thirteen years William Wilde was knighted in 1864, is best known in her own right as a fiery advocate of the Irish nationalist cause and a regular contributor to *The Nation* newspaper. Under the *nom de guerre* "Speranza," the Italian word for "hope" (she was inspired by the Risorgimento and claimed descent from Dante Alighieri), she wrote poetry and pamphlets once described by her editor Charles Gavan Duffy as "vehement."[8] One particularly passionate article, "Jacta Alea Est" ("The Die is Cast"), a revolutionary appeal titled after the Latin phrase used by Julius Caesar after crossing the Rubicon, led to Duffy's prosecution on a felony charge of treason, a hangable offense, and to the suppression of *The Nation* in 1848. From the public gallery at the Duffy trial, Speranza reportedly sprang up and diverted blame to herself: "I am the criminal who, as the author of the article that had just been read, should be in the dock."[9] The prosecution was ultimately abandoned, but the image of Speranza as a fearless advocate and fiercely loyal friend took hold and endured. Her own "courtroom-conscious son," in Richard Ellmann's phrase, would take a similarly courageous stand nearly a half century later. An even eerier parallel is to be found in the 1864 cause célèbre in which Lady Wilde was sued for libel. Responding to demands for money and threats of further exposure from Mary Travers, a young patient of her husband who claimed that he sexually abused her while she was under sedation, Speranza wrote directly to Travers's father to warn him of the "disreputable conduct" of his daughter: "The wages of disgrace she has so basely toiled for and demanded shall never be given."[10] Unlike Wilde, whose 1895 suit for libel against the father of his lover would ultimately produce the evidence that would land him in prison, Travers prevailed, although she was awarded only a farthing in damages by the jury.[11]

Such intensity also characterized Speranza's literary ambitions and her love of gossip, enjoyable conversation, and a good party. Writing to a friend, she declared: "You and other poets are content to express only your own little soul in poetry. I express the soul of a nation. Nothing less would satisfy me, who am the acknowledged voice in poetry of all the people of Ireland."[12] Speranza's grandeur was equaled by her hospitality, the stately Georgian house in Merrion Square being, according to one visitor, "a rallying place for all who were eminent in science, art, or literature."[13] As Lord Alfred Douglas would later remember, "it was a house of opulence and carouse; of late suppers and deep drinking; of careless talk and example."[14] Aphorism was a favorite mode of self-presentation and communion at these gatherings, which both Wilde boys regularly attended. "We live in a bad prosaic age, but not in an age of good prose," Speranza declared, having banned the description of any attendees as "respectable" in her house: "Only tradespeople are respectable."[15] ("I hate being educated," Lady Basildon will later say in *An Ideal Husband*, to which Mrs. Marchmont replies: "So do I. It puts one almost on a level with the commercial classes."[16]) Bram Stoker recalls introducing a female friend as half English and half Irish, a description that was quickly met with this ribald response: "Glad to meet you, my dear. Your English half is as welcome as your Irish bottom."[17] Decamping to London after the death of her husband in 1876, Speranza continued to hold "at-home" hours shrouded in near darkness to hide the effects of aging and her increasingly straitened circumstances and ill health. Still, the "soul of a nation" and her even more famous son, who attended the London as well as the Dublin salons, knew how to talk and to draw a crowd, and this remains the prevailing image of Speranza and her influence to this day.

Less well known, however, is Speranza's more scholarly labor as a self-taught translator. In a flurry of activity after the *Nation* scandal and before her marriage and the birth of three children between 1852 and 1857 (only the two sons, Willie and Oscar, survived childhood), she produced English translations of a number of French and German books, including works by Alphonse de Lamartine and Alexandre Dumas père.[18] The 1849 translation of Meinhold's *Sidonia*, her first, established her name. Coming in at nearly five hundred pages, the volume must have taken considerable effort. Most notably, this work focused the young Elgee's attention not on the promise of the glittering social and literary circles of the day but on a strange and distant past. After having been lost for years, the records of the Pomeranian scandal were discovered on the shelves of the Berlin State Library, and Goethe's brother-in-law, Christian August Vulpius, included Sidonia in his *Pantheon of Famous and Noteworthy Women* in 1812.[19] Meinhold's novelized account would then lead to Speranza's English translation, the popularity and success of which, despite her downplaying of it as merely work she did for pay, became by one critic's estimation unequaled by any other German book in British literary history: "No other German novel has enjoyed the particular kind of artistic *succès d'estime* which this now forgotten Gothic romance enjoyed in its day, or been published in such sumptuous editions."[20] More to the point, the poet and critic Edmund Gosse observed in referencing this volume: "How the attention of Speranza was directed to it I am quite unable to report, but it is hardly a paradox to say that this German romance did not begin to exist until an Irishwoman revealed it to a select English circle."[21]

Meinhold and the Pre-Raphaelite Cult of the Stunner

Nothing about Wilhelm Meinhold's career portended the outsize role that his anti-heroine Sidonia would play in the mid-century Victorian art world or the archetypal figure she would later become in the 1890s, not coincidentally, in the wake of *Dorian*'s publication. Born on the Pomeranian island of Usedom in the Baltic Sea, a site crisscrossed throughout history by the armies of France, Sweden, and Prussia, Meinhold lived as an eccentric and largely underestimated Lutheran clergyman. Yet in the description of him by York Powell as a man "shrewd, obstinate, not to be convinced save by himself, persistent, observant, and keen in feeling and word and deed," a portrait of the artist also emerges.[22] After falling out of favor for his headstrong ways with both his parishioners and authorities, including the king of Prussia, he retired early and died in 1851 at the age of fifty-four. He undoubtedly would have faded into obscurity if it were not for the popularity afforded to him by his English translators, Lucie, Lady Duff Gordon (1821–69), and Jane Elgee.

Sidonia, his second novel after *The Amber Witch*, is a work of historical fiction written in the language of the period that it represents, the 1620s. The novel's initial reviews were quite negative. The archaic language of the original is perhaps one reason why the linguistically streamlined English translation by Speranza met with considerably more success.[23] Other reasons, of course, include Sidonia's viciousness, the gloominess of the novel's theme of sorcery and the occult, and the sympathy it seems to construct for evildoing outsiders—Sidonia, like Dorian, is also a murderer—in short, its apparent amorality. Still, the novel strongly appealed to artistic circles, given Meinhold's scrupulous attention to local detail (the setting of the court of Wolgast is in the same district in which he was born) and the novel's striking visual descriptions and eventful chronicle. No small part of that appeal is also to be found in the novel's eroticism, often combined with violence, and in Sidonia's status as a sexual outlaw in open rebellion to a world of strict convention—the ducal court as image for Victorian London.

The narrative falls roughly into three parts. It follows the free-thinking and ambitious Sidonia to the court of Wolgast, where she falls in love with the prince and several others, is exiled for her libertine ways, and is thought to have cast a spell of sterility on all the young princes, eventually bringing about the extinction of the House of Pomerania. Book One treats her early life and reception at court and is full of the pageant and colorful detail of court life. The conflict between her liberal upbringing in a noble Pomeranian family—she is a "castle and land dowered maiden," she repeatedly insists—and the rigid social structure and ceremonies at court are on full view and lead to her eventual banishment, the subject of Book Two.[24] In exile, Sidonia pursues a life of crime with her lover, the leader of a gang of outlaws who terrorize villages and travelers with thievery and violence. This more fanciful book is shot through with recorded historical detail of Pomeranian life, politics, and the general state of lawlessness at the time, lending the novel the sense of biography and contemporary chronicle, which it purports to be.[25] Book Three covers Sidonia's final years in the convent of Marienfliess and the acts of witchcraft that explain the novel's subtitle—"The Supposed Destroyer of the Whole Reigning Ducal House of Pomerania"—and ultimately led to her execution in Stettin, followed by the burning of her body, as was typical at the time.

In his important review of a 1926 luxury edition of the novel—another indication of its artistic appeal—Edmund Gosse offers a revealing account of the craze for *Sidonia* as well as a retrospective view that reflects the novel's changing fortunes. According to Gosse, Lady Wilde's translation came into Dante Gabriel Rossetti's hands from an Irish acquaintance, probably the poet and diarist William Allingham. Rossetti had a "positive passion" for the book, "referring to and quoting from it incessantly, until he inoculated the whole Preraphaelite circle with something of his own enthusiasm."[26] Rossetti's zeal would lead him so far as to call *Sidonia* the best novel "as regards power and sound style for two ages," an assertion that Gosse only tempers by calling "this sinewy and ferocious narrative" a "very remarkable work."[27] Meinhold's heroine, for Gosse, "makes a splendid fight for life and power."[28] He concludes that the fascination that the romance held over Rossetti and the painters of his school is easily accounted for, noting the affinity between the novel's striking visual details and the Pre-Raphaelites' painterly practice: "There are pictures everywhere in the conduct of the story; every page suggests a brilliantly, rather crudely coloured vignette. The violence of the action lends itself to this pictorial result; we seem less to be listening to a narrative than to be looking on at a series of *poses plastiques*."[29] Gosse's catalog of examples offers a good summary of both the novel's artistic bona fides and Gosse's retrospective appreciation:

> Where Sidonia faints under the excitement of the Lapland drum; where the
> Prince bursts into the chamber in the little tower and finds Sidonia on the
> bed weeping, "in a green velvet robe, laced with gold and embroidered with
> other golden ornaments, and her head crowned with pearls and diamonds";
> where Sidonia is caught with the groom; where she sits spinning, like a Lady
> of Shalott, at the window of her prison at Sastzig Castle, and sees, far below,
> the life of the town and the motion of the boats on the lake—all these episodes,
> and a hundred more, seem ready for the pencil of Millais or Frederick Sandys.[30]

The analogy to the nineteenth century's most painterly poem, Tennyson's "The Lady of Shalott" (1832), underscores the novel's sumptuous visual appeal and its "readiness" for artistic treatment. The preposterousness of the novel's supernatural elements only adds a mystical aspect to the pictorialism for Gosse, who finds in Rossetti's zeal evidence of a class of mind that delights in conjuring "disturbances of the course of nature" but meets "accredited miracles of an apostle" with indifference.[31]

Gosse's insightful review focuses primarily on the role of Rossetti's captivation with Meinhold's novel in conferring on it an "odd value" and "continuity of fame" where it might otherwise have remained obscure.[32] But the influence was wider still and part of a broader interest in not only German Romantic literature but the cruel femme fatale, a figure associated more closely with Wilde's *Salomé* and the end of the century but with a clear foothold in the Pre-Raphaelite cult of the "stunner" in the 1850s. By all accounts, *Sidonia* was required reading for members of the Pre-Raphaelite Brotherhood, the group of English painters, poets, and critics who joined in opposition to what they perceived to be the prevailing frivolity of art of their day, typified by the Royal Academy's promotion of the highly mannered Renaissance master Raphael. That Meinhold was well known beyond this avant-garde artistic circle is evidenced by Charlotte Brontë's reference to Sidonia, without any apparent need for explanation, in her 1853 novel *Villette*.[33] In his *Appreciations* (1889), Walter Pater also casually alludes to "the sorceress of Streckelberg," a reference that assumes familiarity with Meinhold's *Amber Witch*; as he explains in a postscript, the "addition of strangeness to beauty" is what constitutes the romantic character in art, the bearer of that spirit in Germany being, for Pater, none other than Meinhold, "the author of *Sidonia the Sorceress*."[34] Tennyson reportedly said, "I would not have missed it for anything, but I would not read it again for anything."[35] Ruskin suggested to his friend Ellen Heaton that she buy Burne-Jones's *Sidonia* in 1862, but she was too "scandalized" by the subject, which surely would have pleased Rossetti's circle.[36]

The Meinhold mania was no fleeting vogue either. It would return and reach a crescendo in the 1890s for reasons that I will discuss shortly. Morris's lifelong admiration of *Sidonia* led to the 1893 Kelmscott reprint in large quarto, "just as it stands," emphasizing his love of it precisely as an artifact.[37] In the announcement for the book, he credited Lady Wilde's translation for conveying Meinhold's "genius" to the English-speaking world and called it "good, simple, and sympathetic."[38] New editions of *The Amber Witch* also appeared in short order, one printed by the artist and designer Charles Ricketts for the Ballantyne Press in 1894 and another with illustrations by Philip Burne-Jones and dedicated to his mother in 1895.[39] Swinburne listed *Sidonia* among his hundred favorite books and declared it a "real work of genius, but very horrible, the most horrible in literature."[40] Patrick Bridgwater notes that Swinburne discovered *Sidonia* at more or less the same moment as the writings of the Marquis de Sade, further linking the sadomasochism of Meinhold's novel to the Pre-Raphaelite view of women.[41] As the Burne-Jones expert John Christian writes:

> these were no ordinary witches. They were enchantresses whose fatal power lay at least partly in their beauty, and this invokes another aspect of Meinhold's influence, his impact on the circle's cult of the beautiful woman, or in Pre-Raphaelite slang, the "stunner." Here indeed was the writer's true significance so far as these devotees were concerned. By adding a dimension of menace to their worship of female beauty, his book proved a potent source for depiction of the femme fatale, a concept that looms so large in later Pre-Raphaelite and Symbolist imagery.[42]

On this point, Bridgwater sees a "smokescreen" in Rossetti's profession of enjoyment in *Sidonia*'s "sound style," the true source of his attraction being her sadism, an opinion that Mario Praz also expresses in his important early reading: "In Rossetti, there is to be found a conspicuous presence of the sad and the cruel; the Middle Ages are, to him, a legend of blood [. . .]. Sidonia von Bork [. . .], whom Rossetti admired and caused the Pre-Raphaelites to admire, is a cruel, fatal woman."[43]

Especially taken by this "addition of strangeness to beauty" were the Pre-Raphaelite painters, whose work we know Wilde later saw at the Grosvenor and New Galleries in London and wrote about as a journalist in the 1880s. Of particular interest is Burne-Jones's remarkable painting of the uncanny double portrait described in Meinhold's novel and mentioned above. Burne-Jones had met Rossetti in 1856, after which he left Oxford without a degree and moved to London to pursue a career as an artist-craftsman. Enthused by his reading of Meinhold, the artist created a pair of portraits in the style of Rossetti; in addition to *Sidonia von Bork*, there is a pendant of Sidonia's virtuous cousin who is brought to a gruesome death, *Clara von Bork* (1860). In the latter, a clutch of white fledgling doves that Clara holds is menaced by a black cat, Sidonia's witchy familiar, at her feet.

In one of the most gruesome scenes of the novel, Sidonia dances on Clara's coffin as she suffocates inside, begging to be let out, having first been drugged into a death-like state, "stiff and cold as a corpse," in keeping with Gothic convention (I:232). Clara appears to die several times, with periods of silence from within the coffin shortly thereafter met with knocking, pleas for help, terrified cries, and finally "a gurgling sound" (I:233–35). The repetition heightens the horror of the scene and ultimately the impact of the gory aftermath, which seems to arrive gratuitously and unexpectedly:

> It was an easy matter to remove the cover, for the screws were not fastened; but—O God! what has she beheld? A sight that will never more leave her brain! The poor corpse lay all torn and disfigured from the writhings in the coffin, and a blood-vessel must have burst at last to relieve her from her agony, for the blood lay yet warm on the hands as she lifted the cover. But more horrible than all were the fixed glassy eyes of the corpse, staring immovably upon her, from which clear tears were yet flowing, and blending with the blood upon the cheek. (I:235)

Foretelling this gruesome end—the "fixed glassy eyes" of the corpse finding an echo in the set stare of the innocent holding fledgling doves as a predator circles—the von Bork pictures are among Burne-Jones's best-known and most thoroughly documented works. They are displayed prominently in the Tate Gallery and have been exhibited around the world, including in a massive 2013 exhibition at the National Gallery, Washington, the first major survey of

Clara von Bork, 1860 (watercolor and gouache on paper), Edward Burne-Jones. Tate Gallery, London. Bequeathed by W. Graham Robertson, 1948. Photo: Tate

Pre-Raphaelite art in the United States. Although Ruskin's friend Mrs. Heaton found the true-crime aspect of the source material unsuitable, the paintings' provenance reads like a who's-who of nineteenth-century British art collecting. They were first bought from the artist by James Leathart (1820–95), one of the period's new "self-made" industrialists, a lead manufacturer from Newcastle and owner of one of the finest Pre-Raphaelite collections. Upon his death, the works were exhibited by the Goupil Gallery, in London, and purchased by the young aesthete Graham Robertson, who bequeathed the paintings to the Tate in 1948.[44]

The relatively small size of the paintings, at roughly thirteen inches by seven inches each, belies their eerie and unsettling power. The portrait of Sidonia is particularly spine-chilling and significant for the reading of *Dorian* that follows. As Meinhold describes it:

> Sidonia is here represented in the prime of mature beauty—a gold net is drawn over her almost golden yellow hair, and her neck, arms, and hands are profusely covered with jewels. Her bodice of bright purple is trimmed with costly fur, and the robe is of azure velvet. In her hand she carries a sort of pompadour of brown leather, of the most elegant form and finish. Her eyes and mouth are not pleasing, notwithstanding their great beauty—in the mouth, particularly, one can discover an expression of cold malignity. (I:9)

In realizing this description in watercolor, Burne-Jones opts for a starker emotional truth and adds some new touches of his own. Fatally attractive to all the men who see her, his Medusa-like Sidonia stands in the foreground with her back partially turned to the viewer, slyly glancing sideways with her head tilted at a knowing angle. Her abundant hair, a distinguishing feature of all of Rossetti's models (this one is Fanny Cornforth), is bound together with a gilded net, which in her first appearance in the novel attracts a "swarm of bees" that mistake her tresses for flowers (I:21). Her dress, white with a webbed pattern of "knot-fantasies" (*fantasie dei vinci*), snake-like black interlaced bands suggesting a tethering of beauty and evil, echoes the confinement of the hair net, as does the gold neck chain that is described in the novel and that she pulls away from her throat with her hand in a small fist. The design of the dress was taken from Guilio Romano's sixteenth-century *Portrait of Margherita Paleologo*, a pattern that reappears in the costume for Miranda Richardson, who plays a vengeful witch in Tim Burton's 1999 horror film *Sleepy Hollow*, suggesting the long historical arc of Sidonia's popularity.[45] In the bottom right-hand corner of Burne-Jones's *Sidonia*, a large black spider crawls over the artist's signature and date, as if the picture frame itself constituted an expectant web.

Most important for my purposes here, in the upper right-hand corner of Burne-Jones's *Sidonia* appears an inset portrait painted in a different style. According to the art historical record, this portrait depicts the Dowager Duchess of Wolgast, who would not be deceived by her lady-in-waiting, Sidonia, and several of Sidonia's male victims in the doorway, an architectural detail that also seems to be taken from Romano's portrait.[46] In the novel, however, this portrait is described as a later addition depicting Sidonia herself, near the end of her life, in black-and-white execution robes:

> Immediately behind this form there is another looking over the shoulder of Sidonia, like a terrible specter (a highly poetical idea), for this specter is Sidonia herself painted as a Sorceress. [. . .] It is a fearfully characteristic painting, and no imagination could conceive a contrast more shudderingly awful. The Sorceress is arrayed in her death garments—white with black stripes; and round her thin white locks is bound a narrow band of black velvet spotted with gold. In her hand is a kind of work-basket, but of the simplest workmanship and form. (I:9)

This fact is important since even if Wilde was inspired by Burne-Jones's *Sidonia*, he clearly had Meinhold's original description in mind when conceiving of Dorian's portrait double.[47] Interestingly, even though Burne-Jones's version seems to collapse the irreal temporality of Meinhold's fictional portrait by showing Sidonia plotting her next crime in real time in front of the Dowager Duchess and not of an older version of herself, the temporal and iconographic relationship between the two figures remains the same. As Bridgwater observes: "In every detail this [background] figure represents an undoing of the main figure."[48] Only the symbolically evocative colors of black and white remain, further highlighting the contrast between youthful exuberance and the night that awaits. The key difference is that in Meinhold's more imaginative version, and later in Wilde's, there is the Gothic element of doubling and temporal splitting within the pictorial frame. As Ellmann writes, without elaborating: "The search for sources of Wilde's *The Picture of Dorian Gray* is unending, but here is another analogue to the benign portrait of Dorian by Basil Hallward, and the malign one of Dorian as drawn by his own soul."[49]

Portrait of Margherita Paleologo, c.1531 (oil on panel), Guilio Romano (1499–1546), King's Dressing Room, Windsor Castle, Royal Collection Trust. © Her Majesty Queen Elizabeth II 2022

The Male Stunner and Queer Sterility in Wilde

Considering *Sidonia* as a significant context for *Dorian* thus reveals some intriguing lines of connection across national literatures, historical periods, and the sister arts. In the remaining portion of this chapter, I trace several

Miranda Richardson, *Sleepy Hollow*, 1999 (film still), directed by Tim Burton (1958–), Paramount Pictures. ScreenProd/Photononstop/Alamy Stock Photo

important implications of reading Wilde's novel in light of this lesser-known German romance. As we have seen, it suggests the importance of Lady Wilde's intellectual life on young Wilde and on his later writing—not just as the Irish nationalist poet Speranza and convener of a famous Dublin salon—but as a gifted linguist and translator of modern European languages (not just French) and a transnational thinker in her own right. Speranza's work and reputation as a translator of popular Continental fiction might not have stood up as well, but her translation of Meinhold, which was commissioned under unknown circumstances and to which Speranza turned as a kind of remunerative intellectual exercise and possibly as a retreat immediately after her brush with the law in 1848, would clearly affect her impressionable young son.

Recalling this work and its effect on Wilde also suggests the importance of the earlier nineteenth-century romance tradition—and its fascination with the motif of the magical portrait—in addition to the better-known influences of later-century British Aestheticism and French Decadence. In chapter 4, I say much more about this fascination with portraits in examining influential American texts by Edgar Allan Poe and by Henry James, who was himself influenced by Nathaniel Hawthorne's use of the magic-portrait motif in *Twice-Told Tales* (1837/1842) and *The House of the Seven Gables* (1851). I will say here that the connection to *Sidonia* suggests further German contexts, including a genealogy reaching back to Heinrich Heine, whose 1833 story "From the Memoirs of Herr Schnabelewopski," is thought to have also influenced Richard Wagner's opera *The Flying Dutchman* (1843), a work that too features an uncanny portrait. Heine's narrator recounts the fable of the Flying Dutchman, the story of an enchanted ghost ship that can never arrive in port, featuring a mysterious time-worn portrait of the Dutchman as he appeared a hundred years before, an old heirloom of the Scottish family of a young maiden who now awaits him despite the warning that has come down, according to the legend, that "the women of the family must beware the original."[50] Heine writes: "When the man himself makes his appearance, she is startled, but not with fear. He too is moved at beholding the portrait" and "passe[s] into a pathetic mood, depicting [. . .] how his body itself is his living coffin, wherein his soul is terribly imprisoned."[51] The connection between Meinhold's 1847 novel and this 1833 story by Heine and 1843 opera by Wagner merits more scholarship, but here too we have a mysterious portrait that would seem to hold the secret of an "imprisoned soul" whose body, eternally split from "the original," exists outside of time as it is commonly known, and ultimately becomes a "living coffin." The connection suggests an alternative genealogy for *Dorian* to the usual "art for art's sake" story of intellectual lineage from Gautier, Pater, and Huysmans that has been told to date. In an interesting twist that points to a broader timeline still, a popular English production of *Dutchman* reached Dublin in 1877 and is recollected in James Joyce's *Ulysses* (1922) as a "stupendous success" by Bloom.[52]

Of particular importance to Wilde scholarship are several formal aspects of this tradition and of Meinhold's novel especially. The uncanny double portrait of Sidonia is presented in the novel's preface, where we are told that the painting and the book that accompanied it were inherited years later by the narrator of the outer frame narrative. The novel itself comprises a continual circling back to the "original" story via interviews, local lore, and other second- and thirdhand accounts offered to the narrator of the outer frame. As is typical of this common Gothic device, questions about representation and point of view, and about the effect of the preface on the reading of the novel as a whole, are never far away, much as Wilde's epigrammatic preface continually conditions and undercuts readings of *Dorian*, constantly reminding us of its own status as a work of art, a fiction.

Additionally, in describing the double portrait Meinhold emphasizes the different styles of painting held by the artwork. We are told that the earlier portrait of a young Sidonia is in the school of Kranach, and the later one of Sidonia the Sorceress, added after a lapse of many years, is in the school of Rubens. Interestingly, Burne-Jones makes somewhat less of this distinction than Meinhold's novel does, although a flatter, slightly different use of paint is discernable in the upper right-hand corner of the portrait. Without first-hand knowledge of the novel, a viewer might be forgiven for missing it. The change of styles emphasizes the passage of time, of course; it is also reminiscent of the blending of styles that structures Wilde's novel, as discussed in chapter 1, and the queer energies and temporalities that accompany it. The idea for this kind of temporal splitting and genre-blending can, in no small degree, be traced to *Sidonia*'s portrait. More importantly, in *Dorian* Wilde can be seen to intervene in this tradition. He makes his novel's portrait a simultaneous double of the *living* Dorian, who is haunted less by an innocent past and a future seemingly foretold, as in Sidonia's case, as by a displacement of the very passage of time, at least as he lives it. Wilde takes the idea suggested by *Sidonia* and makes it his own, fully realizing it.

The implications are more far-reaching still. In particular, the traces of this Anglo-German context, first on the Pre-Raphaelite Brotherhood and later on Wilde via his mother's translation, lead to a more nuanced understanding of the queer thematics of *Dorian*, the function of the historical past within literary Decadence, and the centrality of translation to that project's transnational aims. First, in drawing a direct line from the Pre-Raphaelite cult of Sidonia to *Salomé*, Wilde's experimental French play about the biblical story first published in 1893, critics rightly see a clear connection to a long nineteenth-century tradition. As Bridgwater writes of *Sidonia*: "For those revolted by Victorian morality the book was like a blast of fresh air, its heroine the very type of the Belle Dame sans Merci [Beautiful Lady without Mercy] who looms so large in imaginative writing from Keats to Wilde and beyond."[53] Importantly, however, the direct line from Keats's merciless "faery's child" to Wilde's *Salomé* skips over an important intermediary.[54] In *Dorian*, Wilde first reconfigures the trope of the femme fatale or erotic stunner as a fatally attractive young man. For conceptual tools, he takes up Sidonia's righteous challenge to the rigid social conventions of the patriarchal court and the Pre-Raphaelites' celebration of her rebellion against bourgeois Victorian morality to wage his own challenge to the prohibition against representing queer desire. Salomé's uncompromising bloodthirst, seen from the perspective of *Sidonia*'s influence, is merely a predictable, even logical—and, by 1893, more conventional—extension of Dorian's earlier Medusa-like deadliness.

Meinhold's Romanticism brings a specific kind of imaginative clarity and affective force to Wilde's challenge to Victorian morality. Themes of sexual transgression, sterility, the fatal power of the erotic stunner, now male, mark Wilde's transposition of Meinhold's heterosexual romance. Like Sidonia, Dorian is of the aristocracy, an insider-outsider in a power structure of which he is both beneficiary and existential threat, and his physical beauty has a disarming effect on men in the novel. The opening chapters of *Dorian* quickly establish this defining feature of Dorian's character, first in a description of Basil's portrait and then in the appearance of Dorian in the flesh. The suggestion of a dangerous social threat linked to his personal beauty appears on the novel's very first page. Immediately following the opening set piece of the saturated and highly charged description of the artist's studio discussed in the first chapter, Wilde writes: "In the centre of the room, clamped to an upright easel, stood the full-length portrait of a young man of extraordinary beauty, and in front of it, some little distance away, was sitting the artist himself, Basil Hallward, whose sudden disappearance some years ago caused, at the time, such public excitement, and gave rise to so many strange conjectures" (5). In moving directly from Dorian's "extraordinary beauty" to the "public excitement" and "strange conjectures" surrounding Basil's past disappearance, this sentence leads the reader to infer a causal relationship between Basil's interest in male beauty and scandal; in this, it both encapsulates the arc of the novel from easel to disappearance and inaugurates the kind of cagey knowing/not-knowing on which its meaning will depend. Basil underscores the sense of erotic threat when, in affirming the essential difference between Dorian and him, he says: "I should be very sorry to look like him. [...] There is a fatality about all physical and intellectual distinction, the sort of fatality that seems to dog through history the faltering steps of kings" (7).[55] From the start, then, the distinctions of beauty and social position are inseparably joined to fatal danger, and the threat of public scandal is foretold in the frame of a portrait in *Dorian* as in *Sidonia*.

Mixed with this distinctive beauty is a wickedness that makes both Sidonia and Dorian dangerous to others and a useful amoral center of their respective novels. They are sympathetic at first but ultimately become horrifying in the relentless and uncompromising selfishness of their actions. Their combination of beauty and amorality, or what Pater termed "the addition of strangeness to beauty," makes Dorian, like Sidonia before him, the perfect inverse of the heroic figure of heterosexual romance and of traditional Victorian novelistic character *tout court*. Their individualistic rebellion against a stifling social structure aligns with the novel tradition at the same time that their Gothic excesses reveal the destructive potential that lies at that tradition's heart. Another word for this phenomenon is Decadence, of course, but it is a defamiliarized Decadence.

When Dorian appears in person in chapter 2 of the novel, Lord Henry has none of the "curious sensation of terror" that overcame Basil when his eyes first met Dorian's at a party (9). As we have seen in the novel's opening paragraph, Wilde codes this frisson both iconographically and syntactically as natural and unstoppable, something occurring from without, a mere predicate, and perhaps in this context, almost otherworldly. "I suddenly became conscious that someone was looking at me," Basil recounts before ultimately affirming that the encounter was not reckless: "It was simply inevitable" (9–10). As if to underscore this point, the bees from the novel's opening paragraph—"shouldering their way through the long unmown grass, or circling with monotonous insistence round the dusty gilt horns of the straggling woodbine"—return no less sensuously or suggestively after Lord Henry delivers his influential panegyric on youth: "After a time the bee flew away. He saw it creeping into the stained trumpet of Tyrian convolvulus. The flower seemed to quiver, and then swayed gently to and fro" (23). This image is one of many that Wilde uses to naturalize the queer sexual desire that circulates so freely in *Dorian's* opening chapters. It is the same natural imagery that attends Sidonia's first appearance, where bees mistake her gilt-netted tresses for flowers and get trapped in the net. That motif, like the one in *Dorian*, prefigures the host of men who will become entrapped by an infamous beauty pursued, Medusa-like, by a swarm of suitors. Wilde complicates the metaphor by combining noticeably multivalent meanings. As an image, the morning glory's "stained trumpet" connotes both anal and phallic sexuality: it is at once a receptacle for the penetrative bee and its own stem, swaying "gently to and fro" after springing free from the encounter. Importantly, in both Meinhold's and Wilde's use of the metaphor, the active agent, a pollinator attracted by a beautiful and innocent "flower," has no consequential effect but a barely perceptible "quiver."

The gender crossing of Wilde's imagining Dorian through the lens of Meinhold's femme fatale has precedent within the novel, as well. Perhaps unwittingly, Basil associates Dorian with the feminine in his oblique reference to Austin Dobson's poem "To a Greek Girl" in chapter 1: "'A dream of form in days of thought':—who is it who says that? I forget; but it is what Dorian Gray has been to me" (12). The speaker of the forgotten Dobson poem hears Autonoë, the Theban princess of the work's title, coming across the years with "bees that hum" as if on the wind, without agency, and seen "only in my dreams."[56] Dorian, whose name is Greek for the Hellenic people speaking the Doric dialect of Greek, represents to Basil that classical ideal of feminine beauty that must remain hidden in a dream-world of imagination, which is certainly aligned with the reason that Basil gives for refusing to exhibit his work: "I have put too much of myself into it," he claims (6). Wilde writes: "As the painter looked at the gracious and comely form he had so skillfully mirrored in his art, a smile of pleasure passed across his face, and seemed about to linger there. But he suddenly started up, and, closing his eyes, placed his fingers upon the lids, as though he sought to imprison within his brain some curious dream from which he feared he might awake" (5). Just as tremendous personal beauty is coupled with fear and "strange conjectures" in this novel, signs of pleasure quickly lead to a "curious" dream-space that must protect it. Dorian's suggestion of "a new manner in art" to Basil is again articulated in an agentless construction: "Some subtle influence passed from him to me" (12, 13). And it results in a fatal attraction: "As long as I live," Basil tells Lord Henry, "the personality of Dorian Gray will dominate me" (14).

Dorian sees his own beauty, revealed to him by Basil's portrait and Lord Henry's admiration, in these same fatal terms. When he first sees his image, he draws back from the canvas, his cheeks flushing for a moment with pleasure: "A look of joy came into his eyes, as if he had recognized himself for the first time" (24). But then, just as quickly, he remembers Lord Henry's speech about youth, and realizes that he too will become old: "As he thought of it, a sharp pang of pain struck through him like a knife, and made each delicate fibre of his nature quiver. [. . .] He felt as if a hand of ice had been laid on his heart" (25). Foretelling of Dorian's stabbing the portrait at the novel's conclusion and his own injunction against Basil's ripping up the canvas because it would be "murder," the sting of the figurative knife is followed by the same word used to describe the effect of the bee on the receptive flower—"quiver"— right after Lord Henry's speech. Dorian's self-conscious intimation of a fatal dimension to the beauty captured by his portrait, his feeling of an icy chill come over his petrified heart, leads him to strike the Faustian bargain that will change the course of his life and the novel: "If it were I who was to be always young, and the picture that was to grow old! [. . .] I would give my soul for that!" (25). Wilde's nod to Goethe's *Faust* is obvious, but it is the lesser-known

German text, *Sidonia*, that makes the connection to the Medusa myth clear. When the picture begins to alter in his body's place, it is a "touch of cruelty in the mouth" that Dorian first sees (78). This closely parallels the "expression of cold malignity" to be found in Sidonia's mouth in Meinhold's description of her portrait (9).[57] As Swinburne wrote of the Medusa, "many names might be found for her."[58] Wilde, pointing back to Sidonia, imagines that one of those names is Greek and a man's.

The danger of Dorian's beauty is no mere abstraction or a question of potential either. In full destructive swing, Dorian's effect on other young men's lives is described in terms of fatality throughout the novel. Dorian at first attributes this quality to the medium itself; in refusing to sit for Basil again, he explains: "There is something fatal about a portrait. It has a life of its own" (100). But it is the license that he takes in living as he wishes in Victorian London—or, more properly, the social rules that structure the very need for "license" and secrecy—that causes harm to the young men he encounters. Rumors begin to circulate first: "His extraordinary absences became notorious, and, when he used to reappear again in society, men would whisper to each other in corners, or pass him with a sneer, or look at him with cold searching eyes, as though they were determined to discover his secret" (120). These "whispered scandals," however, only increased his "strange and dangerous charm" in the eyes of many (120). When Dorian runs into Basil in a London street eighteen years later, the situation has become more serious. Basil eventually comes to the point:

> Why is your friendship so fatal to young men? There was that wretched boy
> in the Guards who committed suicide. You were his great friend. There was
> Sir Henry Ashton, who had to leave England, with a tarnished name. You and
> he were inseparable. What about Adrian Singleton, and his dreadful end? What
> about Lord Kent's only son, and his career? I met his father yesterday in St.
> James's Street. He seemed broken with shame and sorrow. What about the
> young Duke of Perth? What sort of life has he got now? What gentleman would
> associate with him? (127)

Suicide, forced exile, blackmail, ruined reputations, broken families, and stalled careers: the catalog of Dorian's effects on young men over the years parallels Sidonia's in its severity and devastating repetitiveness. For her, too, a parade of suitors meets an untimely and horrific demise, to which the narrator of that novel laments symptomatically: "What calamities may be caused by the levity and self-will of a beautiful woman!" (61).

For Dorian, like Sidonia, this was but the beginning of the tragedy. The particularly gruesome scene in which Dorian repeatedly stabs Basil Hallward to death recalls, in several key formal aspects, a harrowing scene of heartless violence and gore from *Sidonia*—the previously mentioned scene in which Sidonia dances on her virtuous cousin's coffin as she suffocates to death inside. First, for all their lethal violence both murders take considerable time to complete. Death is drawn out and seems to happen several times only for it to be revealed that the victim is still alive, increasing and prolonging the horror of the scene. After delivering what seems like it would be a fatal blow, Dorian must stab Basil multiple times: "He rushed at him, and dug the knife into the great vein that is behind the ear, crushing the man's head down on the table, and stabbing again and again. [. . .] Three times the outstretched arms shot up convulsively, waving grotesque stiff-fingered hands in the air. He stabbed him twice more, but the man did not move" (134). Sidonia's cousin's suffocation is similarly protracted, as we have seen, the grim episode also ending with a disfigured and bloody body: "The poor corpse lay all torn and disfigured from the writhings in the coffin, and a blood-vessel must have burst at last to relieve her of her agony for the blood lay yet warm on her hands" (I:235). At times, the outlandishness of the violence and the repeated, unsuccessful attempts to kill—the convulsive arms, the grotesque hands, a burst blood vessel—verges on bathos but both deaths end awfully: with "a gurgling sound" and "the horrible sound of someone choking on blood" (*Sidonia* I:235, *Dorian* 134).

It is important to note that these "idols of perversity," to use Bram Dijkstra's provocative phrase, also carry a queer valence.[59] To the expectations of heterosexual romance plot they bring an eroticism that is marked by its "sterility," in the language of both novels, as by its flagrant seriality; it is without apparent direction or teleology. Marked as outsiders by supernatural phenomena, both Dorian and Sidonia remain oblique to heterosexual romance when they are not actively opposing it. Dorian's bargain concerning the portrait operates as a kind of sorcery or magic spell, even if, like so much else in the novel, the painting's transformation seems to happen without any agency at all. Sidonia is notorious for being, as the novel's subtitle reminds us, the "destroyer" of the reigning house of Pomerania. The preface's opening lines reinforce the centrality of sterility in offering it as a reason for her unparalleled celebrity among all the trials for witchcraft: "She was accused of having by her sorceries caused sterility in many families, particularly in that of the ancient reigning house of Pomerania, and also of having destroyed the noblest scions of that house by an early and premature death" (I:7). Sterility, following Sidonia's refusal to abide by the rules of the court and her vengeful spells in the aftermath of her exile, is the novel's first concern; it is even worse, it would seem, than cruelty and murder.

Wilde places a parallel emphasis on sterility, as both an aesthetic end—*"All art is quite useless,"* his preface announces—and, by extension, as a figure for the erotic energies circulating among the novel's non-reproductive men. The substitution of the aesthetic for the homoerotic and, as we have seen, the anxious attempt by Wilde's editor to contain any breaches, become especially clear in the instances where the word "sterile" appears in the text. In the first case, responding to Dorian's charge of having been poisoned by the yellow book Lord Henry once gave him, the aesthete replies: "My dear boy, you are really beginning to moralize. [. . .] You and I are what we are, and will be what we will be. As for being poisoned by a book, there is no such thing as that. Art has no influence upon action. It annihilates the desire to act. It is superbly sterile" (183). Aimed at critics of "poisonous" art, a favorite charge of moralistic criticism, Lord Henry's refutation of any outcome from art, harmful or otherwise, reinforces the aesthetic philosophy of the novel's preface and elaborates Wilde's strategy for defending the 1890 edition of his book in the press; it is not by chance that both the preface and Lord Henry's denial of the dangerous effects of literature were added at the same time, in the 1891 edition.[60] The second instance, suppressed by Stoddart even in the 1890 edition, exposes the novel's use of the aesthetic to veil the homoerotic romance at its heart. After Basil confesses to Dorian all that is to be found in the portrait—"every flake and film of colour seemed to me to reveal my secret" (98)—there seems to Dorian to be "something infinitely tragic in a romance that was at once so passionate and so sterile" (*CW* 93).[61] Sterility here marks a kind of passionate romance, not its absence; it is both an unconventional or "tragic" quality inherent in some relationships among people who "are what we are" and the source of a dangerous threat in these novels—to a patriarchal heteronormative social structure as to a ruling family in need of heirs.

Meinhold's weird fictional account of a moral panic concerning a dangerously excessive feminine sexuality thus echoes throughout Wilde's novel that instigated a moral panic not unrelated to that same misogyny half a century later, when queer male sexuality was imagined as both an overdetermined "tragic" femininity and a sterility. No small part of Dorian's transgression is his standing in for the femme fatale—indeed, showing it to be a role, in the strong sense, to be occupied—and the effect that he has, through no doing of his own (or of others, it turns out), on other men. The implications of *Dorian*'s debt to and interventions in the German Romantic tradition are more far-reaching than might initially appear. Wilde clearly reworks the double portrait and the themes of the dangerous erotic stunner and queer sterility found in *Sidonia* to his own ends in *Dorian*. As this book argues, no one source or context is all defining in this notoriously allusive novel. But what might have seemed at mid-century to be a quaint romantic look back at an antiquated past in Meinhold and in the Pre-Raphaelite Brotherhood's cult of *Sidonia*, had become by the 1890s a full-blown archetypal figure: the dangerous eroticism of the femme fatale of *Salomé* and, as I have been arguing here, even earlier, of the male stunner in *Dorian*. This is important and not merely interesting in that it shows the full extent to which literary Decadence entails not a degradation or decay of the past, as its contemporary critics famously claimed and its proponents strategically celebrated, but, crucially, a reuse of the past that attempts to reposition and thus revise it for the present. It comprises a highly curated archive of materials placed in new, often startling and generative relation to one another.

What emerges from this quirky comparison, then, is an early iteration in practice of the idea of tradition that T. S. Eliot would theorize several decades later in "Tradition and the Individual Talent" (1919). For Eliot, tradition famously involves that "historical sense" that is sensitive to both the pastness of the past and its presence. Wilde's notorious allusiveness suddenly appears an advantage in this light:

> Not only the best, but the most individual parts of [the artist's] work may be those in which the dead poets, his ancestors, assert their immortality most vigorously. [. . .] What happens when a new work of art is created is something that happens simultaneously to all the works of art which preceded it. The existing monuments form an ideal order among themselves, which is modified by the introduction of the new (the really new) work of art among them.[62]

Wilde's resurrection of elements of the romance that he so loved as a child and that the Pre-Raphaelites had celebrated before him is, then, best understood as a reciprocal relation. It involved an archivist's sense and collection of a history that is both past and present; and it effects a highly creative and radically new sense of the archive that could not exist before it. That is to say, *Sidonia* is both recollected by Wilde's novel as well as repositioned and re-signified within a longer and more geographically expansive literary history. When the old order is met with novelty, for Eliot:

the *whole* existing order must be, if ever so slightly, altered; and so the relations, proportions, values of each work of art toward the whole are readjusted; and this is conformity between the old and the new. Whoever has approved this idea of order, of the form of European, of English literature will not find it preposterous that the past should be altered by the present as much as the present is directed by the past.[63]

It is not merely that *Sidonia* influenced Wilde as it is that *Dorian* changes how we read Meinhold—indeed, that reading them together changes what "influence" means.

Wilde's Decadent archival practice, however, goes even further than Eliot's renovating idea of tradition in one important respect: its transnationalism. Not a literary-historical project as such, Wilde's Decadence is archival more out of practical necessity—a concern for recollecting the forms of the past in order to reimagine them for a new present. Eliot's sense of tradition is more purely historical, although it conceives of history as recursive and ever changing. To the extent that its remit extends outward in space, it includes a pan-European literary tradition. Yet within that tradition it reinscribes the national literatures to which individual authors exclusively belong: "The historical sense compels a man to write not merely with his own generation in his bones, but with a feeling that the whole of the literature of Europe from Homer and within it the whole of the literature of his own country."[64] As we have seen, Decadence's impulse is to disregard if not erase the need or desirability of national boundaries, the key prepositions being "across" and "beyond," not "from" or "within."

For this reason, translation across languages and cultures is as important a theoretical concern as transmission across time. Stefano Evangelista's location of the birth of Decadence in Baudelaire's 1856 and 1857 translations of Poe's tales speaks to the importance of translation as a Decadent literary form in its own right and as a forger of transnational alliances that opened up, in Evangelista's words, "an extraterritorial space of artistic freedom [. . .] where future decadent writers could now also claim citizenship."[65] That the imaginative ground for that space was already being prepared in Jane Elgee's 1849 translation of a little-known German terror tale and Rossetti's fascination with its spectral painterliness from the early 1850s only adds to the foundational importance of translation to literary Decadence. Crossing boundaries between languages, time periods, and artistic forms, the case of Wilde's reinvention of Sidonia in Dorian reveals connections that have previously only been glimpsed. Attending to these connections as part of the central impulse of Decadence rather than as quirks of literary history illuminates the avant-garde quality of Wilde's reinvention of past forms. It also reveals the unruly Decadent transnationalism that an explicitly modernist historical sense, in Eliot, would soon distance itself from and leave to the side of the road of "progress."

PART THREE

NETWORKED FORMS

CHAPTER FOUR

Transatlantic Forebears

Painted Betrayals in Hawthorne, Poe, and James

Most genealogies of literary Decadence refer to, if not begin with, the writings of Edgar Allan Poe, so it is perhaps no surprise to see his name appear in this study. As mentioned in chapter 3, Poe's legacy is central to a view of a transnational Decadence in particular, as his tales extended across and found new life beyond national borders in the translation of his books into many languages. As Stefano Evangelista has argued, Baudelaire's encounter with Poe provides a foundational example by which we can see that nineteenth-century Decadence "was truly born in translation."[1] Making the contemporary case for translation as a creative and experimental literary form of its own, Arthur Symons called Baudelaire's translations of Poe's *Tales* "better than a marvelous original."[2] Stéphane Mallarmé followed Baudelaire's example in the 1880s, focusing instead on translating Poe's poetry, so that when writers such as Wilde, Symons, and Vernon Lee drew on Poe's works, in Evangelista's words, "it was no longer simply the American writer they were evoking but the one that had been made more precious by the French patina, the translated and de-territorialized Poe created by the French decadent poets."[3]

In addition to the unpredictable effects of translation's movement back and forth between English and target-language worlds, John Paul Riquelme has also found the influence of Poe, whom he calls "the most echoic stylist among earlier prominent figures in the Gothic tradition," at the level of the original language.[4] For example, the effect of the consonance in Wilde's opening passage about the laburnum ("blossoms [...] laburnum [...] branches [...] bear [...] burden [...] beauty [...] birds") finds one potential origin in the beginning of the first sentence of Poe's "The Fall of the House of Usher" ("During the whole of dull, dark, and soundless day [. . .]") or the title of the story discussed in this chapter, "William Wilson."[5] Jamil Mustafa has documented the haunting of Wilde's poem "The Harlot's House" (1885) by the ghosts of Poe and Baudelaire, including a gender-shifting substitution of "Harlot" for "Prince" in the manuscript, which Mustafa reads as invoking Poe's Prince Prospero and "The Masque of the Red Death."[6] And of particular interest for this chapter, Kerry Powell has placed *Dorian Gray* at the pinnacle of what he calls the nineteenth-century "mania" for fiction about magic portraits popularized by Poe and others, which was especially acute in the 1880s and 1890s but is now largely forgotten.

This chapter expands upon Poe's centrality to transnational Decadence by deepening the sense of his influence on Wilde within a wider network of specifically US contexts: the commissioning of *Dorian* by the American editor J. M. Stoddart for *Lippincott's Monthly Magazine* and a US tradition of magic-picture narratives that Wilde would have known would ensure his story's appeal to a transatlantic audience, even if memory of his 1882 North American tour had by then begun to fade. These narratives include Nathaniel Hawthorne's "The Prophetic Pictures" (1837) and "Edward Randolph's Portrait" (1838), Poe's "William Wilson" (1839) and "The Oval Portrait" (1842), and Henry James's artist tales, "The Story of a Masterpiece" (1868) and "The Liar" (1888). As we will see, whether Wilde knew of each and every one of these tales is less important than the fact that the tradition as a whole clearly informs his narrative and formal choices in *Dorian*, especially in the way that the stories problematize and undercut the moralizing logic by which they seem to work.[7] In addition to assimilating his *Lippincott's* readers' preferences and expectations, I suggest, Wilde learned from his American predecessors how to use formal complexity against a moralistic national sentiment. Poe's weighty influence on transnational Decadence can be seen to derive not only from the import of his translations or reuse of the linguistic patterns of the original; it is also to be found in the broader understanding that Poe offered Wilde of the formal tradition of his American forebears' magic-picture tales.

In taking a close look at the forms that Wilde found circulating from the other side of the Atlantic in the mid- to late 1800s and the practices that they offer for challenging the literary, social, and moral status quo while remaining publishable in the contemporary Anglo-American literary marketplace, a key question emerges. Why did Wilde choose this particular tradition—the magic-picture story—for his only novel, a work that went further than any mainstream text in English up to that point to raise the specter of homosexuality? In addressing this question, I suggest that an emphasis on the formal aspects of Wilde's US sources, rather than purely on the national or contemporaneous qualities of these texts, throws light on *Dorian*'s challenge to the moralizing logic by which it would also seem to operate. The magic-portrait tradition was interesting to Wilde precisely for this reason: by choosing it to give shape to his ingenious story that speaks of the love that dare not speak its name, he was ensuring a proliferation of possible meanings and interpretive challenges. As a result, for more than a century, those looking for a simple one-dimensional parable, as well as those sensitive to the complexities and deep ambivalences of the story, have been able to find their readings in this novel.

To establish the connections across these short narratives, this chapter provides some necessary background about plot and narration before expanding on the larger implications for reading *Dorian*, the text that remains this tradition's chief export and high-water mark. Indeed, its success has eclipsed the influential work that preceded it. We know, however, that Wilde devoured the popular fiction of his day, greatly admired Poe, and owned multiple copies of his works.[8] Also, he chided James for writing fiction "as if it were a painful duty," regarding him as one of those authors "one ought to read" but was "not bound to like."[9] Still, he was impressed by the ghost story *The Turn of the Screw* (1898), describing it in a letter to Robert Ross as a "most wonderful, lurid, poisonous little tale," and adding: "James is developing, but he will never arrive at passion, I fear."[10] As critics have long held, James was himself influenced by Hawthorne's use of the magic-portrait motif, and Poe was an early reviewer and critic of Hawthorne's tales.[11] Joining this tradition in writing his story of a transmogrifying canvas for *Lippincott's* must have felt like a rite of literary initiation for Wilde. The formal resonances and homologies within this tradition accrue to something like evidence and have significant implications for how we read the novel. In particular, the narrative complexity of each tale belies a seeming moral clarity and points to an additional need to read against the grain of *Dorian*'s ostensibly inevitable, strongly moralizing ending—namely, the scene in which, by stabbing his disfigured portrait, that "most magical of mirrors," Dorian kills himself and thus is properly punished, according to convention, for his transgressions (91). Rather, close attention to the novel's formal features—inherited, in part, from its American precursors—reveals it to be not only a cautionary tale, but also—crucially—a cautionary tale about reading for cautionary tales.

Prophetic Pictures, Profligate Liars: Magic Portraits before Wilde

Before delving into this archive, a few points about the chapter's larger argument will be useful to keep in mind. First, Wilde's sourcing of his novel in such a rich tradition of popular storytelling suggests, as Kerry Powell has convincingly written, not so much a case of derivativeness or plagiarism as a canny piecing together, reimagining, and putting to new use an entire tradition that has since been ignored or oversimplified by critics. For Powell, the key insight is that Wilde made ingenious use of an entire lexicon of motifs associated with the magic-picture tradition, rather than any one or more precedents—so much so that we tend to remember *Dorian* today only in unique terms, but essentially out of context. Powell writes: "Gathering his materials from the tradition at large rather than from any one or even a few sources, Wilde constructs a work of tighter structure, greater power, and more teasing subtlety than any other work of its kind. His novel can thus be viewed as both a compendious and consummate expression of a literary tradition whose outlines have been largely forgotten by us, but which flourished in the popular literature of the [nineteenth] century especially."[12] Building on Powell, my contention is that Wilde annexed this broader tradition for strategic reasons and put it to particular uses, not the least of which was to furnish a model for how to transgress and yet persist in publishing a novel that dared to speak of illicit homosexual desire, as explored in chapter 1. The focus on identifying ever more "overlooked" sources of Wilde's novel has revealed many interesting points of connection but risks missing the larger import of Wilde's strategic use of the magic-picture tradition as a whole. At least part of why Powell is correct when he notes that "in *Dorian Gray* there is much of importance which cannot be accounted for by reference to any single source" is that Wilde's novel makes use of the magic-picture tradition's formal logic of epistemological uncertainty and ironic reversal as well as, or even more than, any of its individual component parts.[13]

Second, the texts by Hawthorne, Poe, and James discussed below are important contexts for Wilde, then, not because any one text is a lynchpin to understanding the genesis or meaning of *Dorian Gray* but because, taken together, they point to a certain feeling for form—a consistency not only of motifs, themes, situations, and character types, but of narrative structures and techniques that cut against the conventional morality that the stories would seem to purport to uphold. Understanding both the thematic and narrative affinities between the earlier nineteenth-century magic-picture tradition and Wilde's novel, as well as Wilde's innovations to this tradition, has significant implications for how we read *Dorian*, and especially what we make of the famous ending. Rather than accumulate ever more definitive sources for the novel, then, the goal here is to trace the implications of sourcing this novel that we thought we knew within a tradition that has been largely forgotten.

In each of the two volumes of Hawthorne's *Twice-Told Tales* (1837, 1842) there is a story about portraiture's supernatural, almost monstrous power to reveal character and the otherwise hidden truths that determine future lives. "The Prophetic Pictures" (1837) recounts the tale of Walter Ludlow and his fiancée Elinor, who, on the eve of their marriage, have their portraits made by an artist said to paint "not merely a man's features but his mind and heart," catching "the secret sentiments and passions" and throwing them upon the canvas "like sunshine—or perhaps, in the portraits of dark-souled men, like a gleam of internal fire."[14] They both witness a change in their portraits as the artist works, ostensibly revealing their "inmost soul" and a future prophecy: in hers, a glint of grief and terror, and in his, a look of wild passion (463). The artist then shows Elinor a crayon sketch of two figures in some kind of horrific action (purportedly the cause of the change in the portraits), suggesting that he could always alter the expression in the portraits or the action in the sketch, but "would it influence the event?" (464). Elinor demurs. The couple is married, the portraits hung. Elinor eventually drapes a curtain of purple silk over them (as Dorian will do, too) under the pretense of protecting the portraits from dust, and time wears on. The artist remains cold-hearted: "He had caught from the duskiness of the future—at least, so he fancied—a fearful secret, and had obscurely revealed it on the portraits" (466).

The "coming evil" foreshadowed by the artist eventually comes to pass when he visits the couple at home: Elinor sees an increasing wildness in Walter's expression as her own face assumes a look of terror, as in the portraits. Walter then tries to stab Elinor to death. The sketch, "with all its tremendous coloring, was finished" (469). The artist intercedes in his own vision and stops the scene, asking Elinor: "Did I not warn you?" She replies: "You did. [. . .] But—I loved him" (469). The story concludes with a question: "Is there not a deep moral in the tale? Could the result of one, or all our deeds, be shadowed forth and set before us, some would call it Fate, and hurry onward, others be swept along by their passionate desires, and none be turned aside by the PROPHETIC PICTURES" (469). The idea of the portrait as both revealer and repository of the true self, which can only be caught up to in real life in a moment threatening death—by stabbing—can thus be traced back at least as far as Hawthorne's strange tale. The story's "deep moral"—not to be swept along by "passionate desires" but to heed all warnings—would seem to anticipate, structurally, at least, the cautionary tale of Dorian's final demise, an excess prolonged, captured in a work of art, and ultimately held to account.

Similarly, "Edward Randolph's Portrait" (1838) features an otherworldly portrait that offers a dreadful warning. This time, instead of gleaming, brand-new images concealed by a silk curtain until a moment of horrific revelation in which life catches up to the artist's prevision, the mysterious picture in this later story is ancient and obscure, blackened by years of hanging in a colonial Boston province-house. The narration is now first-person and framed by the outer narrator's retelling of the legend of a canvas dark with age, damp, and smoke, recounted by an old denizen of the province-house, Mr. Bela Tiffany. "Time had thrown an impenetrable veil over it," he begins, "and left to tradition, and fable, and conjecture, to say what had once been there portrayed" (641–42). Alice Vane, a young niece of a provincial captain (who shares a surname with Dorian's fleeting love interest, Sibyl), becomes interested in restoring the picture. Lieutenant-Governor Hutchinson informs her that it was once a portrait of Edward Randolph, the much-despised British colonial administrator jailed during the 1689 Boston revolt. "And yet," Alice wonders, "may not such fables have a moral?" (645). If the visage is so dreadful, it would do well to be visible to rulers, as a reminder of "the awful weight of a People's curse" (645). "Come forth, dark and evil Shape," she beckons. "It is thine hour!" (646).

The portrait's dark revelation is soon at hand. During a debate among selectmen about the presence of British troops in the town, the restored painting is unveiled, showing the "terrors of hell" upon Randolph's face, intensified by the passing of time, a "dreadful effigy" (649). "Be warned then!" Alice says. "He trampled on a people's rights. Behold his punishment—and avoid a crime like his!" (649). But defying the warning and the picture, "which seemed, at that moment, to intensify the horror of its miserable and wicked look," Hutchinson signs the colonial decree (650). In the morning, the picture goes dark again; as for Hutchinson, on his deathbed, he "complained he was choking with the blood of the Boston Massacre" and there was "a likeness in his frenzied look to that of Edward Randolph" (650–51). "Did his broken spirit feel, at that dread hour," the old man's story concludes, "the tremendous burthen of a People's curse?" (651). As in "The Prophetic Pictures," "Edward Randolph's Portrait" thematizes art's affinity with revelation, truth, and prophecy and ends with the suggestion of a conventional "moral" that reverses the forces put in motion by the denial of art's powerful warnings within the narrative just told—Elinor's demurring, Hutchinson's willful defiance. It is a narrative arc that will be elaborated much more complexly (and artistically) by Wilde, but it served as a germ and a scaffold for a tradition of nineteenth-century writing about magical portraits that followed, the bulk of which these tales predate by several decades.

In his 1842 review of Hawthorne's tales, Poe commends their beauty and originality but laments their "mysticism" and overt didacticism, by which, he fears, "the *obvious* meaning [. . .] will be found to smother the *insinuated* one" and the "moral [. . .] will be supposed to convey the *true* import of the narrative."[15] This review will be especially useful for thinking about the supposed "moral" of the ending of Wilde's novel with regard to this tradition, but, for his part, Poe wrote several magic-picture stories to his own liking. His tales "William Wilson" (1839) and "The Oval Portrait" (1842) take up Hawthorne's subject while moving away from the didacticism and allegory with which he found fault. In "William Wilson," portraiture is a metaphor rather than a prop. The titular first-person narrator is stalked and tormented from early childhood by a tireless doppelgänger.[16] The "second William Wilson" who somehow goes undetected as his supernatural double by everyone else, has the same name, the same birthdate, is of the same height, has the same stature and appearance, copies his dress, appropriates his gait and general manner, and arrives at boarding school on the same day as the narrator. The only difference is that he speaks only in a whisper. He is a "perfect imitation," copying not just the letter "which in a painting is all the obtuse can see" but "the full spirit of the original" (632).

The rest of the tale recounts the lengths to which the "portrait" hounds the "original," driving him into a "vortex of thoughtless folly," a "miserable profligacy," and "rooted habits of vice" (634). Repeated confrontations in which his "rival" thwarts his plans to do mischief by exposing the narrator's "true character" (including his penchant for intoxication, cheating at cards, and seducing married women), followed by flights to new cities away from his "evil destiny" and inevitable rediscoveries by his "tormentor," culminate in a final episode in which the two spar to the death (631, 638, 639). After stabbing his double fatally, a large mirror suddenly appears and reflects his own image, but as his double now, "with features all pale and dabbled in blood" (641). "It was my antagonist," he declares (641). But the double no longer speaks in a whisper, and it is the narrator himself who feels that he is speaking: *"In me didst thou exist—and, in my death, see by this image, which is thine own, how utterly thou hast murdered thyself"* (641). Competing guises, an overweening egotism, an extravagant decadence, and the stabbing of one's image-conscience, which ironically turns out to be the means of one's own destruction: the date is 1839, yet the shape of Dorian Gray's story is already apparent here.

Turning from the idea of living "portraiture," "The Oval Portrait" tells the story of an actual painting that purportedly came to life at the expense of its sitting subject. Here a wounded first-person narrator and his valet break into an abandoned chateau to take shelter for the night and discover a great number of paintings. A chance repositioning of the candelabrum throws light on a portrait of a young girl, which seems to "dissipate the dreamy stupor" and "startle [him] at once into waking life" (290–91). What he sees is the "true secret" of the painting's effect: despite the "peculiarities" of the design and of the frame, reminding him it is "a thing of art" and not "a living person," he finds the "spell" of the picture in "an absolute life-likeliness of expression" (291). On the bed pillow he discovers a small volume that "purported to criticise and describe" the paintings, which both relates the history of the oval portrait and comprises the final words of the tale (290). A painter marries a young woman, and, in bringing her portrait to life, slowly, unwittingly, kills her. The story concludes without ever returning to the outer frame narrative: "For one moment, the painter stood entranced before the work which he had wrought; but in the next, while yet he gazed, he grew tremulous and very pallid, and aghast, and crying with a loud voice, "This is indeed Life itself!" turned suddenly to regard his beloved:—*She was dead!*" (292).

Poe's "Oval Portrait" thus fantasizes a dangerous zero-sum game of the artist's power to transfer "life-likeliness" from the sitting subject to the work of art in a way that betrays the living human for an aesthetic ideal, the model for the copy. Unbeknownst to the painter, "the tints which he spread upon the canvas were drawn from the cheeks of her who sat beside him" (292). This game works somewhat differently in *Dorian*, with the picture taking on the physical signs of the experiences Dorian hungrily pursues with seeming impunity, but both literalize the idea of art as the transfer of life to canvas. Dorian's stabbing of the canvas, his final attempt to save himself from the moral calculus exacted by the portrait, results in a violent reversal. The painting reverts back to its original pristine state, and Dorian's dead body lies on the floor, "withered, wrinkled, and loathsome of visage" (188). In Poe's tale, life is taken from the model by an artistic monomania and perhaps by the artistic process itself; in Wilde's version, the model's life is taken when he tries to reverse his own fateful wish to have the painting take on secret, moralizing meanings of its own.

James's artist tales "The Story of a Masterpiece" (1868) and "The Liar" (1888) also make use of the motif of the uncanny portrait in ways that Wilde's later and more famous example echoes. Both stories concern an artist involved in a love triangle and the stabbing of a picture that betrays a secret truth about its subject. In "The Story of a Masterpiece," the wealthy John Lennox is engaged to the penniless Marian Everett, who used to be engaged to a young artist named Stephen Baxter until she jilted him (and several others). Lennox meets Baxter by chance in a studio he shares with a mutual artist friend and is struck first by the artist's face—an interest quickly displaced onto his artwork: "'A man with that face,' he said to himself, 'does work at least worth looking at.'"[17] Then, he quickly notices the likeness to his fiancée of the subject of one of his paintings. Lennox learns of their past connection, but not of their engagement, and invites Baxter to paint Marian's portrait. "Without malice," the omniscient narrator tells us, Baxter infuses into the commissioned picture something of his bitter disappointment and the "force of characterization" and "depth of reality" that his knowledge of Marian's past indiscretions (and her lie of omission in hiding their own past engagement from Lennox) yields: "His genius had held communion with his heart and had transferred to canvas the burden of its disenchantment and its resignation" (233–34). The result is a "masterpiece" but betrays a "heartlessness" and lack of seriousness that Lennox had always suspected in Marian:

> It seemed to Lennox that some strangely potent agency had won from his mistress the confession of her inmost soul, and had written it there upon the canvas in firm yet passionate lines. Marian's person was lightness—her charm was lightness; could it be that her soul was levity too? Was she a creature without faith, and without conscience? (232)

Lennox falls out of love but plans to go ahead with the wedding anyway. When the portrait arrives from the framer's, he sees no other choice but to destroy the evidence of Marian's deceit:

> He looked about him with an angry despair, and his eye fell on a long, keen poignard, given to him by a friend who had bought it in the East, and which lay as an ornament on his mantel-shelf. He seized it and thrust it, with barbarous glee, straight into the lovely face of the image. He dragged it downward, and

made a long fissure in the living canvas. Then, with half a dozen strokes, he wantonly hacked it across. The act afforded him an immense relief. (241)

A short postscript to this climactic scene confirms their ensuing marriage: "I need hardly add that on the following day Lennox was married," but not before locking the library door and keeping the fate of the picture a secret until after the honeymoon: "He had the key in his waistcoat pocket as he stood at the altar" (241).

The homologies between this early James story's use of a powerfully revealing portrait and Wilde's version—the "strangely potent agency" that forces a "confession" of the "inmost soul," a "living canvas" secreted away in a locked room to silence the shocking story it tells and ultimately stabbed in a desperate attempt to escape it—can also be found in the later story "The Liar," in which James reuses the motif with several important variations—namely, the artist's model here is male and he slashes his own portrait. As in the earlier story, an artist, Oliver Lyon, sees an old flame, Everina Brant, at a dinner party at an estate where he has been invited to draw the owner's portrait. Everina is now married to Colonel Capadose, who, in the presence of everyone, tells outlandish untruths that implicate his wife in his dishonesty, since she is forced to go along with her husband's "queer habit" of lying.[18] Soon, Lyon agrees to paint Capadose's portrait and, full of the anger and resentment of a rejected suitor, plans to unmask him in the process and to force Mrs. Capadose to confess her dissatisfaction with her choice of husband. When the portrait is completed, the Capadoses visit the artist's studio when he is supposed to be out of town; however, when Lyon returns unexpectedly, he overhears the couple through a curtain. Startled by their cries and his own painting's "look of life," Lyon struggles to take in the incredible scene:

> The Colonel turned away and moved rapidly about the room, as if he were looking for something; Lyon was unable for the instant to guess his intention. Then the artist said to himself, below his breath, "He's going to do it a harm!" His first impulse was to rush down and stop him; but he paused, with the sound of Everina Brant's sobs still in his ears. The Colonel found what he was looking for—found it among some odds and ends on a small table and rushed back with it to the easel. At one and the same moment Lyon perceived that the object he had seized was a small Eastern dagger and that he had plunged it into the canvas. He seemed animated by a sudden fury, for with extreme vigour of hand he dragged the instrument down (Lyon knew it to have no very fine edge) making a long, abominable gash. Then he plucked it out and dashed it

again several times into the face of the likeness, exactly as if he were stabbing a human victim: it had the oddest effect—that of a sort of figurative suicide. (362–63)

The Capadoses cover their crime together, by blaming a drunken artist's model whom they had declined to give money, a performance that made Lyon's "whole vision crumble—his theory that [Everina] had secretly kept true to herself" (369). Instead, Mrs. Capadose, whose husband "had trained her too well," has the parting shot, telling Lyon: "For you, I am very sorry. But you must remember that I possess the original!" (371).

With their theme of portrait painting as a form of exposure, their anxious fantasies about a strangely imbued "living canvas," and the not-so-thinly-veiled romantic triangles and erotic rivalries, these American stories form a remarkably coherent narrative tradition of uncanny portraits that predates Wilde and would have been known to many of his *Lippincott's* readers. This tradition further suggests a different genealogy through which to read *Dorian Gray*, one in which formal resonances are also intimately connected to thematic concerns. For these stories' use of the motif of the magical portrait is only the most obvious feature that they share. Through various narrative techniques, they all also undercut their own authority, highlighting the lack of reliability of the text itself and, thus, dramatizing the need to read the subject of the fiction as a formal problem as well.

Didactic Narrators, Unreliable Morals

Poe's criticism that the "moral" of Hawthorne's fiction threatens to be too easily confused with the "*true* import of the narrative" signals an important difference between what the tales purport to be saying and what else they might also "insinuate" or come to mean.[19] Indeed, it is characteristic of the US magic-picture tradition that Wilde takes hold of in 1890 for the narrative to turn in on itself, and against its own apparent didacticism. I argue below that the playful equivocations of these formal somersaults—to transgress and yet to be seen to be moralizing—are precisely what attracted Wilde to this tradition and what he exploits so effectively. First, it will be helpful to show how consistently earlier nineteenth-century magic-picture fiction relies on formal tricks such as framing and unreliable first-person narration, to undercut the seemingly obvious "deep morals" of their endings. Even the earliest of the stories, the tales by Hawthorne that are the most open to the charge of didacticism, dramatize the need to read closely for form. For instance, "The

Prophetic Pictures," an otherwise straightforward third-person omniscient narrative, couches its moral about passion's blinding qualities in a negative question—"Is there not a deep moral in the tale?" (469). The ambivalence of this question can also be found in what comes of another crucial question in the story, when the artist offers to change the frightened look in Elinor's portrait or the hideous action in his prophetic sketch: "But would it influence the event?" he asks (464). In fact, the foreseen stabbing of Elinor by her husband Walter turns out not to have been preordained, since it does not happen, and it is the artist himself who stops Walter's hand; he turns out to be at least as deluded as Walter in his belief in art's power to affect the destinies of its subjects—or "so he fancied," the narrator recalls (466). The reader arrives at this realization only after the power of the artist to reveal "true character" and acquire "influence over their fates" is already established, then reinforced by the artist's monologue about his godlike powers. But the ambiguity resonates long after the story's ending, further complicating the otherwise obvious message. For the question "Is there not a deep moral in the tale?" also asks: "Is there?"

The warning of "Edward Randolph's Portrait" not to trample on a people's right—"to avoid a crime like his!" (649)—is also complicated by the form of a question. In his dying hour, Lieutenant-Governor Hutchinson, who ignored the portrait's warning, exhibits "a likeness in his frenzied look" to that of Edward Randolph: "Did his broken spirit feel, at that dread hour, the tremendous burthen of a People's curse?" (650–51). Because this tale is a frame narrative, the ambivalence of the inner narrator Bela Tiffany's question about Hutchinson is compounded by the outer first-person narrator's story of hearing the story "babbled" to him (651). When he first comes across Tiffany in the province-house, he notes that the whiskey punch he is drinking acts as a "solvent upon his memory" so that it "overflowed" with stories (641). Introducing the narrative that he then hears from Tiffany about the mysterious black portrait, the first-person narrator admits that while it is "as correct a version of the fact as the reader would be likely to obtain from any other source," it has a "tinge of romance approaching to the marvelous" (641). Likewise, at the conclusion of "this miraculous legend," his final paragraph details the lack of any proof that there was ever any such portrait and drifts off into the anticlimax of a blinding snowstorm on his return home instead, further obfuscating the status of Tiffany's story and undercutting its power as a cautionary tale or anything more than a "marvelous" fiction (651).

As we have seen, Poe eschewed the didacticism of a stated "moral" in creating his tales, preferring an ironic, if no less fantastical, reversal at the conclusion of "William Wilson." The message spoken by his double as Wilson looks into the mirror at his bloodied figure, feeling as if it were himself speaking, is that the copy and the original were one; in killing his double, Wilson has killed himself. As a first-person narrator, however, Wilson is anything but reliable. He is, by his own admission, the heir of a "family character" prone to an "imaginative" and "easily excitable temperament," which has intensified with age, becoming "a cause for serious disquietude" to his friends (626). He is so ashamed of the "detestation of [his] race" as to withhold his real name; "William Wilson" is a mere approximation, we are told, and hence a double fiction (626). Having developed a clear picture of an encroaching insanity in his adolescence, the story of his double then becomes increasingly suspect. His monomania is such that he is not disabused of his fantasy by the fact that those around him do not see the other Wilson as an extraordinary double, only as a possible relation. His language for Wilson—his "namesake" (629), "rival" (631), "tormentor" (639), "arch-enemy and evil genius" (639)—mirrors his growing hysteria. At the same time, it becomes increasingly clear that the story of the double actually enables the narrator to displace blame and not take responsibility for his own extravagance; he is the victim, persecuted by another. The psychologically unstable narrator thus casts the entire story of a "second William Wilson," as well as his sanity, into question. The story's ostensible message—that our conscience, or that which thwarts our baser impulses, is essential to our very existence—remains clear, but it becomes subordinated to the expression of an all-consuming paranoid monomania. The telling of the story upstages the story told.

Similarly, in "The Oval Portrait" Poe's first-person narrator is physically wounded, mysteriously, a fact that from the story's opening line casts some doubt on his mental state and his observations of the chateau and its treasure trove of art. In addition, Poe's disturbing fantasy of a murderous artistic monomania here relies on a story-within-a-story framing device. The history of the oval portrait is related by another text, the small volume on the bed pillow that only "purport[s]" to tell the truth; it is a story within a story whose climactic moment also concludes the outer frame narrative itself: *"She was dead!"* the narrator and the reader discover at the same moment (290, 292). Thus, the "spell" of the picture and its ability to expose the "truth" of its creation depend upon a questionable first-person narrator and a text within the text that comes to the narrator secondhand.

Like Poe's tales, "The Liar" shifts the reader's interest—and suspicion—

elsewhere through narration, to the story of the story's telling. In his narrative of 1888, James revises the more conventional third-person omniscient treatment of his earlier 1868 tale "The Story of a Masterpiece," now using his famed center of consciousness method of narration to place the story firmly within the limited point of view of the character of the portraitist himself.[20] Offering an anatomy of the obsessively jealous spurned lover, "The Liar" makes the story told from Lyon's perspective increasingly suspect, raising the question of who exactly the liar is (the analogy to fiction and to James himself is never far away here). The artist Lyon's bitter resentment, his own deviousness and questionable motivations for trying to expose his old lover's complicity in her husband's pathological lying to make her regret spurning him, and his spying and cynical lie of omission in allowing the guilty couple to give an excuse he knows to be untrue gradually become even more interesting, and more disturbing to the reader, than the actual subject of the story being narrated. The other interesting revision that James makes between 1868 and 1888 is in who stabs the exposing portrait: in "The Story of a Masterpiece," Marian's fiancé Lennox does the honors, whereas in "The Liar," the subject of the portrait, Colonel Capadose himself, destroys his own image—"a sort of figurative suicide," in the words of the story, and an important precursor to Wilde's treatment of the subject two years later.

Killing the Past in *Dorian Gray*

In *Dorian*, Wilde transcends this earlier tradition's use of stark narrative framing and first-person monologue; indeed, part of what makes the novel so remarkable is its refusal of the tradition's more obvious devices in preference for even more sophisticated and stealth inventions. Rather than merely imitate the tradition, Wilde again takes it up in order to transform it. It is precisely by formal means that *Dorian* troubles any simplistic understanding of what Poe called the "moral" as opposed to the "*true* import of the narrative." To signal that something more complicated than a mere cautionary tale is at stake in the novel, Wilde's clever use of hybrid genres heightens the sense of artifice and the critical distance between what is being said and what is meant throughout. As discussed in chapter 1, the novel's inventive design hinges on the key moment of the supernatural transformation of the portrait relatively early on, and the picture's acquisition of magical properties sharply divides the book into two parts: a homoerotic-Bildungsroman first part, in which Dorian seems to be on a path of self-discovery, and a paranoid-Gothic second part that forecloses that possibility and safely reinscribes the novel within conventional Victorian morality. The urban Eden of the novel's opening scene, in which Dorian's youthful beauty appears in the luminous, fragrant, all-male space of the artist's garden studio gives way to the hiding of the portrait behind an ornate Spanish screen and satin pall and then removing it entirely to an old, disused schoolroom upstairs, where it remains locked away until Dorian's fateful confrontation with it in the novel's final scene.

The novel's ending would seem to ask us to reconfirm Dorian's death as his just desserts. But the dramatic shift out of the Bildungsroman narrative and into one of Gothic horror raises more questions than it answers and is never quite forgotten. For one, it invites an awareness of the impossibility of the homoeroticism that saturates the opening chapters and the subsequent effects of its repression on Dorian's character. The genre shifting that occurs at the moment of the portrait's magical transformation interrupts the self-development narrative and yet is the very means of its persistence. Throughout the rest of the novel, the self-development narrative initiated in the novel's opening scenes acts as an ever-present reminder of a counterfactual otherwise: what if things happened or could happen differently, or perhaps, at least, what if Dorian had acted differently? The recursive reading process that results is not unlike that triggered by the more overt narrative techniques used by Hawthorne, Poe, and James to create ambiguity in their fiction or to suggest ambivalence in their own stance, causing the reader to go back and reconsider. Part of the mysterious power of Wilde's contribution to this lineage is the forcefulness of the novel's ending—the obvious moral that hedonism must be paid for and there is no separating one from one's conscience. Yet there is a lasting sense that there is much more to it than that. The novel's hybrid form provides important clues as to how to read it, and how not to. For one, the strategic blending of diametrically opposed genres makes it nearly impossible to read the "moral" of Dorian's fate as a simple cautionary tale. The moralizing story of the picture's transformation and Dorian's ultimate destruction at the end necessarily co-opts and screens the incipient homoeroticism of the beginning, as was required at the time; yet, the homoeroticism is registered nonetheless and never really disappears, a canny use of uncanny generic conventions on Wilde's part.

At the level of narration, Wilde eschews Poe's troubled first-person narrator and James's center of consciousness method in favor of a clever use of point of view. Wilde's use of focalization, or shifting into the subjective point of view from the narrator to a character or characters, is less robust than James's. But Dorian is portrayed vividly by the third-person omniscient narrator, in part, so he can be better held up to scrutiny. The interest in Dorian's narrow consciousness that especially marks the novel's Gothic descent invites us to question his behavior on slightly different grounds from the moral—namely, that it is Dorian's belief that art holds a message of any kind that the novel criticizes. *"There is no such thing as a moral or an immoral book,"* Wilde writes in his preface. *"Books are well written, or badly written. That is all"* (3). Yet it is precisely this maxim that Dorian ignores in turning to Basil's portrait for reasons other than aesthetic, and in falling under the influence of Lord Henry's yellow book and beautiful phrases, which are flung out artistically to dazzle and perhaps to inspire similar acts of creativity but not necessarily to be acted upon, literally. Lord Henry himself doesn't even act on them. "The aim of life is self-development," he says, after all (18). Bound by conventions, Dorian looks for an end in art beyond the beauty and pleasure that are so clearly written there, and this too is what the story of his demise seems to caution against. The external third-person narrative point of view curbs any potential identification and helps reinforce the reader's growing skepticism of the reading practices that Dorian exemplifies.

Interestingly, the rare moments of free indirect discourse in the novel occur when the narrative shifts briefly into Lord Henry's perspective. We saw an example of this in chapter 2, in the moment where readers are let into the aesthete's thoughts after hearing the romantic story of Dorian's parentage—"Yes; it was an interesting background. It posed the lad" (33). This use of free indirect style happens twice more, at the very moment when Lord Henry first meets Dorian in person: "Lord Henry looked at him. *Yes, he was certainly wonderfully handsome,* with his finely curved scarlet lips, his frank blue eyes, his crisp gold hair. There was something in his face that made one trust him at once. All the candour of youth was there, as well as all youth's passionate purity. One felt that he had kept himself unspotted from the world. *No wonder Basil Hallward worshipped him"* (17; emphasis added).

Of course, it is also the reader who meets Dorian through this description, so perhaps it makes sense to have the narration shift into a more subjective style. But its rarity in the novel makes the shift conspicuous nonetheless. Compare the description of Dorian's dawning recognition a few pages later of a "secret cord that had never been touched before, but that *he felt* was now vibrating and throbbing to curious pulses" (19; emphasis added). After Lord Henry speaks to him of "passions that have made you afraid, thoughts that have filled you with terror, day-dreams and sleeping dreams whose mere memory might stain your cheek with shame—" the narrator remains stubbornly present in the description of Dorian's response: "Yes; there had been things in *his* boyhood that *he* had not understood. *He* understood them now. Life suddenly became fiery-coloured to *him*. It seemed to *him* that *he* had been walking in fire. Why had *he* not known it?" (20; emphasis added). And again, when Lord Henry muses on the chance effect of his words on the younger man, the narration slips momentarily into free indirect discourse to give us a glimpse of his thoughts seemingly unmediated by the narrator: "He had merely shot an arrow into the air. Had it hit the mark? *How fascinating the lad was!*" (20; emphasis added).

That the novel's few instances of free indirect discourse happen on the occasion of Lord Henry's meeting Dorian thus conditions both our view *of* him and *how* we view him. Rather than an intimately focalized view from his subjective consciousness, we get an external picture—another portrait of sorts—from the narrator or, briefly, from Lord Henry's point of view, the very party whose views Dorian so unthinkingly accepts as his own, and to such calamitous effect. This subtle difference of narrative perspective makes a profound difference in how we read the novel, and Dorian's character in particular. Whereas Lord Henry's (and the reader's) introduction to Dorian is privileged with the closer, more subjective narrative style of free indirect discourse, not even Dorian's expanding consciousness in the opening self-development narrative is afforded the same benefit, nor is it once his consciousness narrows in the Gothic degeneration portion that concludes the novel. The only exception is the pivotal scene between the two halves when Dorian sees the mark of cruelty in the portrait and he realizes that his "mad wish" that the portrait age in his place has come true: "It was certainly strange. [...] Cruelty!" (78). But the use of free indirect discourse here is so slight and fleeting that it also works to highlight how little unmediated sense of Dorian's consciousness we have. Thus, we are discouraged from identifying with Dorian from the start; critical distance is largely maintained. He is then scrutinized for sacrificing his own self-development—Lord Henry's stated ideal—to his devotion to Lord Henry. As readers, we are invited to see him critically, as someone who doesn't think for himself more than as someone who is "immoral," at least at first. The novel's narrative perspective reinforces this view in keeping him an objectively described character firmly within the gaze of others, including readers, throughout.

I suggested at the start that the American precursors to Wilde's now more famous work shed new light on *Dorian Gray* as a formal achievement and offer another means of resisting the seduction of the parable-like simplicity of the novel's powerful conclusion, with Dorian paying the ultimate price for his "sins" despite his attempts to "kill the past" by stabbing the picture, "this monstrous soul-life" (187). The narrative complexities of these thematically linked works have highlighted several ways that Wilde's novel also uses formal devices to problematize the moralizing logic by which it seems to work. Although these formal interventions are subtler than his American predecessors' reliance on more conspicuous narrative framing and unreliable first-person narration, they can and should be understood as part of a transformation of the well-worn earlier tradition, an annexation by which Wilde can be seen both to borrow from and yet transcend his sources, to make something strikingly original and ever more complex, artistically and philosophically.

However we read the novel, the magic-picture tradition out of which Wilde is writing makes it clear that questions of form are as important to its interpretation as themes and characters are—indeed, that form is often central to the interpretation of its themes and characters. As its American predecessors help us to see, the novel invites us to question the beliefs and actions of its main character, as well as the larger structuring devices of the multiple genres that come to bear on the story told—indeed, of what a story could tell in 1890s Britain and America—and this becomes an important part of its meaning. This kind of formalist reading of the novel does not depend on a close comparison of the narratives by Poe, Hawthorne, and James that I have been discussing. But seeing *Dorian* as part of this other genealogy makes such a reading all the more possible, historically specific, and perhaps more necessary than ever. As the transnational dimensions of Decadence come into clearer view, the link between Wilde and his US contexts beyond his 1882 North American lecture tour lends more credence to Poe's centrality but also, more surprisingly perhaps, to Hawthorne's and James's supporting roles, and to a more nuanced and complex reading of *Dorian's* notoriously tricky ending.

CHAPTER FIVE

Epigrammatic Inheritance

Peacock, Meredith, and the Forgotten English Lineage

> "You would sacrifice anybody, Harry, for the sake of an epigram."
> "The world goes to the altar of its own accord," was the answer.
>
> Oscar Wilde, *The Picture of Dorian Gray* (172)

When Lord Henry flings that most Meredithian word—the "world"—back at Dorian, he does more than perhaps even he knows. To be sure, he deflects the personal attack that would see him as a singularly cruel aggressor: as Henry sees it, he is merely a participant-critic of a style of mass self-sacrifice before the altar of art. With the word "world," however, he also invokes an older tradition of English comedy, theorized by George Meredith in his "Essay on Comedy" (1877), that conceives of society as regulated by the iron laws of laughter, or what Meredith termed "the uses of comedy in teaching the world to understand what ails it."[1] So far, I have focused primarily on Wilde's inheritance from the Gothic, historical romance, and subgenres like the magic-picture story, with all their melodrama, melancholy, gore, and ability to eclipse otherwise dominant forms like the Bildungsroman. One of the oddest aspects of *The Picture of Dorian Gray*, however, is just how funny a novel it is. In this chapter, I consider the profound impact of Meredith's thought on Wilde's writing. In particular, I suggest that Wilde's canny use of epigrammatic speech—both to confront an enervated Victorian social conservatism and to counterbalance that negative critique with a dandified character's decisive action—can be traced back to an older experimental English tradition that culminated in Meredith's fiction but is largely forgotten today.

The epigram and the ethical interventions of the dandy characterize both writers' wit. A self-consciousness about the form's razor-edge can also be detected in each. "You cut life to pieces with your epigrams," Dorian at one point complains to Lord Henry (84). In Meredith's 1879 novel *The Egoist*, the scholar Vernon Whitford similarly protests to his future father-in-law, who has a passion for wine: "You destroy the poetry of sentiment, Dr. Middleton."[2] "To invigorate the poetry of nature," he replies (368). This impulse not just to criticize but to "invigorate"—if not the "poetry of nature" of the heavily satirized Dr. Middleton, then certainly a critical function that tears itself free from the bonds of "sentiment"—points to a significant, if somewhat counterintuitive link. For tracing the impact of Meredith's imagination on Wilde complicates the standard view that Wilde readily joined with his contemporaries in offering a largely unfavorable, if good-humored, assessment of his predecessor, Meredith, the "last Victorian," in each of several key critical writings. It also underscores the generative quality of Meredith's influential formal experiments, as well as Wilde's feel for literary history in his creative attempts to reinvent the social world.

By way of conclusion, then, I demonstrate that reading *Dorian* through a transnational lens reveals a key additional context: an alternative literary history within the supposed "home" context itself. That is, looking aslant of Victorian Aestheticism also provides a fuller view of Wilde's English literary context and the tricky and sometimes inconvenient knowledge that his backward glances can occasion. Specifically, tracing Wilde's use of the epigram form to the experimental "conversation novels" of Thomas Love Peacock and George Meredith yields, on the one hand, an understanding of the significance of these earlier writers' experiments in literary form and style—an "otherwise" that has been mostly left to the side of the road of "progress" and the rise of realism—and a deeper sense of Wilde's interventions in literary history, on the other hand. Transnationalism's decentering effects help to uncover *Dorian*'s links to an earlier comic tradition that have for too long been overshadowed.

Meredith's "Unique Perversity": A "Difficult Case"

In his Clark Lectures of 1969, the writer and critic V. S. Pritchett offered this useful and time-tested perspective about George Meredith: "At any time during the last forty years it has been pretty safe to put on superior and evasive airs and to say that 'no one reads him.' [. . .] But there is no doubt that Meredith not only is but always *was* a difficult case."[3] To illustrate his point, Pritchett cites the critic of the *Athenaeum*, who might stand in for an entire history of critical abuse in writing, in 1891: "It is becoming a common experience to meet cultivated persons who gravely assure us that Meredith is our greatest living novelist. . . . To us this vogue is inexplicable. . . . So far from being a great novelist, he does not seem to us to possess the qualifications which go to the making of a capable novelist of even the second rank, and, even if those qualifications were his, their effect would be ruined by a literary manner which even in these days of affectation and strain is of unique perversity."[4] To be sure, Meredith also enjoyed a number of distinguished admirers, but even they mustered only qualified praise and a series of backhanded compliments. E. M. Forster's oft-repeated gibe about "the home counties posing as the universe" in Meredith's fiction was followed by the less well-known words: "And yet he is in one way a great novelist. He is the finest contriver that English fiction has ever produced."[5] For his part, Henry James equivocated—noting Meredith's tendency to "shirk every climax, dodge round it, and veil its absence in a fog of eloquence"—before finally arriving at the somewhat snide conclusion: "Meredith did the best things best."[6]

At the center of these embarrassed relations among old masters lies the question of Meredith's ungovernable wit, his subversion of the contemporary tyranny of common sense that his experimental comic novels sought to disturb and undo, in particular, regarding the social inequality of the sexes. "Comedy," as he writes with illuminating clarity in his 1877 essay on the subject, "is an exhibition of [women's] battle with men, and that of men with them."[7] One point of connection in this now-familiar terrain that seems to remain curiously understated in the criticism is the echo of Meredith's flamboyant nonconformity—his "unique perversity," to reclaim the epithet—in the writings of one whose celebrated wit also sought to challenge the inequality of the sexes and would soon eclipse the notoriety of Meredith's own: Oscar Wilde. The critical reticence is found on all sides: in Wilde studies, there is perhaps an embarrassment in the backward glance at a Victorian source like Meredith (who himself can be seen to have been looking back to the eighteenth century); and in Meredith studies there is perhaps a squeamishness in locating his wit (and, by extension, his concept of the dominant tradition of the English novel) as an important source of Wilde's queer style.

Lines of Transmission: Meredith and Wilde in Dialogue

Wilde's best-known assessment of Meredith appears in "The Decay of Lying" (1889):

> Ah! Meredith! Who can define him? His style is chaos illumined by flashes of lightning. As a writer he has mastered everything except language: as a novelist

he can do everything, except tell a story: as an artist he is everything except articulate. Somebody in Shakespeare—Touchstone, I think—talks about a man who is always breaking his shins over his own wit, and it seems to me that this might serve as the basis for a criticism of Meredith's method. But whatever he is, he is not a realist. Or rather I would say that he is a child of realism who is not on speaking terms with his father.[8]

Consistent with the hedging to be found in both the abuse and the praise of Meredith, Wilde's assessment gestures ironically in two opposing directions at once: toward an overweening excess—"everything" that Meredith "has mastered," "can do," and "is" as an artist—as well as toward a debilitating lack—"everything except" those qualities usually associated with literary style. If "breaking his shins over his own wit" provides a keenly perceptive and memorably witty phrase capturing a crucial aspect of Meredith's writing in a single stroke—indeed, as one of Meredith's own characters might do—Wilde's most biting criticism comes in the form of a mocking comment on and imitation of his predecessor's unusual style and syntax: "By its means he has planted round his garden a hedge full of thorns, and red with wonderful roses" (*DL* 81). Wilde, of course, wins in being the most ruthlessly devious critic, although perhaps imitation truly is the highest form of flattery. In "The Critic as Artist" (1890), he offers a somewhat more positive evaluation of Meredith's style in comparing it with that of Robert Browning, if at the latter's expense: "Meredith is a prose Browning, and so is Browning."[9]

What, if anything, do these witticisms reveal about Meredith, Wilde, and the lines of transmission between these two writers? What does it mean that Wilde's various assessments all appear in the form of dialogic essays, "The Decay of Lying" and "The Critic as Artist" being not straight criticism but fictional performances enacted by two characters, or critical positions, in dialogue? Wilde describes Meredith as "a child of realism who is not on speaking terms with his father": How might this turn of phrase be seen to betray both an inheritance and an anxious relation between Wilde himself and Victorian forebears like George Meredith? Or, perhaps more aptly, to take up Kevin Ohi's recent incitement to rethink dominant reproductive models of transmission, how might the points of contact between Meredith and Wilde articulate an alternative, non-Oedipal, non-agonistic model of literary history?[10] In looking forward to and harnessing more market-friendly forms, Wilde would outlast, if not outlive, Meredith, but the debt is as evident as it is mutually revealing. Below I suggest two important areas in which there

Epigrammatic Inheritance *111*

appears to be much Meredith in Wilde, areas adumbrated by the formal echoes of their devotion to the epigram. The first concerns both writers' self-conscious identification with Celtic traditions—Meredith's family origins were Irish and Welsh, not English—in particular, that of preferring romance over realism. This is to find additional support, on slightly different grounds, for Katarzyna Bartoszyńska's persuasive argument that "a new global literary history demands a more rigorous formalism"—that is, a "weak theory of the novel" that is not coterminous with the rise of realism in England but accommodates seemingly unimportant, experimental, or peripheral works, as well.[11] The second area that I explore has to do with the related issues of the development of an epicene style, including an ironic, almost-camp, cross-gender identification with, or at least great pleasure taken in, the figure of the Victorian *grande dame*, and of both writers' overt feminism, most notably in the key figure of the female dandy.

If this argument returns to the now somewhat routine view that any history of modernism is incomplete if it does not grant a place in the tradition to Meredith, it does so with caution. Donald Fanger's influential 1960 article finding a similar kind of "stylistic indigestion" in the writings of both Meredith and James Joyce, for example, claims that Meredith boldly uses the interior monologue in a sustained way as early as 1891, in his "remarkable if vexing" novel *One of Our Conquerors*.[12] But in uncovering compelling new links in the tradition of the modern novel, Fanger too quickly concludes that Joyce's achievement marks the "extreme perfection" of Meredith's "innovations."[13] Margaret Harris has rightly warned against this kind of anticipatory logic that often attends the identification of precursors, a logic that can obscure more than it illuminates. In this case, it risks obscuring that Meredith had his own style, which, considered on its own terms, was emphatically not a failure or a false start on the road to *Ulysses*; in the case of another frequently pejorative comparison, with Henry James's advanced use of highly articulate narrative filters, the logic of anticipation risks failing to see that, in Harris's words, "an important part of Meredith's aim is to show his characters struggling to achieve articulateness."[14]

In finding in Meredith an important antecedent to Wilde, then, I heed Harris's good warning not to suggest some direct, linear progression from early experiment to eventual perfection. Rather, I reconsider Wilde's own apparently disparaging mentions of Meredith in light of their formal complexity and explore figures used expansively and expertly by Meredith that have nonetheless, through a trick of time and modern celebrity culture, become nearly synonymous with Wilde alone. In a concluding section, I reflect on the more diffuse, non-dyadic, intergenerational aspect of this lineage by considering Wilde protégé Richard Le Gallienne's little-known 1890 book on Meredith and the broader implications of this inheritance. Meredith did not anticipate Wilde so much as hang back, indifferent to public opinion and literary canons alike, producing his own highly individual work "for his own pleasure," as Wilde himself would later recognize, all the while collecting perennial circles of acolytes and belated lovers of his works.[15]

Beautiful Lies, Experimental Forms: Wilde's Dialogic Essays as "Comedies in Narrative"

In addition to being an inspired piece of writing, "The Decay of Lying" is Wilde's impassioned argument against realism and its "careless habits of accuracy" in favor of "Lying in art," of exaggeration—"not simple truth but complex beauty"—in short, of romance (*DL* 76, 75, 85). It is not surprising, then, that Meredith makes a significant appearance. Vivian, the main speaker of the dialogue, says of Meredith: "Whatever he is, he is not a realist. [...] By deliberate choice he has made himself a romanticist" (*DL* 81). Joseph Bristow and Rebecca N. Mitchell write of this moment with revealing clarity: "Here, then, for Wilde the spirit of Romanticism is not a temporal quality but rather an aspect of the creative imagination."[16] As Vivian notes of the imperatives of the inventive mind: "No great artist ever sees things as they really are. If he did, he would cease to be an artist" (*DL* 97). Indeed, one of Meredith's defining traits as a novelist is the refusal of the concrete, the particular, the real, in favor of the abstract, the mythic, the ideal—or, what he called "Poetic Romance."[17] In Meredith, characters are presented in recognizable, contemporary scenes, but they more often function in the service of a larger Idea—the idea of the Ordeal in *The Ordeal of Richard Feverel* (1859) or of the rich and ruling classes' Egoism in the England of the 1870s in *The Egoist: A Comedy in Narrative* (1879), for example. The Comic Spirit itself achieves a kind of Platonic ideal: she appears as a figure within *The Egoist* and is even linked to the narration itself when, in the very last words of the novel we are told, "she compresses her lips" (425). Meredith's and Wilde's rejection of the need to represent reality as it is currently lived, in favor of imagining it as it might be—or might already be, in embryo, if only the poet would show us—can be traced to Pater's call in his famed conclusion to *The Renaissance* to make the most of the interval that remained to us by "intellectual excitement": "To burn always with this hard, gem-like flame, to maintain this ecstasy is suc-

Epigrammatic Inheritance   113

cess in life."[18] By contrast, Sir Willoughby Patterne, the perfect "pattern" gentleman lampooned in *The Egoist*, is shown to be a lethal bore to the woman who is to marry him and thus become the prisoner and subject of his habitual pride: "Miss Middleton caught the glimpse of his interior from sheer fatigue in hearing him discourse of it. What he revealed was not the cause of her sickness—women can bear revelations—they are exciting: but the monotonousness. He slew imagination" (325). In *Diana of the Crossways* (1885), the narrator, recalling Pater's opposition of momentary "ecstasy" to a "stereotyped world," offers this ironic explanation for why Lady Wathin could dispense with witty men and women at her table: "The intrusion of the spontaneous on the stereotyped would have clashed."[19]

Wilde's famous words about Meredith are often taken to be representative of his own views—and it is difficult not to read the aesthetes of the dialogic essays, Vivian and Gilbert, as mouthpieces for the author himself. But the form of the dialogue is crucial to interpretation: by self-consciously presenting a scene between two fictional characters, it enacts the very anti-realist mode that it would seem merely to be describing. One need only note that the essay that Vivian reads is titled "The Decay of Lying: A Protest," whereas Wilde's more detached title is "The Decay of Lying: An Observation," to mark the ironic distance between character and author. For Wilde, the protest against realism—and, significantly, the faults that the speaker Vivian finds with Meredith—are presented in dialogue with a conventionally minded auditor, the result being a synthesis or "observation" that undercuts the very authority it is at the same time asserting. It is itself a beautiful lie, a fiction, and a very Meredithian move.

Meredith himself published some stand-alone dialogues, and his first father-in-law, the novelist and poet Thomas Love Peacock (1785–1866), was probably the most adept master of the dialogue as a form. In what follows, I take a brief detour through this earlier tradition to better account for the resources that Wilde found in Meredith. Peacock's formal innovations, like his son-in-law's, were ahead of their time, and his commercial success never caught up to his critical reputation. As Rebecca N. Mitchell notes, "while his fiction drew heavily on romantic and Gothic tropes, Peacock's idiosyncratic novels brim with epigrammatic dialogue structured explicitly like a play."[20] The resonance of Peacock's style is perhaps most explicit in Meredith's "Up to Midnight," a series of dialogues published in the *Graphic* from December 1872 to January 1873; however, as Mitchell argues, "the extended passages of sharp, finely observed dialogue in *The Egoist* equally hearken back to Peacock's example."[21] Peacock himself is clearly the model for the character Dr. Middleton, the elderly scholar and parodied connoisseur of wine, in that novel.

"Up to Midnight" comprises a series of five wide-ranging conversations on contemporary topics among a group of gentlemen gathered by their host Sir John Saxon. The lines offer a sense of excited talk about the wider world, crackling with spontaneity if not always with clarity. Take, for example, this rapid-fire exchange concerning the retention of India between Mr. Finistare, who plays the pessimist, and Mr. Brighton, who plays the optimist, which quickly pivots to another subject, in turn:

> "What a price we pay for India," said Mr. Finistare. The Doctor perceived his error immediately; for a serious word had to be guarded by all the might of the members to keep it out of the clutches of Optimy and Pessimy. He tried to retract. Unfortunately, Mr. Brighton was too quick for him.
>
> MR. FINISTARE. "I can prove that it is matter of anxiety to those who use foresight."
>
> MR. BRIGHTON. "Why do your weeping before a tear is due?"[22]

Or, take the beginning of the second installment, when the prospect of a fresh polar expedition yields this interchange:

> "I would get up at any hour this year to find a frost," said Sir John.
> "The North Pole decidedly wants doctoring," observed Mr. Helion.
> "Yes, if you like," said Dr. Anthony, "but whether a couple of whalers of Dundee can do it is another question."
>
> MR. HELION. "Homœopathic doses are popular."
> THE DOCTOR. "Nothing is more popular than humbug."
> MR. HELION. "Luckily Brighton is not here to hear you."
> SIR JOHN. "Nor my daughters. They dose their little ones every other night with globules and tinctures, after a mighty deal of consultation. The homœopathic books are big, whatever the dose may be."[23]

Or, finally, take the banter about the common sense of various nation's characters in the third installment by Sir Patrick, the Celtic counterpart to Sir John's "Saxon" inheritance, and Mr. Helion, who, in accord with his name, shines additional light:

> SIR PATRICK. "French common sense always seems to be playing like the porpoise, and exhibiting a lively, a rounded, and a glistening spine as it rolls over and over; but you never see it when you require it, and it won't come to a call."
> MR. HELION. "Irish common sense, you mean?"

SIR PATRICK. "I said French; and I should be sorry to correct you in the good
ancient fashion, common in schools, when my state demanded a teacher with
a ready hand and a swing to it."[24]

Drawn from current affairs and social mores of the 1870s, the subjects of
these dialogues are Meredith's, but the style of brilliant talk rushing to catch
up with itself is Peacock's.

The conversation found in Peacock's satirical novel *Nightmare Abbey* (1818),
his third and best known, offers a brief illustration. The aim of Peacock's
satire, a roman à clef in which contemporary figures are meant to be discernable, is to critique modern literature's excessive gloom, "the morbid anatomy
of black bile" to be found in the fashionable vogue for romances and German
tragedies, which Peacock sees as poisoning the reading public.[25] This heavily
ironized mixture of gloom and comedy redounds in *Dorian*'s combination of
the Gothic and the satirical, too, as we have seen. As Peacock wrote to his
friend Percy Bysshe Shelley, he wanted "to bring to a sort of philosophical
focus a few of the morbidities of modern literature and to let in a little daylight
on its atrabilarious [gloomy] complexion."[26] The novel's plot, to the extent that
it can be said to have one, concerns the romantic illusions and prospects of
Scythrop Glowry (a thinly veiled Shelley), son and heir of Christopher Glowry,
Esquire, who is host to many visitors at his remote family seat in Lincoln-
shire, Nightmare Abbey. The talk of these guests, who come to enjoy the freely
flowing wine and endless debate, often overwhelms the narrative, however,
and the form of the novel becomes predominantly dialogue. For instance,
when the poet Mr. Cypress (a Byronic figure) comes one last time to partake
of the "morbid hospitality of the melancholy dwelling" of Nightmare Abbey,
the guests offer toasts that are perfectly in keeping with their characters:

MR GLOWRY.

You are leaving England, Mr Cypress. There is a delightful melancholy in
saying farewell to an old acquaintance, when the chances are twenty to one
against ever meeting again. A smiling bumper to a sad parting, and let us all be
unhappy together.

MR CYPRESS (filling a bumper).

This is the only social habit that the disappointed spirit never unlearns.

THE REVEREND MR LARYNX (filling).

It is the only piece of academical learning that the finished educatee retains.

MR FLOSKY (filling).

It is the only objective fact which the sceptic can realise.

SCYTHROP (filling).

It is the only styptic for a bleeding heart.

THE HONOURABLE MR LISTLESS (filling).

It is the only trouble that is very well worth taking.

MR ASTERIAS (filling).

It is the only key of conversational truth.

MR TOOBAD (filling).

It is the only antidote to the great wrath of the devil.

MR HILARY (filling).

It is the only symbol of perfect life. (107)

Here the characters reveal themselves and the various types that they represent wholly through their speech, as in a play. The seemingly circuitous exchanges lead to new points of view; sharp repartee becomes an antidote to the immersion in "gloomy reverie," misanthropy, and self-isolation brought about by modern literature, "a blight on the human soul" (72). The multivocal intellectual community forged in dialogue provides the corrective for such "morbidities," satirized by the responses to Mr. Hilary's rejection of the present day's "conspiracy against cheerfulness" by each of the guests, now well into the Madeira but still in character:

MR TOOBAD.

How can we be cheerful with the devil among us!

THE HONOURABLE MR LISTLESS.

How can we be cheerful when our nerves are shattered?

MR FLOSKY.

How can we be cheerful when we are surrounded by a reading public, that is growing too wise for its betters?

SCYTHROP.

How can we be cheerful when our great general designs are crossed every moment by our little particular passions?

MR CYPRESS.

How can we be cheerful in the midst of disappointment and despair?

MR GLOWRY.

Let us all be unhappy together. (113)

Meredith's influential style is thus Peacock's updated for a new age, a bulwark for the bright comic spirit of the dinner table against the solipsism and melancholic paralysis that both authors satirize.

Seen in this light, Wilde's dialogic essays—contrived, ironic, seemingly insular, insistently self-reflexive—take on some of the cast of the "comedies in narrative" of Peacock and Meredith. Yet, in making them his own, Wilde queers this tradition. In a knowing nod to comedy's conventional resolution in the union of marriage, the narrative arcs of Wilde's dialogues also conclude with scenes of seduction that bring the two male interlocutors together in a call to leave the enclosed, civilized space of the library for the outdoors. In "Decay," Vivian invites Cyril out onto the terrace, where the relations governing nature and art are self-consciously upended in the crepuscular light: "At twilight nature becomes a wonderfully suggestive effect, and is not without loveliness, though perhaps its chief use is to illustrate quotations from the poets" (*DL* 103). "Come! We have talked long enough," he implores (*DL* 103). In "Critic," Gilbert invites Ernest down into the London street, which is aestheticized by the description of the light of dawn: "How cool the morning air is! Piccadilly lies at our feet like a long riband of silver," he entices (*CA* 206). "A faint purple mist hangs over the Park, and the shadows of the white houses are purple. It is too late to sleep. Let us go down to Covent Garden and look at the roses. Come! I am tired of thought" (*CA* 206). Cloistered contemplation is here opposed to the social pleasures of "nature," the terrace and the street—the "roses" in the market also metonymically suggesting the street life stirring awake (or waking still) in one of London's most notorious red-light districts, where prostitutes were commonly known as "flower sellers." The flower market at Covent Garden is also, of course, the scene of Dorian Gray's nocturnal meanderings, so illicit they are only mentioned elliptically. It is also presumably the scene of Wilde's early 1881 poem "Impression du Matin" in which a "Thames nocturne" yields an impressionist morning scene, with the dome of St. Paul's looming in the distance and a lone figure who "loitered beneath the gas lamps' flare, / With lips of flame and heart of stone."[27] As a formal device, the union of the aesthete and his more conventionally minded interlocutor brings both the comedy and the essay (if not the night) to a close, and a modern Platonic dialogue thus merges with a camp discourse on love.

Ironically, then, it is when Wilde's highly quotable—and portable—criticisms of Meredith seem at their most trenchant that they are actually, in the experimental form of a fictional "comedy in narrative," most indebted to his predecessor. If, on one level, Wilde would seem to be merely having a laugh at Meredith's expense in these critical essays, a closer reading also suggests an acknowledgment of an intellectual debt and a lineage, if not the presence of a coconspirator. One need only see a list of books submitted by Wilde to the Prison Governor, at Reading Gaol, in 1897, to know that the admiration of Meredith ran deeper than his fictional characters' glib view of him: he requested Meredith's "Essay on Comedy" and his novel *The Amazing Marriage* (1895) be sent to him.[28] We also know from a letter written a month later to Robbie Ross, one of Wilde's few longtime friends who stood by him during his trial and imprisonment, that the novel "charmed" him.[29] That word's oldest form, of course, derives from magic: to attract, fascinate, and delight; but also, to cast a spell on, to influence.[30]

The Epigram as "Weapon of Estrangement": The Dandy's Alternative Vision and Ethics

If a commitment to romance—to contriving and thus remaking instead of merely reflecting the social world—led to a practice of generic experimentation for Meredith and Wilde alike, both men were also great friends of women, and they put their formal experiments in the service of a steadfast devotion to the equality of the sexes. Their brand of romance had a radical edge to it. Indeed, the beginnings of the epigrammatic epicene style that has since become so closely associated with Wilde are already clearly on display in Meredith: most notably, in his witty, clear-sighted women, but also, more generally, in the very serious thought that Meredith gives, like Wilde after him, to concepts of sincerity and frivolity, nature and artifice, and surface and depth. Two prominent examples will serve to illustrate the various types: namely, the *grande dame* of *The Egoist*, Mrs. Mountstuart Jenkinson, and the eponymous female dandy of *Diana of the Crossways*.

Like the great ladies of Wilde's later society comedies, Mrs. Mountstuart Jenkinson is "a lady certain to say the remembered, if not the right, thing": "Again and again was it confirmed on days of high celebration, days of birth or bridal, how sure she was to hit the mark that rang the bell; and away her word went over the county: and had she been an uncharitable woman she could have ruled the county with an iron rod of caricature, so sharp was her touch" (10). Mrs. Mountstuart holds sway over her social world—and over the text—with her brilliant phrasemaking, authorizing her own kind of power: to discern individual character, to name it, and to harness it to social convention. Especially germane to her social power are her epigrammatic sayings for the main characters of *The Egoist*, which "see in embryo" what is latent in the individual and in the plot of the novel itself. Meredith writes: "Her saying of Laetitia Dale: 'Here she comes, with a romantic tale on her eyelashes,' was a portrait of Laetitia. And that of Vernon Whitford: 'He is a Phoebus Apollo turned fasting friar,' painted the sunken brilliancy of the lean long-walker and scholar at a stroke. Of the young Sir Willoughby, her word was brief [. . .]: *You see he has a leg*" (10–11). Of Willoughby's potential match, Clara Middleton, Mrs. Mountstuart proclaims, "a dainty rogue in porcelain": "his companion picture," but "one of that sort" (37, 38). Mrs. Mountstuart's perceptive one-liners bring into consciousness what can only be glimpsed; they seem to set things in motion for having been uttered. What at first appears to be the power of perception turns out to be the power of suggestion, as well, for each of Mrs. Mountstuart's epigrammatic pronouncements foretells of the plot's climax and resolution.[31] And yet, "like all rapid phrasers, Mrs. Mountstuart detested the analysis of her sentence. It had an outline in vagueness, and was flung out to be apprehended, not dissected" (39).

This is precisely the kind of authoritative, pithy wit—what Len Gutkin has aptly characterized as the "aggressivity of epigrammatic speech" in Meredith—with which Wilde will soon make his name.[32] Like Wilde's Lady Bracknell, whose interview of Jack as a potential son-in-law in Act I of *The Importance of Being Earnest* has become perhaps the best-known example of the form, Mrs. Mountstuart's satire is mordant and withering; she is funny because, in scrutinizing and identifying types, she, too, reveals herself to be a type—she is also "one of that sort." Another is Victoria Wotton, Lord Henry's wife in *Dorian Gray*, or as Bartoszyńska aptly calls her, his "beard."[33] She leads what seems to be an entirely independent life as one half of a marriage of convenience. Her passion "was never returned," the narrator tells us, and so "she had kept all her illusions" (41). A "curious woman, whose dresses always looked as if they had been designed in a rage and put on in a tempest," she has a weakness for pianists: "two at a time, sometimes, Harry tells me. I don't know what it is about them. Perhaps it is that they are foreigners. [. . .] Even those that are born in England become foreigners after a time, don't they? It is so clever of them, and such a compliment to art" (41). Her queer fashion matches a rapier wit—she plays with a long tortoiseshell paper-knife during this awkward exchange with Dorian, her husband's latest friend—and she eventually leaves Lord Henry, one might say like the "bad habit" that he claims married life is, for a Chopin specialist (178). Aligned with satiric, poetic, idealist tendencies rather than with the protocols of realist character, these discerning phrasemakers are the engines of a variety of English comedy that Wilde so appreciated in Meredith, and so memorably, consummately, made his own. Born out of despair—a "despair of the present (not the past) and the desire to destroy it" as Carolyn Lesjak has cogently argued—the epigram has a radical potential as a form: it "marks the borders of what is considered thinkable and, in so doing, makes alterable those very borders."[34] For both Wilde and Meredith before him, the epigram was a "weapon of estrangement."[35]

In addition to the epigrammatic wit of powerful, sharp-tongued women of the world, Meredith also makes use of the younger female dandy to disturb the era's assumptions and beliefs about gender and marriage, a full decade before Lady Henry runs off with her Chopin specialist and Wilde's subsequent society comedies of the 1890s take the West End by storm. The exemplar of this type is, of course, Diana of the Crossways, herself an authoress and clever wit—"the starry she," in the words of the novel.[36] Like Mrs. Mountstuart, Diana is known for her epigrams and has the ability to parry men and rule a social scene: she can talk. It is only the "hateful yoke" of marriage that constrains her: "It was her marriage; it was marriage in the abstract: her own mistake and the world's clumsy machinery of civilization: these were the capital offenders: not the wife who would laugh ringingly, and would have friends of the other sex, and shot her epigrams at the helpless despot."[37]

Like Wilde's dandies, male and female—Lord and Lady Henry, Algernon Moncrieff, Lord Goring, Mabel Chiltern—Diana plays the role of detached artist, offering an oblique angle from which to see the conventional world, at once inside it and dismantling it by creating an alternative vision and ethics. This epigrammatic detachment, as Amanda Anderson has persuasively argued, makes the dandified character an ideal participant-critic: "self-conscious, artful, committed to demystification, at the center of the conversation yet to the side of cultural norms, drawing both gasps and admiration, intervening by forcing a mode of detached irony to subvert the 'natural' assumptions of his interlocutors."[38] The dandy's formal signature, the epigram, "enacts an *ironic* detachment," but also "serves to express the radically individual, and so perfectly embodies the coincidence of detachment and self-realization, the two elements that Wilde's criticism sought persistently to hold together."[39] Importantly, for Anderson this character type also evinces a movement in Wilde, in which free-floating negative critique takes on something of an ethical form— local moments in the drama that are represented as both "ethical interventions that will benefit others" and "heightened instances of self-realization on the part of the dandy."[40] For instance, when Lord Goring injects pragmatic counsel and judgment into the Chilterns' marriage at the end of *An Ideal Husband* (1895), Wilde's stage direction reads: *"pulling himself together for a great effort, and showing the philosophy that underlies the dandy.*"[41] The critical intervention of the dandy, therefore, is both aesthetic and ethical, the negative critique of the generalizable and endlessly transferable epigrams tempered by a healthy dose of local, situated pragmatism in the drama—an effortful pulling together of the "philosophy" of the dandy in key strategic moments.

Readers of *The Egoist* and *Diana of the Crossways*, in which "pattern" husbands are thrown over by independent New Women, thus might experience a kind of déjà vu at Mabel Chiltern's line at the conclusion of *An Ideal Husband*: "An ideal husband! Oh, I don't think I should like that. It sounds like something in the next world. [. . .] He can be what he chooses. All I want is to be . . . to be . . . oh! A real wife to him."[42] (Notably, Wilde's play, like Meredith's *Diana*, also hinges on the revelation of a Cabinet secret, providing another intriguing connection between these works at the level of plot.) The ethical charge of Wilde's heroic dandies is demonstrated by Mabel and Lord Goring's revitalizing effect on the conventional marriage of the Chilterns, evinced by the play's last line, in which Lady Chiltern declares: "For both of us a new life is beginning."[43] Here, as in Meredith, the comic ending, which is really the mark of a new beginning, shows the dandy to be an ethical actor as well as an epicene. This ethical charge is precisely what Lord Henry's misappropriations of Pater and Dorian's feeble imitations both lack in *Dorian*, as we have seen. Their misguided experiments only end in tragedy.

For Diana, and, before her, Mrs. Mountstuart and Clara Middleton in *The Egoist*, asserting a woman's independence and intelligence through a keen wit also has a leveling and revitalizing function. At the conclusion of *Diana*, in lamenting to her dear friend the loss of Percy Darcier, the one who got away, and asking whether marriage to the eminently rational Englishman Tom Redworth will be "the end of [her]," Diana (who is Irish) says, "I wanted a hero, and the jewelled garb and the feather did not suit him," to which her friend replies: "No; he is not that description of lay-figure. [. . .] Here is a true man; and if you can find me any of your heroes to match him, I will thank you."[44] As in Wilde's later play, this revaluation of the old "ideal" in light of a newly transformed "real"—this exchange of the "pattern" for the "true man"—also has a revitalizing effect; however, because this is Meredith, the effect is registered not by a representative couple like the Chilterns but abstractly, by national culture writ large: "Old Ireland won't repent it," Diana's friend tells her upon entering the churchyard, to which she rejoins at the sight of the beaming bridegroom, advancing: "A singular transformation of Old England!"[45]

"Flashing a Picture in a Phrase": Le Gallienne's Meredith via Wilde

One of the many cruel ironies of Wilde's untimely death in 1900 at the age of forty-six is that the lines of transmission between these two great writers were interrupted and ultimately cut short. It is revealing, however, that Wilde's own devotee, the Liverpudlian poet Richard Le Gallienne, who styled himself after Wilde's celebrated image to the extent that his relatively straitened circumstances would allow, published a work of literary criticism titled *George Meredith: Some Characteristics* (1890).

The book was his first serious foray into criticism, an attempt to escape his apprentice existence in Liverpool through literature, a study of the work of his early hero—not his friend Wilde but the elder master George Meredith. This decision might simply be chalked up to Le Gallienne's youthful ambition, an attempt to gain the attention of Meredith, at the time an influential publisher's reader and tastemaker. But it also speaks to the existence of an affective network of writers and readers that circulated between and among generations and social stations.[46]

In this little-known book, Le Gallienne writes self-consciously as "a lover of the works" from the first page, but it would be a mistake to dismiss this effort as mere hero-worship.[47] His readings of the major and minor works are attentive and often perceptive, and that discernment is especially important given the contrast they create with the prevailing critical view of many of his contemporaries. Here, Le Gallienne, follower of Wilde, attempts to make his name by openly declaring his allegiance to his mentor's predecessor, Meredith: "The passion of his genius is, indeed, the tracing of the elemental in the complex; the registration of the infinitesimal vibrations of first causes, the tracking in human life of the shadowiest trail of primal instinct, the hairbreadth measurement of subtle psychological tangents: and the embodiment of these results in artistic form" (2).

Indeed, it is in Le Gallienne's defense of Meredith's peculiar style, in which he will strikingly recall Wilde's language of "chaos illumined by flashes of lightning," that he is most insightful and convincing. In the "essential quality" of "great metaphor" and the quality of "flashing a picture in a phrase, of, so to say, writing in lightning," Le Gallienne asks: "Who are Mr. Meredith's rivals?" (5). He continues: "So convincing is it too that often as it flashes its light upon some hidden track of thought, or inaccessible lair of sensation, it hardly seems to be metaphor at all, but the very process of thought and feeling literally described. The distinction between objective and subjective is overlapped, and we seem to see matters of spirit and nerve with our very physical eyes" (5). Seeing "with our very physical eyes" what had before remained in a "hidden track of thought" or "inaccessible lair of sensation" is for Le Gallienne the gift of Meredith's often difficult style. "In short," he writes, "his imagination is subtle enough to embody the workings of imagination in others" (7). He is a realist "as all the great artists have been," not after the "modern pattern" but "after the manner of poets" (11). Le Gallienne concludes, echoing Meredith's Vernon Whitford: "It would be impossible to think more ruthlessly than Mr. Meredith, he has been ever resolute in tearing from life every vestige of sentimentality, yet it has been to leave us with all the deeper impression of its high and mystic significance" (12). Or, as Dorian and Lord Henry will say: "You cut life to pieces with your epigrams." / "The world goes to the altar of its own accord." In these lines, which Wilde added to the 1891 revision of *Dorian* a year after Le Gallienne's book on Meredith was published, the epigrammatic inheritance between and among these writers comes full circle.

That Le Gallienne's reading of Meredith was influential to Wilde as he revised his novel is also borne out by a letter that Wilde sent the younger writer in December 1890. It is vintage Wilde—charming, self-dramatizing, fulgent, flirtatious, and certainly something of a performance. Interestingly, Wilde returns the lightning metaphor that Le Gallienne almost surely borrowed from Wilde's own comment about Meredith in "Decay of Lying," using it now to praise Le Gallienne himself:

> It is a wonderful book, full of exquisite intuitions, and bright illuminating thought-flashes, and swift, sudden, sure revelations, a book behind which there is a soul-temperament, and thought shows itself stained by colour and passion, rich and Dionysiac and red-veined, while the aesthetic instinct is immediate in its certainty, and has that true ultimate simplicity that comes, like the dawn, out of a complex night of many wandering worlds. I knew the book would be excellent, but its fine maturity amazes me; it has a rich ripeness about it. You have realised yourself in it.[48]

Thought "stained by colour and passion," "Dionysiac and red-veined," with simplicity that comes "like the dawn, out of a complex night of many wandering worlds": Wilde's letter to Le Gallienne is effusive, full of sensuality, and dense with inside references, including the light of dawn in Piccadilly at Cyril's invitation to "Come! I am tired of thought" in "The Critic as Artist," the stained "lips of flame" of the lone figure who loitered "beneath the gas

Oscar Wilde, 1882 (albumen silver print), Napoleon Sarony (1821–96). Metropolitan Museum of Art, New York. Gilman Collection, Purchase, Ann Tenenbaum and Thomas H. Lee Gift, 2005

Richard Le Gallienne, 1888 (Woodburytype), Alfred Ellis (1854–1930). Wikimedia Commons

126 *Networked Forms*

lamps' flare" at daybreak in "Impression du Matin," and Dorian Gray's secretive nighttime worlds of wandering. The entire body of the letter operates as a self-referential hall of mirrors in which the individual "self" becomes blurred by the recirculation of images, allusions, and textual borrowings back and forth between sender, receiver, and fictional texts. Before reclaiming a discrete individual identity by signing "OSCAR," Wilde teasingly embraces Le Gallienne, warm lips to shut eyes: "I hope the laurels are not too thick across your brow for me to kiss your eyelids."[49]

"An Incomparable Novelist"

As is notoriously the case with any question of literary influence and transmission, it is difficult to know exactly how direct or powerful an effect Meredith's "unique perversity" had on Wilde and Le Gallienne, or whether Meredith was just in the air of the 1880s and 1890s. But from all the available evidence—in Wilde's essays, letters, reading lists, comedies, and a book by his literary disciple—what is clear is that reading the seemingly dismissive lines about George Meredith in Wilde's dialogic essays as if they were simply or straightforwardly his views, instead of in complex relation to Wilde's own art, is to patronize both Meredith and Wilde. Moreover, it risks overlooking the importance of Meredith as a literary predecessor of Wilde: a fellow Celt dedicated to poetry and romance, disdainful of the overfed and brutal English ruling classes, and hopeful to bring about a transformation in the roles of both men and women.

But perhaps it is right to allow Wilde, finally, to speak for himself. In the "The Soul of Man under Socialism" (1891), a work not complicated by the dialogic comic-narrative form of "The Decay of Lying" and "The Critic as Artist"—also written a year after Le Gallienne's celebratory book and in the same year as Meredith's evisceration by the critic of the *Athenaeum*—Wilde wrote:

> One incomparable novelist we have now in England, Mr George Meredith. There are better artists in France, but France has no one whose view of life is so large, so varied, so imaginatively true. There are tellers of stories in Russia who have a more vivid sense of what pain in fiction may be. But to him belongs philosophy in fiction. His people not merely live, but they live in thought. One can see them from myriad points of view. They are suggestive. There is soul in them and around them. They are interpretative and symbolic. And he who made them, those wonderful quickly-moving figures, made them for his own

pleasure, and has never asked the public what they wanted, has never cared
to know what they wanted, has never allowed the public to dictate to him or
influence him in any way but has gone on intensifying his own personality, and
producing his own individual work. At first none came to him. That did not
matter. Then the few came to him. That did not change him. The many have
come now. He is still the same. He is an incomparable novelist.[50]

More philosophical and "imaginatively true" than "better" writers in France
and Russia, Meredith transcends national categories with his formal experimentation, "intensifying his own personality" as Lord Henry advocates, without emptying the experiment of thought the way that Dorian does. Wilde's
evident esteem for Meredith, on view in this passage in his own essayistic
voice rather than mediated by one of his characters in the more contrived
dialogues, suggests a profound inheritance. This lineage has been largely
obscured, however, by a focus on the clearer, more intuitive importance of a
predecessor and mentor like Pater and of Wilde's more contemporary, proximate contexts.

In many ways, this concluding discussion of the long reach of Meredith's
earlier experiments in literary form and style returns us recursively to my
original argument in chapter 1 that *Dorian* should be read in light of its formal innovations, including its satiric use of the epigram, not just its thematic
incitements—indeed, that those two things are not at all separate phenomena. To that argument and its implications, we can now add a new comprehension of the novel. Wilde's queer formalism derived from a self-conscious
awareness of writing himself into, and out of, a transnational field—one that
simultaneously included past writers in the English context, we can now see,
who had tried to break the mold, not just those whose Aestheticism *Dorian*
so clearly echoes in its themes and content. This is perhaps to return on somewhat different grounds to the idea articulated by Wilde's Meredithian dandy,
Victoria Wotton, that all artists become foreigners after a time: "Even those
that are born in England."

Coda

This book has focused on origins—of ideas, tropes, and forms—that made up the life of a book before its tumultuous publication and klieg-lit aftermath. The alternative archive that it begins to reconstruct suggests ever widening circles of influence and sometimes startling lines of connection across and among those networks. Indeed, it points to even more work to be done, both within these networks and beyond the retrospective question of influence. As I suggested in the preface, this work includes the unfinished and necessary task of undisciplining the archives and "decolonizing" Wilde, a writer who criticized and, in many ways, transcended national and imperial paradigms but also sometimes trafficked in, unconsciously or uncritically, Western and colonial fantasies about the Other. Understood in this light, the novel's well-documented Orientalism and the blatantly anti-Semitic description of Mr. Isaacs, the man who owns the East End theatre where Dorian meets Sibyl Vane, are only the most glaringly obvious examples. The description of Mr. Isaacs is spoken by Dorian, it is true, so perhaps it is meant to comment on the narrowness of his character—Wilde himself was great friends with Jewish women such as Ada Leverson and Sarah Bernhardt. But the language is so awful, and remains otherwise unqualified or uncritiqued in the novel, that it perhaps does not matter whose words they are.[1]

There are other troubling moments, as well, moments that are focused through Dorian's consciousness but remain very much in the narratorial voice. Take, for instance, the description of Dorian's habit of collecting "from all parts of the world the strangest instruments that could be found either in the tombs of dead nations or among the few savage tribes that have survived contact with Western civilizations" (114). At once seemingly laudatory and stigmatizing in the way of much colonial thinking about the colonized, the sentence makes an object of the "strangest instruments" while subordinating the indigenous people who made and played them. It does this both linguistically, through the exoticizing and plural "dead nations" and "savage tribes" (whereas Dorian is the individual subject, the expert collector-connoisseur), and grammatically, through an entombing syntax of indirection: "*from* all parts of the world," "*in* the tombs of," and "*among* the savage tribes." Here Wilde can be seen to be a product of his times and, in particular, of a pervasive fascination with the decline of empires within literary and artistic Decadence; as the editors of *Volupté* have rightly noted, "much European decadent art and literature has been entranced by settler-colonial fantasies of extinct and vanishing peoples."[2]

The serial list of examples that follows this moment in the novel is often read as a formal aspect of the lengthy chapter 11's cataloging of Dorian's obsessive descent into an all-consuming hedonism, but its content is often glossed over as so much extravagance. (As with the long chapter's many other catalogs, the tedium of the list form makes it almost unreadable.) Beyond its formal interest, however, the catalog of instruments continues to exoticize indigenous people and to foreground the object's fascination for the Western individual (and presumably for the reader): the "mysterious" *juruparis* of the Rio Negro Indians, the "shrill cries" of Peruvian earthen jars, the Chilean flutes of human bones, the "harsh *ture*" of Amazonian tribes, the "doleful sound" of the drums covered with the skins of serpents in the Mexican temple, and so on (114).

This passage is itself an echo of the key scene early in the novel in which Lord Henry, "in his low, musical voice," says: "The bravest man among us is afraid of himself. The mutilation of the savage has its tragic survival in the self-denial that mars our lives. We are punished for our refusals" (19). Here the "savage" is imagined as natural Man, the distant, atavistic heart of our human-animal constitution, an idea that would become so central to the project of European modernism, the timescale now Darwinian. But ultimately it is a trope (literally, a "turning away"), useful primarily for modern European self-definition ("*our* lives," "*we* are punished") and in this particular case for propagating Decadent notions of cultural and imperial decline. The conclusion of the catalog recalls Lord Henry's idea and makes the function of the list clear: "The fantastic character of these instruments fascinated [Dorian], and he felt a curious delight in the thought that Art, like Nature, has her monsters, things of bestial shape and with hideous voices" (114). Dorian eventually bores of these musings (not nearly soon enough) and goes to the opera to hear Wagner's *Tannhäuser*, finding in that "great work of art" a presentation of the "tragedy of his own soul," what Lord Henry had called the "tragic survival" of the "mutilation of the savage," the repressive self-denial that is the supposed inheritance of the modern subject (114).

Thus, even though Wilde's novel can be profitably traced to a wider set of intellectual sources, as I have argued, *Dorian* leaves its own lingering questions as to what a transnational Decadence can come to mean. It is perhaps the rethinking of the novel by contemporary global artists, freed from its historical biases and blind spots and able to exert a vision and an epistemology of their own, that offers the most revealing lines of sight, however. Wilde suggested as much in his preface, at least, when he wrote: *"The critic is he who can translate into another medium or a new material his impression of beautiful things"* (3).

At the start of this book, I mentioned the British-Nigerian artist Yinka Shonibare's rendering of Wilde's novel in photography as an example of how it lives on in the global cultural imagination. Shonibare's *Dorian Gray* (2001) also makes an important intervention. The series of twelve photographic prints revisits the novel through a sequence of intensely concentrated visual fragments. With this formal choice, Shonibare is able to distill the narrative into representative moments while also selecting and sequencing these moments to his own ends. An Englishman of African descent with a paralytic disability, Shonibare himself appears as Dorian in the series, playing the Victorian dandy at cross-purposes with the conventional, bourgeois, heterosexual, now explicitly white, and able society that he criticizes and seeks to transform.

This Dorian appears first as an image on an easel, then alone before his own reflection; next, in a top hat, with Sibyl Vane and Victorian society; in the London fog with a man crossing behind him and then confronting him face to face; in the act of murdering Basil; in a state of increasing social isolation; in a confrontation with his distorted image; and finally, as a dead body discovered by others. The effect of the fragmentation, selection, and sequencing of images, the substitution of a Black Dorian, and the overall chiaroscuro of the Hollywood-Gothic styling is as playful and knowing as it is striking.

The two most intriguing prints are the second and tenth, where Shonibare's Dorian stands before his own image. In the second scene, Dorian stares directly at himself with a pensive tilt of the head, the light falling sharply on one side of his face in the "portrait" but leaving his actual image obscured

Scene 2 of *Dorian Gray*, 2001 (resin print), Yinka Shonibare CBE (1962–). © Yinka Shonibare CBE. All rights reserved, DACS/ARS, NY 2023. Photo: The Jack Shear Collection of Photography at the Tang Teaching Museum, Skidmore College, 2017.25b

and slightly blurry, with the back of his head to the viewer. Further contrast is provided by this Dorian's blackness and his tuxedo's white shirt and by the empty geometric space of the paneled room behind him, set off by the ornate border of the gilt frame. Like Wilde's novel, Shonibare's reimagining is a play of dark and light, presence and absence, embodiment and the devastating effects of its negation. Brilliantly, Shonibare swaps the novel's painting, that "most magical of mirrors" (91), for an actual mirror, the reflected "picture" a self-portrait, no longer a projection of the artist and his medium but a questioning of the very status of the self and perhaps of the photographic process itself.[3]

Scene 10 of *Dorian Gray*, 2001 (lambda print), Yinka Shonibare CBE. © Yinka Shonibare CBE. All rights reserved, DACS/ARS, NY 2023. Photo: The Jack Shear Collection of Photography at the Tang Teaching Museum, Skidmore College, 2017.25j

As in Alfred Lewin's 1945 black-and-white film adaptation of the novel, which this series also invokes, Dorian's fully disfigured portrait appears in vivid color. In Lewin's film, only the earlier scene in which the portrait is first revealed to Dorian also appears in color, briefly, whereas Shonibare's tenth scene stands alone in such distinction.[4] As Robert Stilling has noted, "Shonibare alters this later Technicolor moment not to reveal the supernatural degradation of the painting but Dorian's embodiment of his own moral degeneracy."[5] For the purposes of my reading, this scene depicts a suspended moment in the transfer of self and image that the novel imagines to occasion Dorian's death and the reversion of soul to body in the moment of the portrait's stabbing. Interrupting the novel's zero-sum logic of reversals, Shonibare's Dorian stares at himself appraisingly, much as he did in the earlier scene, the side of his face now fully illuminated. Instead of dying immediately, what he sees in the reflected image is the same as the now-transformed physical body that stands before it—decaying skin, grey hair, all the ravages of time apparent: he is a man of this world, not impervious to it. Thus, Shonibare's photograph momentarily interrupts the seeming inevitability of the novel's conclusion, opening the space for a crucial insight. Two prints later, the last in the series, a disfigured Dorian lies dead on the ground as he does at the novel's conclusion. But for an instant, captured by the camera and foregrounded by the sole color print, we glimpse what Wilde also suggests but is unable to depict as directly in the form of a novel: that Dorian's story is not so much about monstrosity as it is about "what monstrous laws have made monstrous and unlawful" (19), the effects of the suppression of certain bodies, desires, and ways of being. Here we are finally given access to some measure of Dorian's interiority: he sees himself and what has happened to him, for a moment released from the magic portrait's moralizing logic and the loaded language of "degeneracy." As Shonibare's reimagining helps to highlight, Wilde's narrative ultimately—cannily, strategically—indicts the conventional world that can only see Dorian as aberrant, rather than indict Dorian as an individual.

Shonibare's series thus powerfully appropriates and transforms *Dorian Gray*. It holds up a mirror to the original novel and to what a novel can (and cannot) do. Importantly, it gives priority to Black vision and knowledge in creating space for new comprehensions of a "classic" nineteenth-century English novel. For this, Shonibare's *Dorian Gray* is rightly considered one of the most important and generative of the novel's contemporary global resonances. At the same time, as I hope this book has suggested, it reflects and extends Wilde's own transnational impulses and citational methods, recollecting distant and diffuse forms in order to imagine them anew—a complex, vital dynamic in his aesthetic and formal practice that has a rich archive and an inheritance of its own.

NOTES

Preface

1. Thackeray, "A May-Day Ode," 39. This poem was originally published in *The Times*, 30 April 1851.

2. Sharpe, *In the Wake*, 13; Chatterjee, Mireles Christoff, and Wong, "Introduction: Undisciplining Victorian Studies," 369–70. A version of this essay was also published in the *Los Angeles Review of Books*, 10 July 2020.

3. Chatterjee, Mireles Christoff, and Wong, "Introduction," 370. Important exceptions, the editors note, include Dickerson's *Dark Victorians*, Hack's *Reaping Something New*, Lee's *American Slave Narratives and the Victorian Novel*, and Lootens's *The Political Poetess*. I would add the important and sometimes overlooked work in Irish studies on the difficult, overlapping histories of race, racialization, colonialism, and imperialism. See, for example, Cleary's *Outrageous Fortune* and "Misplaced Ideas?," Martin's "Victorian Ireland," and O'Malley's work in progress on John Mitchel and points of contact between Irish nationalism and US white supremacist violence in the 1850s. See also Betensky's illuminating and now foundational essay, "Casual Racism in Victorian Literature."

4. Chatterjee, Mireles Christoff, and Wong, "Introduction," 375, 376; emphasis my own. See also Banerjee, Fong, and Michie, "Widening the Nineteenth Century."

5. Mufti, "Hating Victorian Studies Properly," 401. By "proper hatred" Mufti refers to the operation by which one's love of something—a "product of being formed by" that something—allows one to "articulate its negation," for example, the way in which Trinidadian historian C. L. R. James's love of Victorian culture allowed him to articulate West Indian independence (396, 401).

6. On the emergence of a new Decadence studies, see Kaye's review of Sherry and Potolosky and Volpicelli's "The New Decadence."

7. Thain provides an especially useful overview of the contours and stakes of this methodological turn toward the transnational and transhistorical in a review of Bizzotto and Evangelista's volume *Arthur Symons*.

8. See, for example, the journal *Volupté: An Interdisciplinary Journal of Decadence Studies*; professional organizations such as the British Association of Decadence Studies and the Aestheticism and Decadence Caucus of NAVSA; special issues like Denisoff's "Global Decadence" and "Scales of Decadence"; and companions and edited collections

with titles heavy on big nouns: Desmarais and Weir's *Decadence and Literature*; Alex Murray's *Decadence: A Literary History*; and Hext and Murray's *Decadence in the Age of Modernism*. Several new biographies highlighting Wilde's global and Decadent networks have provided further detail and enticements. See Mendelssohn's *Making Oscar Wilde* and Sturgis's *Oscar Wilde: A Life*.

9. Potolsky, *The Decadent Republic of Letters*, 6.

10. Gagnier, *Literatures of Liberalization*, 136.

11. Evangelista, "Transnational Decadence," 330, 316. Two further studies appeared as I was finishing the writing of this book: Freedman's *The Jewish Decadence* charts a diasporic history and Fieni's *Decadent Orientalisms* examines East-West discourses of obsolescence and decline in the imperial imagination. Lavery's *Quaint, Exquisite* also takes up late nineteenth-century East-West encounters and the "Japanese vellum" luxury editions of Wilde in particular, finding in the idea of Japan an animating force in late-Victorian and modernist aesthetics (74–78).

12. Evangelista, "Transnational Decadence," 318.

13. Evangelista, "Transnational Decadence," 330.

14. Denisoff notes the positive valence of the phrase "a straying aside" as capturing "the author's own vagabondage and slant poetics" and reflecting the vitalizing queer, global, and eco-studies approaches to Decadence of the past decade. A winking reference to Wilde's 1895 conviction for "gross indecency" might still be detected in Symons's lines immediately preceding: "No doubt perversity of form and perversity of manner are often found together, and, among the lesser men especially, experiment was carried far, not only in the direction of style." See Denisoff, "Review," 686; and Symons, *The Symbolist Movement in Literature*, 7.

15. Symons, "The Decadent Movement of Literature," 170, 169.

16. As Bizzotto and Evangelista note, Symons made his more radical stance clear elsewhere, in reference to his own work. For example, in the preface to the second edition of his *London Nights* (1895/1897), he asserts: "I contend on behalf of the liberty of art, and I deny that morals have any right of jurisdiction over it. Art may be served by morality, it can never be its servant" (xiii–xiv); quoted in Bizzotto and Evangelista, eds., *Arthur Symons*, 2.

17. Cohn's reading of Wilde's "playful sociology of imitation" in light of Gabriel Tarde's writings is exemplary. Cohn, "Oscar Wilde's Ghost," 474.

18. Bristow and Mitchell, *Oscar Wilde's Chatterton*, 18. The authors question in particular the conclusions of Saint-Amour's *The Copywrights* and Guy's "Self-Plagiarism, Creativity, and Craftsmanship in Oscar Wilde," 17.

19. Bristow and Mitchell, *Oscar Wilde's Chatterton*, 20, 21.

20. Eliot, "Tradition and the Individual Talent," 14. Riquelme also notes the connection between Wilde and Eliot: "In the case of both writers, their modernist, anti-Romantic borrowings are intentional, motivated, and, because of the new implications of the repeated language, creative" (621).

21. I have in mind here, of course, Potolsky's *Decadent Republic of Letters*, Sherry's *Modernism and the Reinvention of Decadence*, Mahoney's *Literature and Politics of Post-Victorian Decadence*, Stilling's *Beginning at the End: Decadence, Modernism, and Postcolonial Poetry*, and Gagnier's books *Literatures of Liberalization* and *Individualism, Decadence, and Globalization*.

22. Mahoney's work on such twentieth-century figures as the Harlem Renaissance

illustrator Richard Bruce Nugent, who drew heavily from Wilde and the Decadent illustrator Aubrey Beardsley in his images of queer desire, and the Sri Lankan writer Lionel de Fonseka has begun to expand the archive of post-Victorian Decadence. Mahoney, "Taking Wilde to Sri Lanka and Beardsley to Harlem" and *Queer Kinship after Wilde.*

23. Chatterjee, Mireles Christoff, and Wong, "Introduction," 383.

24. Chatterjee, Mireles Christoff, and Wong, "Introduction," 383.

Introduction

1. According to the *Index Translationum* published by the United Nations Educational, Scientific, and Cultural Organization (UNESCO), Wilde's novel was translated over three hundred times into more than forty languages ranging from Albanian to Yiddish between 1979 and 2009 alone, the years for which the records have been digitized. For a detailed account of the European translations of individual works by Wilde between 1889 and 2008, see Barnaby, "Timeline of the European Reception of Oscar Wilde," which includes translations into regional and minority languages such as Basque, Breton, Chuvash, Scottish Gaelic, and West Frisian. Major non-European target languages listed by UNESCO include Arabic, Chinese, Farsi, Hebrew, Japanese, Korean, and Sinhala.

2. Sinfield, *The Wilde Century*, 2.

3. Wilde, *A Woman of No Importance*, 132.

4. Conan Doyle, *Memories and Adventures*, 73.

5. Jane Francesca Wilde, "Letter to Oscar Wilde"; quoted in Ellmann, *Oscar Wilde*, 320.

6. Quoted in *The Picture of Dorian Gray*, Norton Critical Edition, 372; from Mason, *Oscar Wilde*, 75–76. The author of the unsigned review was identified decades later as the writer and journalist Charles Whibley (1859–1930); see Haslam, "Revisiting the 'Irish Dimension,'" 268. Throughout this book, bracketed ellipses indicate my omission of quoted text; all other ellipses are in the original material.

7. Cook, *London and the Culture of Homosexuality, 1885–1914*, 50–51.

8. The practical difficulties, not to mention indignities, of medically proving sodomy were brought into public view in the earlier 1870 scandal of Ernest Boulton and Frederick Park, otherwise known as Fanny and Stella, the performers who were arrested for wearing women's clothing in public and subjected to unauthorized and inconclusive anal examinations by the police surgeon. See Cook, *London and the Culture of Homosexuality, 1885–1914*, 15–18; William Cohen, *Sex Scandal*, 73–129; and Joseph, *Exquisite Materials*, chapter 1. Efforts to change the law allowing for the death penalty for sodomy were successful only in 1861, although they were nearly successful much earlier in the period, in 1841. See Charles Upchurch's *"Beyond the Law."*

9. For the authoritative account and transcript of Wilde's criminal trials, see Bristow's forthcoming book *Oscar Wilde on Trial.*

10. Ellmann, *Oscar Wilde*, 314.

11. On the Oxford scandal involving Pater and an undergraduate known as the "Balliol Bugger," William Money Hardinge, see Inman, "Estrangement and Connection" and the response by Shuter, "The 'Outing' of Walter Pater."

12. Although not explicitly focused on *Dorian Gray*, Evangelista's examination of Wilde's thinking about the philosophy and literary history of cosmopolitanism through

the prism of world literature is indispensable. See *Literary Cosmopolitanism in the English Fin de Siècle*. Evangelista rightly cites Prewitt-Brown's foundational study *Cosmopolitan Criticism* as the fullest exploration of Wilde's engagement with this philosophical tradition.

13. Riquelme, "Oscar Wilde's Aesthetic Gothic," 609.

14. Riquelme, "Oscar Wilde's Aesthetic Gothic," 609.

15. Riquelme, "Oscar Wilde's Aesthetic Gothic," 609.

16. Riquelme, "Oscar Wilde's Aesthetic Gothic," 617.

17. Bristow, "*The Picture of Dorian Gray* and the Aesthetic Tradition," n.p. I am grateful to the author for access to and permission to cite from this forthcoming work.

18. Bristow, "*The Picture of Dorian Gray* and the Aesthetic Tradition," n.p.

19. Bristow, "*The Picture of Dorian Gray* and the Aesthetic Tradition," n.p.

20. Bristow, "*The Picture of Dorian Gray* and the Aesthetic Tradition," n.p.

21. Pater, *The Renaissance*, 189.

22. Bristow, "*The Picture of Dorian Gray* and the Aesthetic Tradition," n.p.

23. Ellmann, *Oscar Wilde*, 47, 301.

24. Smith and Helfand, *Oscar Wilde's Oxford Notebooks*, 141; quoted in Friedman, *Before Queer Theory*, 88. Friedman uses this moment brilliantly to launch his broader argument that Wilde developed his own theory of "erotic negativity" in response to Pater's "vision of the relationship between aesthetics and the metaphysics of the subject" (89). As he himself acknowledges, Friedman is building on scholarship that has taken Pater's sexuality as its explicit focus but that does not place his queerness in relation to the development of his aesthetic philosophy (34). Simon Reader adds credence to the importance of Wilde's notebook jottings in *Notework*. See also Love, "Exemplary Ambivalence," 25; Evangelista, *British Aestheticism and Ancient Greece*, 34; and Michael F. Davis, "Walter Pater's 'Latent Intelligence' and the Conception of Queer 'Theory,'" 262.

25. Other important French contexts include Gautier's preface to *Mademoiselle de Maupin* (1835) and Balzac's *The Wild Ass's Skin* [*La Peau de chagrin*] (1831) and his short story, "Massimilla Doni" (1837). Rachilde's *Monsieur Vénus* (1884), whose main character's name, Raoule, provided an early title for the mysterious book that poisons Dorian (*Le Secret de Raoul*) also deserves wider mention, as Dierkes-Thrun has argued. Dierkes-Thrun, "Oscar Wilde, Rachilde, and the *Mercure de France*." But it is Huysmans's later novel that tends to stand in for the rest, in part because of the clear reference to it as the "yellow book" that Lord Henry gives to Dorian. Sealing the connection to Pater and Huysmans as the most significant contexts for Wilde is the line in *De Profundis*, Wilde's letter from jail, in which he refers to *The Renaissance* as the "book which has had such a strange influence over my life." See Wilde, *De Profundis*, 102.

26. Wilde, *The Picture of Dorian Gray*, ed. Bristow, World's Classics Edition, 108; Huysmans, *Against Nature*, 3. All subsequent page references to these texts appear in parentheses.

27. Bristow, "*The Picture of Dorian Gray* and the Aesthetic Tradition," n.p.

28. Love, *Feeling Backward*, 6.

29. Hammerton, *George Meredith*, 2.

30. V21 Collective, "Manifesto of the V21 Collective."

Chapter 1 • *"Fantastic Shadows"*

1. I am indebted to Joseph Bristow and the members of the 2012 NEH seminar on Wilde at the William Andrews Clark Memorial Library, UCLA, for their observations about this scene.

2. Esty notes a similar quality in Wilde's use of Orientalist tropes to "suspend novelistic time" (Esty, *Unseasonable Youth*, 108). Lavery extends this observation to a contrast with Whistler's aesthetics, which "implicitly took description and narration to be indissociably linked, and took the example of Japan to point to nonlinguistic representations" such as blank space on the page (Lavery, *Quaint, Exquisite*, 65). See also Nunokawa, *Tame Passions of Wilde*, 41–53.

3. Frankel, *The Picture of Dorian Gray*, 5; and Gagnier, *Idylls of the Marketplace*, 59.

4. Sedgwick, *Between Men*, 95, 176; and *Epistemology of the Closet*, especially 48–49 and 131–81.

5. See, for example, Bristow, "'A Complex Multiform Creature'"; Ed Cohen, "Writing Gone Wilde"; Craft, "Come See About Me"; Dellamora, "Representation and Homophobia in *The Picture of Dorian Gray*"; and Nunokawa, "The Disappearance of the Homosexual in *The Picture of Dorian Gray*."

6. Clausson, "'Culture and Corruption,'" 339.

7. Isobel Murray, "Introduction," viii.

8. Clausson, "'Culture and Corruption,'" 363.

9. Clausson, "'Culture and Corruption,'" 363.

10. Oates, "'The Picture of Dorian Gray,'" 421.

11. Ed Cohen, "Writing Gone Wilde," 805. Cohen compares the novel with the pornographic *Teleny* in order to highlight the imperatives and operations of the relatively closeted representation of homoerotic desire in *Dorian Gray*, whereas I focus on competing and interlocking genres within the novel itself and Wilde's strategic use of them across multiple revisions of the text in order to elude the censors.

12. On the queerness of Jamesian style, see especially Kurnick, "What Does Jamesian Style Want?"; Ohi, *Henry James and the Queerness of Style*; and Savoy, "The Jamesian Turn." This work can be seen to extend from Miller, *Jane Austen, or The Secret of Style*. Also relevant to the development of queer formalisms, Helen H. Davis has expanded recent narratological work on *disnarration* (the explicit statement of what did not happen) and *unnarration* (the refusal to state what did happen) to include what she calls "circumnarration," or reporting only obliquely or indirectly or otherwise talking around a subject that is nonetheless made clear; see her essay "'I Seemed to Hold Two Lives.'" I am attempting in this chapter to develop further analytic categories to understand how this phenomenon works in Wilde.

13. For a review of the magic-picture tradition, see Powell, "Tom, Dick, and Dorian Gray"; and chapter 4 of this book for an analysis of the US tradition's impact on Wilde's narrative interests.

14. Pater, *The Renaissance*, 188–89.

15. Sedgwick has written convincingly about this phenomenon of modern culture, when "knowledge meant sexual knowledge and secrets sexual secrets" and "when secrecy itself becomes manifest as *this* secret [of homosexuality]." Sedgwick, *Epistemology of the Closet*, 74; see also 131–81, and Sedgwick, *Between Men*, 94–95.

140   *Notes to Pages 20–32*

16. Savoy takes up these terms via Ed Cohen's *Talk on the Wilde Side*, Dellamora's *Masculine Desire*, Graham's "Henry James's Thwarted Love," and Freedman's *Professions of Taste* to read oblique revelations in James. See "The Queer Subject of 'The Jolly Corner.'"

17. Sedgwick, *Epistemology of the Closet*, 49.

18. Barthes, *A Lover's Discourse*, 42–43.

19. Ellmann, "Introduction," x.

20. Dollimore, *Sexual Dissidence*, 73.

21. Dollimore, *Sexual Dissidence*, 73.

22. Savoy, "The Jamesian Turn," 136. See also Levine, "Strategic Formalism" and *Forms*, as well as new formalist work in the cultural history of imperialism such as Hensley's *Forms of Empire* and Reeder's *The Forms of Informal Empire*.

23. Gagnier, *Idylls of the Marketplace*, 3–4.

24. I have in mind here the processes of writing, (self-)publication, and revision of writers such as Walt Whitman and Emily Dickinson in response to rapidly changing definitions of and attitudes toward homosexuality, but also the changes that a writer like Alfred Tennyson felt he needed to make to his poem *In Memoriam*, to lower the emotional temperature of the homosocial love between him and his friend Arthur Hallam, between the 1850 and 1884 editions. See Moon, *Disseminating Whitman*; Smith, *Rowing in Eden*; and Shatto, "Tennyson's Revisions of *In Memoriam*."

25. Ross, "The Five Faces of Dorian Gray." For a comprehensive treatment of the novel's revision history, see Bristow's 2005 variorum edition and Frankel's 2011 annotated, uncensored edition, as well as Lawler, *An Inquiry into Oscar Wilde's Revisions of 'The Picture of Dorian Gray.'*

26. As Frankel notes, the holograph manuscript bears the stamp of *Lippincott's* London agent and the typescript remained in Stoddart's possession until long after Wilde's death. For more on Wilde's lack of access to the prepublication materials in revising for the single-volume edition, see Frankel's "Textual Introduction," especially 42–44.

27. Wilde, *The Picture of Dorian Gray: The 1890 and the 1891 Texts*, 5, 7. All subsequent page references to this *Complete Works* variorum edition appear in parentheses with the abbreviation *CW*.

28. Ross, "Deceptive Picture," 69.

29. Ironically, Stoddart, an American, largely succeeded in reading his US market well, aided perhaps by the American public's already strong association of Wilde with an effete and flamboyant English Aestheticism since his 1882 North American tour and as a result of his own efforts at rebranding himself in that mold. By all accounts Stoddart neither anticipated nor desired the stanch censorship and long aftermath of scandal that the *Lippincott's* story met with in Britain. In a meeting with Whitman in 1882, Wilde had suggested that America was freer than England, although a sixth edition of *Leaves of Grass* was withdrawn under threat of prosecution only five months later, suggesting that national ties played an important role in determining the level of public tolerance for the flouting of convention, especially on one's perceived home turf. See Ellmann, *Oscar Wilde*, 169–70.

Chapter 2 • Gothic Legacies

1. The connection between Goya's etching and Dorian's allegorical nickname has not, to my knowledge, been noted before. The text included in Goya's "Prado manuscript" is given in both Spanish and English and offers more by way of explanation of the caption: "See here a Calderonian lover who, unable to laugh at his rival dies in the arms of his beloved, and loses her by his daring. It is inadvisable to draw the sword too often. / *Ve aqui un amante de Calderon que por no saberse reir de su competidor muere en brazos de su querida y la pierde por su temeridad. No conviene sacar la espada muy amenudo.*" Goya, *Los Caprichos*, ed. Philip Hofer, plate 10 verso.

2. Wilde, *De Profundis*, 130. The influence of Spanish art is also apparent in Michael F. Davis's reading of Wilde's short story "Birthday of the Infanta" (1891) alongside Diego Velásquez's enigmatic Golden Age painting *Las Meninas* (1656). Michael F. Davis, "Oscar Wilde's *Las Meninas*."

3. See Wilde, *De Profundis*, 275n24.

4. Quoted in "Hasta la muerte (Until death)."

5. Wolf, *Goya and the Satirical Print in England and on the Continent, 1730 to 1850*, especially 17–18.

6. "Hasta la muerte (Until death)."

7. Goya, *Los Caprichos*. S. P. Avery Collection. Gifted by Avery in 1900 after purchase from Rossetti in 1882.

8. Huysmans, *Against Nature*, 83. The enormous popularity of Goya's etchings can be gauged by this line of the novel: "He was captivated by Goya's savage exuberance, by his corrosive, frenzied talent, although the universal admiration which his works commanded today did tend to dampen somewhat his enthusiasm, and it was now many years since he had stopped framing them, for fear that if he were to display them the first imbecile who happened to see them would deem it necessary to proffer some idiotic remarks and to go into carefully studied ecstasies before them" (83). For extensive details on the print runs, costs, and extent of distribution of nineteenth-century editions of Goya, see Glendinning, "Nineteenth-Century Editions of Goya's Etchings."

9. For example, the 1998 Oxford World's Classics and the 2000 Penguin Classics editions of Maturin's *Melmoth* both use works by Goya for their cover illustrations: *Procession of Flagellants* (Academy of San Fernando, Madrid, 1812–19) and *A Monk Talking to an Old Woman* (Art Museum, Princeton University, 1823), respectively.

10. Roditi's book *Oscar Wilde* offered a fascinating early critical appraisal. Roditi writes of the influence as a source of pride and a central motivating force: "Wilde knew *Melmoth* well and was proud of the relationship. [. . .] The magic formula of Dorian Gray's sinister youth was thus an heirloom in Wilde's family, handed down like some choice recipe from old Maturin" (77–79). Ellmann set the tone for much contemporary criticism in noting the importance of Wilde's taking the name of Melmoth after his release from prison; see his *Oscar Wilde*, 6. Milbank links Wilde's adoption of the name of Maturin's doomed anti-hero to his understanding of the sacrificial basis of *Melmoth* in "Sacrificial Exchange and the Gothic Double in *Melmoth the Wanderer* and *The Picture of Dorian Gray*."

11. The effort to rediscover "the Irish Wilde" peaked in the late 1990s following the

142   *Notes to Pages 44–49*

publication of Kiberd's *Inventing Ireland* and McCormack's edited collection *Wilde the Irishman*. Important contributions from the same decade include Coakley, *Oscar Wilde*; Edwards, "The Soul of Man under Hibernicism"; Pine, *The Thief of Reason*; David Upchurch, *Wilde's Use of Irish Celtic Elements in The Picture of Dorian Gray*; and Ní Fhlathúin, "The Irish Oscar Wilde." Subsequent scholarship in this area includes King, "Typing Dorian Gray"; O'Connor, "*The Picture of Dorian Gray* as Irish National Tale"; Killeen, *The Faiths of Oscar Wilde*; and Haslam, "Revisiting the 'Irish Dimension' in Oscar Wilde's *The Picture of Dorian Gray*."

12. Small, *Oscar Wilde*, 7.

13. Bashford, "When Critics Disagree: Recent Approaches to Oscar Wilde," 616–17; King, "Typing Dorian Gray," 22. For an extensive exploration of the question of methods, see Haslam, "The Hermeneutic Hazards of Hibernicizing Oscar Wilde's *The Picture of Dorian Gray*."

14. Bristow's endnote linking the name Daly's to the contemporary American playwright, director, and manager, John Augustin Daly (1838–99), suggests a further historical context and meaning; see Wilde, *The Picture of Dorian Gray*, World's Classics Edition, 226n162.

15. Haslam, "Revisiting the 'Irish Dimension,'" 267.

16. James, "To Mrs. Hugh Bell, 23 February 1892," 373; quoted in Haslam, "'Melmoth' (OW)," 303.

17. Sammells, "Rediscovering the Irish Wilde," 369; and "The Irish Wilde," 41.

18. Walshe, *Oscar's Shadow*.

19. Haslam, "Revisiting the 'Irish Dimension,'" 275. Haslam provides a complete account of this formative debate, which played out in the pages of the anti-Parnellite *Scots Observer* (later the *National Observer*) during the summer and fall of 1890, as well as an interesting discussion of related methodological concerns, including the search for an Irish dimension in Wilde that is "more empirically plausible than those construed and constructed by analogizing strategies" (267).

20. Sedgwick, *Tendencies*, 58–59.

21. Rashkin, *Unspeakable Secrets and the Psychoanalysis of Culture*, 165.

22. Rashkin, *Unspeakable Secrets and the Psychoanalysis of Culture*, 181.

23. Rashkin, *Unspeakable Secrets and the Psychoanalysis of Culture*, 165.

24. Quoted in Rashkin, *Unspeakable Secrets and the Psychoanalysis of Culture*, 165.

25. King, "Typing Dorian Gray," 17.

26. Gramsci is often credited with coining the broader use of the term in relation to cultural hegemony, writing about the proletariat under the duress of censorship in his *Prison Notebooks* (1929–35). Spivak would memorably later insist that "subaltern" is "not just a classy word for 'oppressed'" but rather designates a "space of difference" from the imperial—that is, not the working class in general, but the colonized disenfranchised in particular. See her 1992 interview with Leon de Kock.

27. "Subaltern," *Oxford English Dictionary*.

28. See Rashkin, *Unspeakable Secrets and the Psychoanalysis of Culture*, 192.

29. Not coincidentally, the lead character of Wilde's story "The Portrait of Mr. W. H." (1889), a key fictional precursor to his novel, is also called Erskine and bears the freckles that "run in Scotch families *just as* gout does in English families," a formulation that would seem to suggest some analogic thinking of Wilde's own (304; emphasis added).

Notes to Pages 50–61   143

30. Jones, "Ulster More British Than Britain."

31. Adams, "History as Seduction," 21.

32. Adams, "History as Seduction," 36.

33. Nunokawa, *Tame Passions of Wilde*, 90.

34. Huysmans, *Against Nature*, 3.

35. Sage, "Introduction," xi–xii.

36. Quoted in and translated by Sage, "Introduction," xiv.

37. Maturin, *Melmoth the Wanderer* (Penguin, 2000), 601. All subsequent page references to this edition will appear in parentheses.

38. Ragaz has cautioned that interpretations that rely on the novel's intricate narrative structure must account for the unplanned, chaotic, collaborative piecing together of the manuscript by post evinced in the correspondence between the Dublin-based Maturin and his Edinburgh publisher, Archibald Constable. While in this case the closing of the outer frame narrative is simply a convention, it is important to note that "influence" also sometimes transmits the contingent, material aspects of writing and publication practices. Ragaz, "Maturin, Archibald Constable, and the Publication of *Melmoth the Wanderer*."

39. Of course, the impact was not unidirectional or unique; the rich nineteenth-century tradition of the magic-portrait narrative traced by Kerry Powell, Bellonby, and others was a key source of Wilde's imagination. Indeed, as I note in chapter 4, his novel has rightly been read as a culmination of that tradition; it is the one we still read and teach today. Here I go a step further in arguing that there was something about the Gothic in Ireland at the start of the nineteenth century that especially informed Wilde's narrative interests.

40. Morin, *Charles Robert Maturin and the Haunting of Irish Romantic Fiction*, 147. Answering Ragaz, Morin argues that the novel's paratextual footnotes keep Ireland in mind, if not in view, regardless of how the novel was produced: "Whether Maturin intended to construct his novel in the way we now read it so as to comment allegorically on contemporary Irish society seems, in this context, irrelevant, for such paratextual commentary never relies on the structure of the text for its potency" (147).

41. Morin, *Charles Robert Maturin*, 147.

42. O'Malley, *Liffey and Lethe*, 8.

43. O'Malley, *Liffey and Lethe*, 89–90.

44. O'Malley, *Liffey and Lethe*, 24, 18, 81, 91.

45. Haslam, "Hermeneutic Hazards," 38. This apparent disavowal is its own kind of strategic displacement, of course. As Kiberd has argued, nineteenth-century Ireland functioned as Britain's unconscious (*Inventing Ireland*, 29–30). The lack of explicitly Irish characters and settings is not only the point, then; it also the method.

Chapter 3 • Aesthetic Antecedents

1. Ratchford and McCarthy, *The Correspondence of Sir Walter Scott and Charles Robert Maturin*, 14; original emphasis. Schiller, like Maturin, was also interested in imperial Spain, having written the historical drama *Don Carlos* (1787), about the heir-apparent of Philip II who was given to the Inquisition by his father (who also wanted to marry his lover), which was turned into an opera featuring a chilling auto-da-fé scene by Giuseppe Verdi in 1867.

144   *Notes to Pages 61–67*

2. Wilde, "Some Literary Ladies"; quoted in Wright, *Built of Books*, 41.

3. A notable exception is Isobel Murray's early investigation, which documents the Pre-Raphaelite enthusiasm for *Sidonia* but also endeavors to indicate the unique quality of the book, which Murray calls a "minor masterpiece." Isobel Murray, "*Sidonia the Sorceress*: Pre-Raphaelite Cult Book," 53.

4. Meinhold, *Sidonia the Sorceress*, Kelmscott Press.

5. Christian, "Burne-Jones Studies," 103n3.

6. Tipper, *A Critical Biography of Lady Jane Wilde, 1821?-1896*, 361–62.

7. Wright, *Built of Books*, 41. Wright notes that Wilde's own copy of the Kelmscott *Sidonia* is in the collection of Dartmouth College, 343n11.

8. Wyndham, *Speranza*, 33.

9. Wyndham, *Speranza*, 37.

10. Wyndham, *Speranza*, 84.

11. Ellmann, *Oscar Wilde*, 14–15.

12. Wyndham, *Speranza*, 64.

13. Wyndham, *Speranza*, 68.

14. Douglas, *Oscar Wilde*, 49; quoted in Wyndham, 74.

15. Wyndham, *Speranza*, 70.

16. Wilde, *An Ideal Husband*, 165.

17. Wyndham, *Speranza*, 70.

18. These were Lamartine's *Pictures of the First French Revolution* (1850) and *The Wanderer and His Home* (1851) and Dumas père's *The Glacier Land* (1852).

19. Wyndham, *Speranza*,135; Vulpius, "Sidonia von Borke."

20. Bridgwater, "Who's Afraid of Sidonia von Bork?," 213.

21. Gosse, "Sidonia the Sorceress," 197; see also Melville, *Mother of Oscar*, 54.

22. York Powell, "Wilhelm Meinhold," 120. Bridgwater notes that Powell saw in Meinhold a "type not uncommon in Ireland," suggesting an interesting connection to the Irish route *Sidonia* was to take to reaching English audiences (214).

23. Bridgwater usefully details the novel's contemporary reception; see "Who's Afraid of Sidonia von Bork?," 215–16.

24. Meinhold, *Sidonia the Sorceress*, Aegypan Press, I:67, 137, 239, 262. All subsequent page references will appear in parentheses.

25. Here too we see that, without being realist, the Gothic can "explore the nature of reality and its relationship to both fiction and form," as Bartoszyńska has recently argued in an astute reading of two other ostensibly "peripheral" novels, Maturin's *Melmoth the Wanderer* and the Polish novelist Jan Potocki's *Rękopis znaleziony Saragossie* or *The Manuscript Found in Saragossa* (1804/1810/1847). Bartoszyńska, *Estranging the Novel: Poland, Ireland, and Theories of World Literature*, 74.

26. Gosse, "Sidonia the Sorceress," 195. Gosse borrows the phrase "positive passion" to characterize Rossetti's love of *Sidonia* from Rossetti's brother's memoir. See William Michael Rossetti, *Dante Gabriel Rossetti*, I:101.

27. Gosse, "Sidonia the Sorceress," 198. While reading Rossetti's letters in prison, Wilde would later be delighted to discover that two of the books that fascinated Rossetti as a boy were "my grand-uncle's *Melmoth* and my mother's *Sidonia*." Wilde, "Letter to Robert Ross."

28. Gosse, "Sidonia the Sorceress," 198.

29. Gosse, "Sidonia the Sorceress," 200.

30. Gosse, "Sidonia the Sorceress," 200.

31. Gosse, "Sidonia the Sorceress," 201.

32. Gosse, "Sidonia the Sorceress," 195.

33. The reference appears in the "Malevola" chapter of the novel, when the mysterious portrait on the wall of Mme. Walraven's vanishes and an arched passage suddenly opens up, leading to a strange sorceress-like figure wearing a gown of brocade: "There went that sullen Sidonia, tottering and trembling like palsy incarnate, tapping her ivory staff on the mosaic parquet, and muttering venomously as she vanished." Charlotte Brontë, *Villette*, chapter 34, 466. Bridgwater notes further of the story of the picture on the wall: "The motif of the thwarted lover who becomes a nun is reminiscent of Sidonia, who, like Malevola, is covered in jewels when the reader first meets her in the preface of the novel" (Bridgwater, "Who's Afraid of Sidonia von Bork?," 221).

34. Pater, *Appreciations*, 226, 245. Bridgwater notes that Pater's postscript originally appeared as an essay on "Romanticism" in *Macmillan's Magazine* for November 1876. Bridgwater, "Who's Afraid of Sidonia von Bork?," 226n51.

35. Quoted in Mills, *Sir Edward Cook*, 282n1.

36. Surtees, *Sublime and Instructive*, 251. Christian notes that, in this, the text served much the function of Malory's *Morte d'Arthur* and the poetry of Robert Browning, "two other esoteric literary tastes that the set embraced with relish, providing them with a convenient stick with which to beat the philistine." Wildman and Christian, *Edward Burne-Jones*, 67.

37. Morris, *The Collected Letters of William Morris*, IV:5. Morris explains further in the same letter: "I hate alterations years after the date of the first issue." His failure to mention the title of the book in making his request to Wilde to put his proposal before his mother necessitates a telling postscript: "Just like me! I have not mentioned the name of the book: but no doubt you have guessed that I am writing of Sidonia the Sorceress."

The William Morris Gallery in Walthamstow, London, offers the following connections, as well: "Morris's own writings were influenced by this story and his own novels of the 1890s include many characters clearly inspired by Sidonia. The mistress in 'The Wood Beyond the World' and the Queen of Utterbol in 'The Well at the World's End' are both alluring and charismatic women who are secretly cruel and devious. Many of these novels also include a character inspired by Clara, a faithful and courageous woman who opposes Sidonia and aims to turn her from her wickedness." "Kelmscott Press edition of 'Sidonia the Sorceress.'"

38. Morris, "Brief Description of Wilhelm Meinhold's *Sidonia the Sorceress*"; quoted in Peterson, *A Bibliography of the Kelmscott Press*, 51.

39. Christian, 104, 104n15.

40. *Pall Mall Gazette*, 26 January 1886, 2; quoted in Christian, "Burne-Jones Studies," 104n14 and in Mills, *Sir Edward Cook*, 282n1. Swinburne was also the conduit, along with Pater, for the idea of "art for art's sake," which derives from a movement in France that dates back to Gautier's preface to his 1835 novel *Mademoiselle de Maupin*, where he uses the phrase for the first time (*l'art pour l'art*).

41. Bridgwater, "Who's Afraid of Sidonia von Bork?," 228.

42. Christian also notes an interesting visual counterpart to Meinhold's influence in

Rossetti and his associates' feeling for the work of Albrecht Dürer and other early German engravers. Wildman and Christian, *Edward Burne-Jones*, 68.

43. Bridgwater, "Who's Afraid of Sidonia von Bork?," 218; Praz, *The Romantic Agony*, 226.

44. Wildman and Christian, *Edward Burne-Jones*, 66. See also *Paintings from the Leathart Collection*.

45. Once thought to be a portrait of Isabella d'Este (1474–1539), the Royal Collection Trust explains that "it has been suggested more recently that the portrait may depict Isabella's daughter-in-law, Margherita Paleologo (1510–1566), at the time of her marriage to Federico Gonzaga, 1st Duke of Mantua, in 1531. There is evidence to connect the costume worn here with Isabella d'Este or her circle, which would support either identification." See the catalog entry, "Portrait of Margherita Paleologo."

46. See, for example, Wildman and Christian, *Edward Burne-Jones*, 66; and Wood, *Burne-Jones*, 28. Christian notes the difference between the novel and the painting and suggests that it is merely owing to Burne-Jones's artistic license.

47. Wilde would have had ample opportunity to see the von Bork paintings when they were exhibited at the Burne-Jones retrospective at the New Gallery, in Regent Street, London, in 1892–93. See the provenance for each work in Wildman and Christian, *Edward Burne-Jones*, 66, 70. The New Gallery was founded by the former directors of the Grosvenor Gallery, Joseph Comyns Carr and Charles Edward Hallé, who had resigned in 1887. An important venue for artists of the Pre-Raphaelite and Aesthetic movements, the New Gallery hosted the first exhibition of the Arts and Crafts Society in 1888, which Wilde attended as we know from his anonymous reviews of lectures delivered there, "Mr. Morris on Tapestry," "Sculpture at the Arts and Crafts," "Printing and Printers," "The Beauty of Bookbinding," and "The Close of the Arts and Crafts," for the *Pall Mall Gazette* from November 2 to 30, 1888; reprinted in Wilde, *Miscellanies*, 93–109. Wilde had previously written about Burne-Jones and other Pre-Raphaelite painters in a review titled "The Grosvenor Gallery" for the *Dublin University Magazine* in July 1877; reprinted in Wilde, *Miscellanies*, 5–23.

48. Bridgwater, "Who's Afraid of Sidonia von Bork?," 220.

49. Ellmann, *Oscar Wilde*, 21.

50. Heine, *From the Memoirs of Herr Schabelewopski*, 41.

51. Heine, *From the Memoirs of Herr Schabelewopski*, 41–42.

52. Joyce, *Ulysses*, 591.

53. Bridgwater, *The German Gothic Novel in Anglo-German Perspective*, 378; Keats, "La Belle Dame sans Merci." Keats's ballad's preoccupation with love and death would provide the subject for a number of Pre-Raphaelite paintings of the same title, including those by Arthur Hughes (1863), John William Waterhouse (1893), Henry Meynell Rheam (1901), Frank Dicksee (c. 1901), as well as *Punch* magazine cartoons.

54. Keats, "La Belle Dame sans Merci," 241, line 14. As a result, this trajectory from Keats to *Salomé* also tends to minimize or overlook *Salomé* as a revision of the Medusa myth that ends in someone else's decapitation—a man's.

55. The verb "to dog" appears again in the context of Dorian's nighttime wanderings through dimly lit London streets, further suggesting a link between beauty, sex, and fatality. Purged by Stoddart in the typescript, the censored passage reads: "A man with curious eyes had suddenly peered into his face, and then dogged him with stealthy

Notes to Pages 80–91   147

footsteps, passing and repassing him several times" (Wilde, *The Picture of Dorian Gray: The 1890 and 1891 Texts*, 65). As in chapter 1, all subsequent page references to this *Complete Works* variorum edition appear in parentheses with the abbreviation *CW*.

56. Dobson, "To a Greek Girl."

57. Bridgwater suggests that Pater also had Sidonia in mind when writing of Mona Lisa's "strange" expression, emptied of "Swinburnian savagery of the mouth" but still an "enigmatic reminder of her savage origins." Bridgwater, "Who's Afraid of Sidonia Bork?," 226. Bridgwater refers to Swinburne's description of the Medusa in "Notes on Designs of the Old Masters at Florence": "her mouth crueller than a tiger's, colder than a snake's, and beautiful beyond a woman's. She is the deadlier Venus incarnate." Swinburne, "Notes on Designs of the Old Masters at Florence," 320.

58. Swinburne, "Notes on Designs of the Old Masters at Florence," 320.

59. Dijkstra, *Idols of Perversity*.

60. Mighall provides a useful summary on this point in his edition of the novel. Wilde, *The Picture of Dorian Gray*, Penguin edition, 253n9.

61. Stoddart lowered the emotional temperature by revising this to "a friendship so coloured by romance" and by canceling the explanatory line that followed "my secret": "There was love in every line, and in every touch there was passion" (*CW* 91).

62. Eliot, "Tradition and the Individual Talent," 14, 15.

63. Eliot, "Tradition and the Individual Talent," 15.

64. Eliot, "Tradition and the Individual Talent," 14.

65. Evangelista, "Transnational Decadence," 321.

Chapter 4 • Transatlantic Forebears

1. Evangelista, "Transnational Decadence," 319.

2. Symons, *The Symbolist Movement in Literature*, 165; quoted in Evangelista, "Transnational Decadence," 322.

3. Evangelista, "Transnational Decadence," 321–22.

4. Riquelme, "Oscar Wilde's Aesthetic Gothic," 619.

5. Quoted in Riquelme, "Oscar Wilde's Aesthetic Gothic," 619.

6. Mustafa, "Haunting 'The Harlot's House,'" 62. The lines "Like strange mechanical grotesques, / Making fantastic arabesques" (lines 7–8) further recall, in Mustafa's reading, Poe's *Tales of the Grotesque and Arabesque* (1840).

7. These texts exist within an even larger international orbit, as Bartoszyńska has recently shown in a fascinating reading of *Dorian* alongside a Polish novel about an uncanny portrait and a femme fatale, Narcyza Żmichowska's *Poganka* (*The Heathen*) (1846/1861). Bartoszyńska's interest is not in the question of influence, so she does not mention Poe as a possible link; instead, she explores what the peculiar resemblance between these eccentric narratives tells us about novel form that has been all but erased by the dominant story about the rise of the novel as the rise of realism in England. Bartoszyńska, *Estranging the Novel*, 75–101.

8. Wright, *Built of Books*, 139–40.

9. Wilde, "The Decay of Lying," 77; and *The Complete Letters of Oscar Wilde*, 1118.

10. Wilde, *The Complete Letters of Oscar Wilde*, 1118. As Mendelssohn notes, Freedman has been one of few critics willing to engage seriously with the idea that James actually influenced Wilde, and not just the other way around, analyzing what he calls

the pair's "quarrels of affinity." Mendelssohn, *Henry James, Oscar Wilde, and Aesthetic Culture*, 7; and Freedman, *Professions of Taste*, 171, 201.

11. See especially Matthiessen, who, in arguing that one of the many devices Hawthorne taught James was "the use of a portrait to bring out character," memorably concluded: "The more closely we look at James, the more signs we find of Hawthorne everywhere" (Matthiessen, "James and the Plastic Arts," 535, 537).

12. Kerry Powell, "Tom, Dick, and Dorian Gray," 164.

13. Kerry Powell, "Tom, Dick, and Dorian Gray," 150.

14. Hawthorne, *Tales and Sketches*, 456. All subsequent page references will appear in parentheses.

15. Poe, *Essays and Reviews*, 574–75.

16. Poe, *The Collected Tales and Poems of Edgar Allan Poe*, 626. All subsequent page references will appear in parentheses.

17. James, "The Story of a Masterpiece," 212. All subsequent page references will appear in parentheses.

18. James, "The Liar," 344. All subsequent page references will appear in parentheses.

19. Poe, *Essays and Reviews*, 575.

20. For more on matters of technique and revision in these two stories and on the problem of deceit and truth in James's fiction more generally, see O'Hara, "'Monstrous Levity'" and Lane, "Framing Fears, Reading Designs."

Chapter 5 • Epigrammatic Inheritance

1. Meredith, "An Essay on Comedy and the Uses of the Comic Spirit," 432.

2. Meredith, *The Egoist: A Comedy in Narrative*, 368. All subsequent page references will appear in parentheses.

3. Pritchett, *George Meredith and English Comedy*, 11.

4. Pritchett, *George Meredith and English Comedy*, 11–12.

5. Quoted in Pritchett, *George Meredith and English Comedy*, 12.

6. Quoted in Pritchett, *George Meredith and English Comedy*, 12.

7. Meredith, "An Essay on Comedy and the Uses of the Comic Spirit," 433.

8. Wilde, "The Decay of Lying," 81. All subsequent page references will appear in parentheses after the abbreviation *DL*.

9. Wilde, "The Critic as Artist," 131. All subsequent page references will appear in parentheses after the abbreviation *CA*.

10. Ohi, *Dead Letters Sent*, 7, 21–22.

11. Bartoszyńska, *Estranging the Novel*, 126, 134. Also of interest here is Waldrep's discussion of Disraeli's novel *Vivian Grey* (1826) as a model for *Dorian*, although one well within the mainstream of the silver-fork novel tradition. In yet another connection, Waldrep cites Stanley Weintraub's argument that German Romanticism provides the "glue to hold together" Disraeli's novel. Waldrep, *The Aesthetics of Self-Invention*, 11–12; quoted in Waldrep, *The Aesthetics of Self-Invention*, 12.

12. Fanger, "Joyce and Meredith," 128.

13. Fanger, "Joyce and Meredith," 130.

14. Harris, "'The Fraternity of Old Lamps,'" 283–84.

15. Wilde, "The Soul of Man," 259.

16. Bristow and Mitchell, *Oscar Wilde's Chatterton*, 232–33.

Notes to Pages 112–127   149

17. Quoted in Pritchett, *George Meredith and English Comedy*, 24.

18. Pater, *The Renaissance*, 189.

19. Meredith, *Diana of the Crossways*, 172.

20. Mitchell, "George Meredith's *The Egoist*," 416.

21. Mitchell, "George Meredith's *The Egoist*," 416.

22. Meredith, "Up to Midnight [I]," 582. Although he reaches a less favorable conclusion, Stone's "George Meredith's Neglected *Up to Midnight*" offers a useful overview and reading.

23. Meredith, "Up to Midnight [II]," 606.

24. Meredith, "Up to Midnight [III]," 7.

25. Peacock, *Nightmare Abbey*, 70. All subsequent page references will appear in parentheses.

26. Peacock, *The Letters of Thomas Love Peacock*, I:152.

27. Wilde, "Impression du Matin," 153.

28. Wilde, *The Letters of Oscar Wilde*, 423.

29. Wilde, *The Letters of Oscar Wilde*, 520.

30. "Charm," *Oxford English Dictionary*.

31. For a more detailed discussion of this phenomenon, see my book *Habit in the English Novel, 1850–1900*, 106–12.

32. Gutkin, "The Dandified Dick," 1308. Simon Reader traces *Dorian's* use of epigrammatic speech to the 1870s, as well, but to the form of the documentary fragment developed in Wilde's Oxford notebooks, to fascinating effect. Reader, *Notework*, 126–51.

33. Bartoszyńska, *Estranging the Novel*, 81.

34. Lesjak, "Utopia, Use, and the Everyday," 189.

35. Lesjak, "Utopia, Use, and the Everyday," 189.

36. Meredith, *Diana of the Crossways*, 233.

37. Meredith, *Diana of the Crossways*, 153.

38. Anderson, *The Powers of Distance*, 159.

39. Anderson, *The Powers of Distance*, 158–59.

40. Anderson, *The Powers of Distance*, 160.

41. Quoted in Anderson, *The Powers of Distance*, 160; Wilde's emphasis.

42. Wilde, *An Ideal Husband*, 245.

43. Wilde, *An Ideal Husband*, 245.

44. Meredith, *Diana of the Crossways*, 353–54.

45. Meredith, *Diana of the Crossways*, 364–65.

46. The title page of a presentation copy recently exhibited at the Liverpool Central Library's show "Richard Le Gallienne: Liverpool's Wild(e) Poet" further tells the story of a young author in thrall to an idiosyncratic literary lion and another author who grew up in Liverpool and escaped an apprenticeship life through writing, Thomas Henry Hall Caine, already a friend of Meredith's, to whom Le Gallienne inscribed a copy in 1890.

47. Le Gallienne, *George Meredith*, i. All subsequent page references will appear in parentheses.

48. Wilde, *The Letters of Oscar Wilde*, 277.

49. Wilde, *The Letters of Oscar Wilde*, 277.

50. Wilde, "The Soul of Man," 259–60.

Coda

1. Most people who have read the novel will remember this depiction even at some distance of time. It can be found in chapter 4 of the novel (46–49).

2. "Decolonizing Decadence?" Call for submissions for a special issue of *Volupté*, https://volupte.gold.ac.uk/call-for-submissions-61.

3. Here I agree with Barbara Black, whose writing about the series has been helpful to my thinking, that this is Shonibare's most inspired decision. Black, "On Yinka Shonibare MBE's Reimagining of *Dorian Gray*."

4. The color image, depicted here in black and white, may be found at the Tang Teaching Museum's website. See Shonibare, *Dorian Gray*.

5. Stilling, "An Image of Europe," 309.

BIBLIOGRAPHY

Adams, James Eli. "History as Seduction: Wilde and Fascination of Heredity." In *Wilde's Other Worlds*, edited by Michael F. Davis and Petra Dierkes-Thrun, 19–39. New York: Routledge, 2018.

Anderson, Amanda. *The Powers of Distance: Cosmopolitanism and the Cultivation of Detachment*. Princeton: Princeton University Press, 2001.

Balzac, Honoré de. "Massimilla Doni" [1837]. Translated by Clara Bell and James Waring, https://www.gutenberg.org/files/1811/1811-h/1811-h.htm.

——. *Melmoth Reconcilié* [1835]. Paris: Editions du Seuil, 1968.

——. *The Wild Ass's Skin* [*La Peau de chagrin*, 1831]. Translated by Herbert Hunt. New York: Penguin, 1977.

Banerjee, Sukanya, Ryan D. Fong, and Helena Michie. "Widening the Nineteenth Century." *Victorian Literature and Culture* 49, no. 1 (2021): 1–26.

Barnaby, Paul. "Timeline of the European Reception of Oscar Wilde." In *The Reception of Oscar Wilde in Europe*, edited by Stefano Evangelista, xxi–lxxv. London: Continuum, 2010.

Barthes, Roland. *A Lover's Discourse: Fragments*. Translated by Richard Howard. New York: Hill and Wang, 1978.

Bartoszyńska, Katarzyna. *Estranging the Novel: Poland, Ireland, and Theories of World Literature*. Baltimore: Johns Hopkins University Press, 2021.

Bashford, Bruce. "When Critics Disagree: Recent Approaches to Oscar Wilde." *Victorian Literature and Culture* 30, no. 2 (2002): 613–25.

Beckson, Karl, ed. *Oscar Wilde: The Critical Heritage*. New York: Barnes and Noble, 1970.

Bellonby, Diana. "A Secret History of Aestheticism: Magic-Portrait Fiction, 1829–1929." Doctoral dissertation, Vanderbilt University, 2012.

Betensky, Carolyn. "Casual Racism in Victorian Literature." *Victorian Literature and Culture* 47, no. 4 (Winter 2019): 723–51.

Bizzotto, Elisa, and Stefano Evangelista, eds. *Arthur Symons: Poet, Critic, Vagabond*. Cambridge, UK: Legenda, 2018.

Black, Barbara. "On Yinka Shonibare MBE's Reimagining of *Dorian Gray*." Tang Teaching Museum, Skidmore College, https://tang.skidmore.edu/collection/artworks/506-dorian-gray.

Bridgwater, Patrick. *The German Gothic Novel in Anglo-German Perspective*. Amsterdam: Rodopi, 2013.

152   Bibliography

———. "Who's Afraid of Sidonia von Bork?" In *The Novel in Anglo-German Context: Cultural Cross-Currents and Affinities*, edited by Susanne Stark, 213–28. Amsterdam: Rodopi, 2000.

Bristow, Joseph. "'A Complex Multiform Creature': Wilde's Sexual Identities." In *The Cambridge Companion to Oscar Wilde*, edited by Peter Raby, 195–218. Cambridge: Cambridge University Press, 1997.

———. *Oscar Wilde on Trial: The Criminal Proceedings, from Arrest to Imprisonment*. New Haven: Yale University Press, forthcoming.

———. "*The Picture of Dorian Gray* and the Aesthetic Tradition: Faithful Allusion, Perilous Misquotation." In *The Picture of Dorian Gray in the Twenty-First Century*, edited by Richard A. Kaye. Oxford University Press, forthcoming.

Bristow, Joseph, and Rebecca N. Mitchell. *Oscar Wilde's Chatterton: Literary History, Romanticism, and the Art of Forgery*. New Haven: Yale University Press, 2015.

Brontë, Charlotte. *Villette* [1853]. London: John Murray, 1932.

Burton, Tim, dir. *Sleepy Hollow*, 1999. Paramount Pictures / Mandalay Pictures.

"Charm, v.1." *OED Online*. Oxford University Press, www.oed.com/view/Entry/30764.

Chatterjee, Ronjaunee, Alicia Mireles Christoff, and Amy R. Wong, "Introduction: Undisciplining Victorian Studies." *Victorian Studies* 62, no. 3 (Spring 2020): 369–91.

———. "Undisciplining Victorian Studies." *Los Angeles Review of Books*, 10 July 2020. https://www.lareviewofbooks.org/article/undisciplining-victorian-studies/.

Christian, John. "Burne-Jones Studies," *The Burlington Magazine* 115, no. 829 (February 1973): 92–109.

Clausson, Nils. "'Culture and Corruption': Paterian Self-Development versus Gothic Degeneration in Oscar Wilde's *The Picture of Dorian Gray*." *Papers on Language and Literature: A Journal for Scholars and Critics of Language and Literature* 39, no. 4 (2003): 339–64.

Cleary, Joe. "Misplaced Ideas? Locating and Dislocating Ireland in Colonial and Post-colonial Studies." In *Marxism and Modernity and Postcolonial Studies*, edited by Crystal Bartolovich and Neil Lazarus, 101–24. Cambridge: Cambridge University Press, 2002.

———. *Outrageous Fortune: Culture and Capital in Modern Ireland*. Dublin: Field Day, 2007.

Coakley, David. *Oscar Wilde: The Importance of Being Irish*. Dublin: Town House, 1994.

Cohen, Ed. *Talk on the Wilde Side: Toward a Genealogy of a Discourse on Male Sexualities*. New York: Routledge, 1993.

———. "Writing Gone Wilde: Homoerotic Desire in the Closet of Representation." *PMLA* 102, no. 5 (October 1987): 801–13.

Cohen, William. *Sex Scandal: The Private Parts of Victorian Fiction*. Durham, NC: Duke University Press, 1996.

Cohn, Elisha. "Oscar Wilde's Ghost: The Play of Imitation." *Victorian Studies* 54, no. 3 (Spring 2012): 474–85.

Conan Doyle, Arthur. *Memories and Adventures*. Boston: Little, Brown, 1924.

Cook, Matt. *London and the Culture of Homosexuality, 1885–1914*. Cambridge: Cambridge University Press, 2003.

Craft, Christopher. "Come See About Me: Enchantment of the Double in *The Picture of Dorian Gray*." *Representations* 91, no. 1 (2005): 109–36.

Davis, Helen H. "'I Seemed to Hold Two Lives': Disclosing Circumnarration in *Villette* and *The Picture of Dorian Gray*." *Narrative* 21, no. 2 (2013): 198–220.

Davis, Michael F. "Oscar Wilde's *Las Meninas*: A Portrait of the Artist as a Young Girl." In *Wilde's Other Worlds*, edited by Michael F. Davis and Petra Dierkes-Thrun, 110–33. New York: Routledge, 2018.

———. "Walter Pater's 'Latent Intelligence' and the Conception of Queer 'Theory.'" In *Walter Pater: Transparencies of Desire*, edited by Laurel Brake, Leslie Higgins, and Carolyn Williams, 261–85. Greensboro, NC: ELT Press, 2002.

Davis, Michael F., and Petra Dierkes-Thrun, eds. *Wilde's Other Worlds*. New York: Routledge, 2018.

"Decolonizing Decadence?" Call for submissions for a special issue of *Volupté: Interdisciplinary Journal of Decadence Studies*, https://volupte.gold.ac.uk/call-for-submissions-61.

Dellamora, Richard. *Masculine Desire: The Sexual Politics of Victorian Aestheticism*. Chapel Hill: University of North Carolina Press, 1990.

———. "Representation and Homophobia in *The Picture of Dorian Gray*." *Victorian Newsletter* 73 (Spring 1988): 28–31.

Denisoff, Dennis, ed. "Global Decadence." Special issue of *Feminist Modernist Review* 4, no. 2 (July 2021).

———. "Review of *Arthur Symons: Poet, Critic, Vagabond* by Elisa Bizzotto and Stefano Evangelista." *Victorian Studies* 62, no. 4 (Summer 2020): 686–88.

———, ed. "Scales of Decadence." Special issue of *Victorian Literature and Culture* 49, no. 4 (Winter 2021).

Desmarais, Jane, and David Weir, eds. *Decadence and Literature*. Cambridge: Cambridge University Press, 2019.

Dickerson, Vanessa. *Dark Victorians: Understanding Connections between Black Americans and White Victorian Britons*. Champaign: University of Illinois Press, 2018.

Dierkes-Thrun, Petra. "Oscar Wilde, Rachilde, and the *Mercure de France*." In *Wildes's Other Worlds*, edited by Michael F. Davis and Petra Dierkes-Thrun, 220–41. New York: Routledge, 2018.

Dijkstra, Bram. *Idols of Perversity: Fantasies of Feminine Evil in Fin-de-Siècle Culture*. Oxford: Oxford University Press, 1988.

Dobson, Austin. "To a Greek Girl." In *A Victorian Anthology, 1837–1895*, edited by Edmund Clarence Stedman, 488. Boston: Houghton Mifflin, 1906.

Dollimore, Jonathan. *Sexual Dissidence: Augustine to Wilde, Freud to Foucault*. Oxford: Oxford University Press, 1991.

Douglas, Alfred Bruce. *Oscar Wilde: A Summing-Up*. London: Duckworth, 1940.

Doyle, Arthur Conan. *See* Conan Doyle, Arthur.

Edwards, Owen Dudley. "The Soul of Man under Hibernicism." *Irish Studies Review* 11 (Summer 1995): 7–13.

Eliot, T. S. "Tradition and the Individual Talent." In *Selected Essays*, 13–22. London: Faber and Faber, 1932.

Ellmann, Richard. "Introduction," *The Artist as Critic: Critical Writings of Oscar Wilde*, edited by Richard Ellmann, ix–xxviii. Chicago: University of Chicago Press, 1968.

———. *Oscar Wilde*. New York: Knopf, 1988.

Esty, Jed. *Unseasonable Youth: Modernism, Colonialism, and the Fiction of Development*. Oxford: Oxford University Press, 2011.

Evangelista, Stefano. *British Aestheticism and Ancient Greece: Hellenism, Reception, Gods in Exile*. Basingstoke, UK: Palgrave Macmillan, 2009.

—. *Literary Cosmopolitanism in the English Fin de Siècle: Citizens of Nowhere*. Oxford: Oxford University Press, 2021.

—, ed. *The Reception of Oscar Wilde in Europe*. London: Continuum, 2010.

—. "Transnational Decadence." In *Decadence and Literature*, edited by Jane Desmarais and David Weir, 316–31. Cambridge: Cambridge University Press, 2019.

Fanger, Donald. "Joyce and Meredith: A Question of Influence and Tradition." *Modern Fiction Studies* 6, no. 2 (Summer 1960): 125–30.

Fhlathúin, Máire Ní. *See* Ní Fhlathúin, Máire.

Fieni, David. *Decadent Orientalisms*. New York: Fordham University Press, 2020.

Frankel, Nicholas. "General Introduction" and "Textual Introduction." *The Picture of Dorian Gray: An Annotated, Uncensored Edition*, by Oscar Wilde, edited by Nicholas Frankel, 1–64. Cambridge, MA: Harvard University Press, 2011.

—, ed. *The Picture of Dorian Gray: An Annotated, Uncensored Edition*. Cambridge, MA: Harvard University Press, 2011.

Freedman, Jonathan. *The Jewish Decadence: Jews and the Aesthetics of Modernity*. Chicago: University of Chicago Press, 2021.

—. *Professions of Taste: Henry James, British Aestheticism, and Commodity Culture*. Stanford: Stanford University Press, 1990.

Friedman, Dustin. *Before Queer Theory: Victorian Aestheticism and the Self*. Baltimore: Johns Hopkins University Press, 2019.

Gagnier, Reginia. *Idylls of the Marketplace: Oscar Wilde and the Victorian Public*. Stanford, Stanford University Press, 1986.

—. *Individualism, Decadence, and Globalization: On the Relation of Part to Whole, 1859–1920*. Basingstoke, UK: Palgrave Macmillan, 2010.

—. *Literatures of Liberalization: Global Circulation and the Long Nineteenth Century*. Cham, Switzerland: Palgrave Macmillan, 2018.

Gautier, Théophile. *Mademoiselle de Maupin* [1835]. Translated by Helen Constantine. London: Penguin, 2005.

Glendinning, Nigel. "Nineteenth-Century Editions of Goya's Etchings: New Details of Their Sales Statistics." *Print Quarterly* 6, no. 4 (December 1989): 394–403.

Gosse, Edmund. "Sidonia the Sorceress." In *Leaves and Fruit*, 193–201. London: William Heinemann, 1927.

Goya, Francisco de. *Los Caprichos*. S. P. Avery Collection, New York Public Library, https://digitalcollections.nypl.org/items/510d47dc-86fe-a3d9-e040-e00a18064a99.

—. *Los Caprichos* [1799]. Edited by Philip Hofer. Cambridge, MA: Dover, 1969.

—. *A Monk Talking to an Old Woman*. Art Museum, Princeton University, 1823, https://artmuseum.princeton.edu/collections/objects/32861.

—. *Procession of Flagellants*. Academy of San Fernando, Madrid, 1812–19, https://www.realacademiabellasartessanfernando.com/es/goya/goya-en-el-museo-de-la-academia.

Graham, Wendy. "Henry James's Thwarted Love." In *Eroticism and Containment: Notes from the Flood Plain*, edited by Carol Siegel and Ann Kibbey, 66–95. New York: New York University Press, 1994.

Gramsci, Antonio. *Selections from the Prison Notebooks*, edited and translated by Quintin Hoare and Geoffrey Nowell Smith. London: Lawrence and Wishart, 1971.

Gutkin, Len. "The Dandified Dick: Hardboiled Noir and the Wildean Epigram." *ELH* 81, no. 4 (Winter 2014): 1299–326.

Guy, Josephine M. "Self-Plagiarism, Creativity, and Craftsmanship in Oscar Wilde." *English Literature in Transition, 1880–1920* 41, no. 1 (1998): 6–23.

Hack, Daniel. *Reaping Something New: African American Transformations of Victorian Literature*. Princeton: Princeton University Press, 2016.

Hammerton, J. A. *George Meredith: His Life and Art in Anecdote and Criticism*. New York: Haskell House, 1911.

Harris, Margaret. " 'The Fraternity of Old Lamps': Some Observations on George Meredith's Prose Style." *Style* 7, no. 3 (Fall 1973): 271–93.

Haslam, Richard. "The Hermeneutic Hazards of Hibernicizing Oscar Wilde's *The Picture of Dorian Gray*," *ELT* 57, no. 1 (2014): 37–58.

———. " 'Melmoth' (OW): Gothic Modes in *The Picture of Dorian Gray*." *Irish Studies Review* 12, no. 3 (2004), 303–14.

———. "Revisiting the 'Irish Dimension' in Oscar Wilde's *The Picture of Dorian Gray*." *Victorian Literature and Culture* 42, no. 2 (2014): 267–79.

"Hasta la muerte (Until death)." The Ashmolean Museum, University of Oxford, https://www.ashmolean.org/hasta-la-muerte-until-death#/.

Hawthorne, Nathaniel. *Tales and Sketches*. Edited by Roy Harvey Pearce. New York: Library of America, 1982.

Heine, Heinrich. *From the Memoirs of Herr Schabelewopski* [1833]. Translated by Charles Godfrey Leland and Hans Breitmann [1891]. New York: Mondial, 2008.

Hensley, Nathan K. *Forms of Empire: The Poetics of Victorian Sovereignty*. Oxford: Oxford University Press, 2016.

Hext, Kate, and Alex Murray, eds. *Decadence in the Age of Modernism*. Baltimore: Johns Hopkins University Press, 2019.

Huysmans, Joris-Karl. *Against Nature* [*A Rebours*, 1884]. Edited by Nicholas White and translated by Margaret Mauldon. Oxford World's Classics. Oxford: Oxford University Press, 1998.

Inman, Billie Andrew. "Estrangement and Connection: Walter Pater, Benjamin Jowett, and William M. Hardinge." In *Pater in the 1890s*, edited by Laurel Brake and Ian Small, 1–20. Greensboro, NC: ELT Press, 1991.

James, Henry. "The Liar." In *The Complete Stories of Henry James, Volume III: 1884–1891*, edited by Edward Said, 321–71. New York: Library of America, 1999.

———. "The Story of a Masterpiece." In *The Complete Stories of Henry James, Volume I: 1864–1874*, edited by Jean Strouse, 209–42. New York: Library of America, 1999.

———. "To Mrs. Hugh Bell, 23 February 1892." In *Henry James: Letters, Vol. III: 1883–1895*, edited by Leon Edel. Cambridge, MA: Belknap Press, 1980.

Jones, Gareth. "Ulster More British Than Britain—'Stands Firm as a Rock for the Empire': An Interview with Lord Craigavon." *The Western Mail* (10 March 1934), https://www.garethjones.org/irish_articles/ulster_more_british_than_britain.htm.

Joseph, Abigail. *Exquisite Materials: Episodes in the Queer History of Victorian Style*. Newark: University of Delaware Press, 2019.

Joyce, James. *Ulysses* [1922]. Oxford: Oxford University Press, 1998.

Kaye, Richard A., ed. *The Picture of Dorian Gray in the Twenty-First Century*. Oxford University Press, forthcoming.

———. "Review of Vincent Sherry, *Decadence and the Reinvention of Modernism*, and Matthew Potolsky, *The Decadent Republic of Letters.*" *Modern Language Quarterly* 78, no. 1 (March 2017): 132–37.

Keats, John. "La Belle Dame sans Merci." In *The Complete Poetical Works of John Keats*, 240–42. Boston: Houghton Mifflin, 1900.

"Kelmscott Press edition of 'Sidonia the Sorceress.'" William Morris Gallery, Walthamstow, London. Google Arts and Culture, https://artsandculture.google.com/asset /kelmscott-press-edition-of-sidonia-the-sorceress-kelmscott-press/wAGgDTqZT 1dddg?hl=en.

Kiberd, Declan. *Inventing Ireland: The Literature of the Modern Nation*. Cambridge, MA: Harvard University Press, 1995.

Killeen, Jarlath. *The Faiths of Oscar Wilde: Catholicism, Folklore and Ireland*. Houndsmills, UK: Palgrave Macmillan, 2005.

King, Mary. "Typing Dorian Gray: Wilde and the Interpellated Text." *Irish Studies Review* 9, no. 1 (2001): 15–24.

Kurnick, David. "What Does Jamesian Style Want?" *Henry James Review* 28, no. 3 (Fall 2007): 213–22.

Lane, Christopher. "Framing Fears, Reading Designs: The Homosexual Art of Painting in James, Wilde, and Beerbohm." *ELH* 61, no. 4 (Winter 1994): 923–54.

Lavery, Grace E. *Quaint, Exquisite: Victorian Aesthetics and the Idea of Japan*. Princeton: Princeton University Press, 2019.

Lawler, Donald L. *An Inquiry into Oscar Wilde's Revisions of 'The Picture of Dorian Gray.'* New York: Garland, 1988.

———. "The Revisions of *Dorian Gray.*" *Victorian Institute Journal* 3 (1974): 21–36.

Le Gallienne, Richard. *George Meredith: Some Characteristics, with a Bibliography by John Lane*. London: Elkin Mathews, 1890.

Lee, Julia Sun-Joo. *The American Slave Narratives and the Victorian Novel*. Oxford: Oxford University Press, 2010.

Lesjak, Carolyn. "Utopia, Use, and the Everyday: Oscar Wilde and a New Economy of Pleasure," *ELH* 67, no. 1 (Spring 2000): 179–204.

Levine, Caroline. *Forms: Whole, Rhythm, Hierarchy, Network*. Princeton: Princeton University Press, 2015.

———. "Strategic Formalism: Toward a New Method in Cultural Studies." *Victorian Studies* 48, no. 4 (Summer 2006): 625–57.

Lewin, Alfred, dir. *The Picture of Dorian Gray*, 1945. Metro-Goldwyn-Mayer.

Lootens, Tricia. *The Political Poetess: Victorian Femininity, Race, and the Legacy of Separate Spheres*. Princeton: Princeton University Press, 2016.

Love, Heather. "Exemplary Ambivalence." *Pater Newsletter* 50 (Spring 2007): 25–30.

———. *Feeling Backward: Loss and the Politics of Queer History*. Cambridge, MA: Harvard University Press, 2007.

Mahoney, Kristin. *Literature and Politics of Post-Victorian Decadence*. Cambridge: Cambridge University Press, 2015.

———. *Queer Kinship after Wilde: Transnational Decadence and the Family*. Cambridge: Cambridge University Press, forthcoming.

———. "Taking Wilde to Sri Lanka and Beardsley to Harlem: Decadent Practice, Race, and Orientalism." *Victorian Literature and Culture* 49 (Winter 2021): 583–606.

Martin, Amy E. "Victorian Ireland: Race and the Category of the Human." *Victorian Review* 40, no. 1 (Spring 2014): 52–57.

Mason, Stuart. *Oscar Wilde: Art and Morality* [1912]. New York: Haskell House, 1971.

Matthiessen, F. O. "James and the Plastic Arts." *The Kenyon Review* 5, no. 4 (1943): 533–50.

Maturin, Charles Robert. *Melmoth the Wanderer* [1820]. London: Penguin, 2000.

——. *Melmoth the Wanderer*. Oxford: Oxford University Press, 1998.

McCormack, Jerusha, ed. *Wilde the Irishman*. New Haven: Yale University Press, 1998.

Mendelssohn, Michèle. *Henry James, Oscar Wilde, and Aesthetic Culture*. Edinburgh: Edinburgh University Press, 2007.

——. *Making Oscar Wilde*. Oxford: Oxford University Press, 2018.

Meinhold, Wilhelm. *Sidonia the Sorceress: The Supposed Destroyer of the Whole Reigning Ducal House of Pomerania* [1849]. Translated by Lady Jane Wilde, 2 volumes. Los Angeles: Aegypan Press, 2011.

——. *Sidonia the Sorceress*. Kelmscott Press edition. The William Andrews Clark Memorial Library, University of California, Los Angeles, shelfmark *f PR5809 Z4M5 1893.

Melville, Joy. *Mother of Oscar: The Life of Jane Francesca Wilde*. London: John Murray, 1994.

Meredith, George. *Diana of the Crossways: A Novel* [1885]. In *The Works of George Meredith*, Memorial Edition, 27 vols. London: Constable, 1910–11; volume 16, 1910, reprinted. Detroit: Wayne State University Press, 2001.

——. *The Egoist: A Comedy in Narrative* [1879]. Edited by Robert M. Adams. New York: Norton, 1979.

——. "An Essay on Comedy and the Uses of the Comic Spirit" [1877]. In *The Egoist: A Comedy in Narrative*, 431–50. New York: Norton, 1979.

——. "Up to Midnight [I]." *The Graphic*, 21 December 1872.

——. "Up to Midnight [II]." *The Graphic*, 28 December 1872.

——. "Up to Midnight [III]." *The Graphic*, 4 January 1873.

Milbank, Alison. "Sacrificial Exchange and the Gothic Double in *Melmoth the Wanderer* and *The Picture of Dorian Gray*." In *Shaping Belief: Culture, Politics, and Religion in Nineteenth-Century Writing*, edited by Victoria Morgan and Clare Williams, 113–28. Liverpool: Liverpool University Press, 2008.

Miller, D. A. *Jane Austen, or The Secret of Style*. Princeton: Princeton University Press, 2005.

Mills, J. Saxon. *Sir Edward Cook*. London: Constable, 1921.

Mitchell, Rebecca N. "George Meredith's *The Egoist*." In *Handbook of the English Novel, 1830–1900*, edited by Monika Pietrzak-Franger and Martin Middeke, 415–29. Berlin: De Gruyter, 2020.

Moon, Michael. *Disseminating Whitman: Revision and Corporeality in 'Leaves of Grass.'* Cambridge, MA: Harvard University Press, 1991.

Morin, Christina. *Charles Robert Maturin and the Haunting of Irish Romantic Fiction*. Manchester, UK: Manchester University Press, 2011.

Morris, William. "Brief Description of Wilhelm Meinhold's *Sidonia the Sorceress* and of Lady Wilde's Translation of It for Kelmscott Press Edition, 1893." The William Andrews Clark Memorial Library, University of California, Los Angeles, shelfmark *f PR5809 Z4M5 1893.

———. *The Collected Letters of William* Morris. Edited by Norman Kelvin, 4 volumes. Princeton: Princeton University Press, 2016.

Mufti, Nasser. "Hating Victorian Studies Properly." *Victorian Studies* 62, no. 3 (Spring 2020): 392–405.

Murray, Alex, ed. *Decadence: A Literary History.* Cambridge: Cambridge University Press, 2020.

Murray, Isobel. "Introduction." *The Picture of Dorian Gray*, edited by Isobel Murray, xiii–xxxiii. Oxford: Oxford University Press, 1982.

———. "*Sidonia the Sorceress*: Pre-Raphaelite Cult Book." *The Durham University Journal* 75, no. 1 (December 1982): 53–57.

Mustafa, Jamil. "Haunting 'The Harlot's House.'" In *Wilde's Other Worlds*, edited by Michael F. Davis and Petra Dierkes-Thrun, 60–84. New York: Routledge, 2018.

Ní Fhlathúin, Máire. "The Irish Oscar Wilde: Appropriations of the Artist." *Irish Studies Review* 7, no. 3 (1999): 337–46.

Nunokawa, Jeff. "The Disappearance of the Homosexual in *The Picture of Dorian Gray*." In *Professions of Desire: Lesbian and Gay Studies in Literature*, edited by George E. Haggerty and Bonnie Zimmerman, 183–90. New York: Modern Language Association, 1995.

———. *Tame Passions of Wilde: Styles of Manageable Desire.* Princeton: Princeton University Press, 2003.

O'Connor, Maureen. "*The Picture of Dorian Gray* as Irish National Tale." In *Writing Irishness in Nineteenth-Century British Culture*, edited by Neil McCaw, 194–209. Aldershot, UK: Ashgate, 2004.

O'Hara, Daniel T. "'Monstrous Levity': Between Realism and Vision in Two of Henry James's Artist-Tales." *The Henry James Review* 28, no. 3 (Fall 2007): 242–48.

O'Malley, Patrick R. "'Citizens' and 'Slaves': John Mitchel and the Polemic of White Grievance." CUNY C19 Conference, 7 May 2021, The Graduate Center, CUNY, New York. Panel on Populism and Nationalism.

———. *Liffey and Lethe: Paramnesiac History in Nineteenth-Century Anglo-Ireland.* Oxford: Oxford University Press, 2017.

O'Toole, Sean. "*Dorian Gray*'s Generic Hybridity and the Aesthetics of Queer Form." In *The Picture of Dorian Gray in the Twenty-First Century*, edited by Richard A. Kaye. Oxford University Press, forthcoming.

———. "Epigrammatic Inheritance: 'Writing in Lightning' in Meredith, Wilde, and Le Gallienne." *Yearbook of English Studies* 49 (2019): 155–72.

———. *Habit in the English Novel, 1850–1900: Lived Environments, Practices of the Self.* Basingstoke, UK: Palgrave Macmillan, 2013.

———. "Oscar Wilde's American Forebears: A Genealogy of Form for Reading *The Picture of Dorian Gray*." In *Wilde's Other Worlds*, edited by Michael F. Davis and Petra Dierkes-Thrun, 40–59. New York: Routledge, 2018.

Oates, Joyce Carol. "'The Picture of Dorian Gray': Wilde's Parable of the Fall." *Critical Inquiry* 7, no. 2 (Winter 1980): 419–28.

Ohi, Kevin. *Dead Letters Sent: Queer Literary Transmission.* Minneapolis: University of Minnesota Press, 2015.

———. *Henry James and the Queerness of Style.* Minneapolis: University of Minnesota Press, 2011.

Paintings from the Leathart Collection. Newcastle-upon-Tyne: Laing Art Gallery, 1968.

Pater, Walter. *Appreciations.* London: Macmillan, 1889.

——. *The Renaissance: Studies in Art and Poetry; The 1893 Text.* Edited by Donald L. Hill. Berkeley: University of California Press, 1980.

Peacock, Thomas Love. *The Letters of Thomas Love Peacock.* Edited by N. A. Joukovsky. 2 volumes. Oxford: Clarendon Press, 2001.

——. *Nightmare Abbey* [1818]. Edited by Lisa Vargo. Peterborough, ON: Broadview, 2007.

Peterson, William S. *A Bibliography of the Kelmscott Press.* Oxford: Clarendon Press, 1984.

Pine, Richard. *The Thief of Reason: Oscar Wilde and Modern Ireland.* Dublin: Gill and Macmillan, 1995.

Poe, Edgar Allan. *The Collected Tales and Poems of Edgar Allan Poe.* New York: Modern Library, 1992.

——. *Essays and Reviews.* Edited by G. R. Thompson. New York: Library of America, 1984.

——. *Tales of the Grotesque and Arabesque.* 2 volumes. Philadelphia: Lea and Blanchard, 1840.

"Portrait of Margherita Paleologo." Catalog entry, Royal Collection Trust, https://www .rct.uk/collection/405777/portrait-of-margherita-paleologo.

Potolsky, Matthew. *The Decadent Republic of Letters: Taste, Politics, and Cosmopolitan Community from Baudelaire to Beardsley.* Philadelphia: University of Pennsylvania Press, 2013.

Powell, Kerry. "Tom, Dick, and Dorian Gray: Magic Picture Mania in Late Victorian Fiction." *Philological Quarterly* 62, no. 2 (Spring 1983): 147–70.

Powell, York. "Wilhelm Meinhold." *The Pageant* (1896): 119–28.

Praz, Mario. *The Romantic Agony.* London: Fontana, 1960.

Prewitt-Brown, Julia. *Cosmopolitan Criticism: Oscar Wilde's Philosophy of Art.* Charlottesville: University of Virginia Press, 1997.

Pritchett, V. S. *George Meredith and English Comedy: The Clark Lectures for 1969.* New York: Random House, 1969.

Rachilde [pseudonym of Marguerite Eymery Vallette]. *Monsieur Vénus: A Materialist Novel.* Translated by Melanie Hawthorne. New York: Modern Language Association, 2004.

Ragaz, Sharon. "Maturin, Archibald Constable, and the Publication of *Melmoth the Wanderer.*" *The Review of English Studies* 57, no. 230 (June 2006): 359–73.

Rashkin, Esther. *Unspeakable Secrets and the Psychoanalysis of Culture.* Albany: SUNY Press, 2008.

Ratchford, Fannie Elizabeth, and William Henry McCarthy, eds. *The Correspondence of Sir Walter Scott and Charles Robert Maturin* [1937]. New York: Garland, 1980.

Reader, Simon. *Notework: Victorian Literature and Nonlinear Style.* Stanford: Stanford University Press, 2021.

Reeder, Jessie. *The Forms of Informal Empire: Britain, Latin America, and Nineteenth-Century Literature.* Baltimore: Johns Hopkins University Press, 2020.

"Richard Le Gallienne: Liverpool's Wild(e) Poet." Exhibition at the Hornby Library, Liverpool Central Library, 5 August–31 October 2016. Curated by Margaret Stetz and Mark Samuels Lasner.

Riquelme, John Paul. "Oscar Wilde's Aesthetic Gothic: Walter Pater, Dark Enlightenment, and 'The Picture of Dorian Gray.'" *Modern Fiction Studies* 46, no. 3 (Fall 2001): 609–31.

Roditi, Edouard. *Oscar Wilde* [1947]. New York: New Directions, 1986.

Romano, Giulio. *Portrait of Margherita Paleologo*, c.1531. King's Dressing Room, Windsor Castle, Royal Collection Trust.

Ross, Alex. "Deceptive Picture: How Oscar Wilde Painted Over 'Dorian Gray.'" *New Yorker*, 8 August 2011: 64–70.

——. "The Five Faces of Dorian Gray." *New Yorker Page-Turner Blog*, 2 August 2011, http://www.newyorker.com/books/page-turner/the-five-faces-of-dorian-gray.

Rossetti, William Michael. *Dante Gabriel Rossetti: His Family Letters, with a Memoir.* London: Ellis and Elvey, 1895.

Sage, Victor. "Introduction." *Melmoth the Wanderer*, by Charles Robert Maturin, vii–xxix. London: Penguin, 2000.

Saint-Amour, Paul. *The Copywrights: Intellectual Property and the Literary Imagination.* Ithaca, NY: Cornell University Press, 2003.

Sammells, Neil. "The Irish Wilde." In *Approaches to Teaching the Works of Oscar Wilde*, edited by Philip E. Smith II, 35–41. New York: Modern Language Association, 2008.

——. "Rediscovering the Irish Wilde." In *Rediscovering Oscar Wilde*, edited by Constantin-George Sandulescu, 362–70. Gerrards Cross, UK: Colin Smythe, 1994.

Savoy, Eric. "The Jamesian Turn: A Primer on Queer Formalism." In *Approaches to Teaching Henry James's 'Daisy Miller' and 'The Turn of the Screw,'* edited by Kimberly C. Reed and Peter G. Beidler, 132–42. New York: Modern Language Association, 2005.

——. "The Queer Subject of 'The Jolly Corner.'" *Henry James Review* 20, no. 1 (Winter 1999): 1–21.

Schiller, Friedrich. *Don Carlos and Mary Stuart.* Translated by Hilary Collier Sy-Quia and Peter Oswald. Oxford: Oxford University Press, 1996.

Sedgwick, Eve Kosofsky. *Between Men: English Literature and Male Homosocial Desire.* New York: Columbia University Press, 1985.

——. *Epistemology of the Closet.* Berkeley: University of California Press, 1990.

——. *Tendencies.* Durham, NC: Duke University Press, 1993.

Sharpe, Christina, *In the Wake: On Blackness and Being.* Durham, NC: Duke University Press, 2016.

Shatto, Susan. "Tennyson's Revisions of *In Memoriam.*" *Victorian Poetry* 16, no. 4 (Winter 1978): 341–56.

Sherry, Vincent. *Modernism and the Reinvention of Decadence.* Cambridge: Cambridge University Press, 2014.

Shonibare, Yinka. *Dorian Gray*, 2001. The Jack Shear Collection of Photography at the Tang Teaching Museum, Skidmore College, https://tang.skidmore.edu/collection ?series=Dorian%20Gray#browse.

Shuter, William F. "The 'Outing' of Walter Pater." *Nineteenth-Century Literature* 48, no. 4 (March 1994): 480–506.

Sinfield, Alan. *The Wilde Century: Effeminacy, Oscar Wilde, and the Queer Movement.* New York: Columbia University Press, 1994.

Small, Ian. *Oscar Wilde: Recent Research. A Supplement to "Oscar Wilde Revalued."* Greensboro, NC: ELT, 2000.

Smith, Martha Nell. *Rowing in Eden: Rereading Emily Dickinson.* Austin: University of Texas Press, 1992.

Smith, Philip E., and Michael S. Helfand. *Oscar Wilde's Oxford Notebooks: A Portrait of a Mind in the Making.* Oxford: Oxford University Press, 1989.

Spivak, Gayatri Chakravorty. "Interview with Gayatri Chakravorty Spivak: New Nation Writers Conference in South Africa." Interviewed by Leon de Kock. *ARIEL: A Review of International English Literature* 23, no. 3 (1992): 29–47; https://web.archive.org/web/20110706205400/http:/ariel.synergiesprairies.ca/ariel/index.php/ariel/article/viewFile/2505/2458.

Stilling, Robert. *Beginning at the End: Decadence, Modernism, and Postcolonial Poetry.* Cambridge, MA: Harvard University Press, 2018.

——. "An Image of Europe: Yinka Shonibare's Postcolonial Decadence." *PMLA* 128, no. 2 (2013): 299–321.

Stone, James S. "George Meredith's Neglected *Up to Midnight.*" *ESC: English Studies in Canada* 2, no. 1 (Spring 1976): 61–82.

Sturgis, Matthew. *Oscar Wilde: A Life.* London: Head of Zeus, 2018.

"Subaltern, n. and adj." *OED Online*, Oxford University Press, www.oed.com/view/Entry/192439.

Surtees, Virginia, ed. *Sublime and Instructive: Letters from John Ruskin to Louisa, Marchioness of Waterford, Anna Blunden, and Ellen Heaton.* London: Michael Joseph, 1972.

Swinburne, Algernon Charles. "Notes on Designs of the Old Masters at Florence." In *Essays and Studies*, 314–57. London: Chatto and Windus, 1875.

Symons, Arthur. "The Decadent Movement of Literature" [1893]. In *The Symbolist Movement in Literature*, edited by Matthew Creasy, 169–83. Manchester, UK: Carcanet, 2014.

——. *London Nights* [1895]. Second edition, revised. London: Leonard Smithers, 1897.

——. *The Symbolist Movement in Literature* [1899]. Edited by Matthew Creasy. Manchester, UK: Carcanet, 2014.

Thackeray, William Makepeace. "A May-Day Ode." In *Ballads*. London: Bradbury & Evans, 1855.

——. "A May-Day Ode." *The Times*, 30 April 1851.

Thain, Marion. "Review of Elisa Bizzotto and Stefano Evangelista, eds. *Arthur Symons: Poet, Critic, Vagabond.*" *Comparative Critical Studies* 17, no. 1 (2020): 161–64.

Tipper, Karen. *A Critical Biography of Lady Jane Wilde, 1821?-1896: Irish Revolutionist, Humanist, Scholar and Poet.* Lewiston, NY: Edwin Mellen Press, 2002.

United Nations Educational, Scientific, and Cultural Organization. *Index Translationum*, https://www.unesco.org/xtrans/bsform.aspx.

Upchurch, Charles. *"Beyond the Law": The Politics of Ending the Death Penalty for Sodomy in Britain.* Philadelphia: Temple University Press, 2021.

Upchurch, David. *Wilde's Use of Irish Celtic Elements in The Picture of Dorian Gray.* New York: Peter Lang, 1992.

162   Bibliography

V21 Collective. "Manifesto of the V21 Collective: Ten Theses," http://v21collective.org
/manifesto-of-the-v21-collective-ten-theses/.

Verdi, Giuseppe. *Don Carlo* [1867 as *Don Carlos*]. Recorded August 1970. EMI, compact
disc.

Volpicelli, Robert. "The New Decadence." *Modernism/modernity* 26, no. 1 (2019):
213–18.

Volupté: Interdisciplinary Journal of Decadent Studies, https://volupte.gold.ac.uk.

Vulpius, Christian August. "Sidonia von Borke." In *Pantheon berühmter und merkwürdi-
ger Frauen*, 69–88. Leipzig: Hahnsche Verlagsbuchhandlung, 1812.

Wagner, Richard. *The Flying Dutchman* [1843]. Recorded April-May 1994. Sony Classical, compact disc.

Waldrep, Shelton. *The Aesthetics of Self-Invention: Oscar Wilde to David Bowie*. Minneapolis: University of Minnesota Press, 2004.

Walshe, Éibhear. *Oscar's Shadow: Wilde, Homosexuality and Modern Ireland*. Cork:
Cork University Press, 2011.

Wilde, Jane Francesca. "Letter to Oscar Wilde, June 1890." The William Andrews
Clark Memorial Library, University of California, Los Angeles, box MS. Wilde 71,
folder 4–11.

Wilde, Oscar. *The Complete Letters of Oscar Wilde*. Edited by Merlin Holland and
Rupert Hart-Davis. New York: Henry Holt, 2000.

——. *The Complete Works of Oscar Wilde*. Series edited by Ian Small, 11 volumes to
date. Oxford: Oxford University Press, 2000 and continuing.

——. "The Critic as Artist" [1890]. In *Criticism: Historical Criticism, Intentions, The
Soul of Man*, edited by Josephine Guy. *The Complete Works of Oscar Wilde*, volume
4, 123–206. Oxford: Oxford University Press, 2007.

——. *Criticism: Historical Criticism, Intentions, The Soul of Man*, edited by Josephine
Guy. *The Complete Works of Oscar Wilde*, volume 4. Oxford: Oxford University
Press, 2007.

——. *De Profundis; Epistola: In Carcere et Vinculis* [1897]. Edited by Ian Small. *The
Complete Works of Oscar Wilde*, volume 2. Oxford: Oxford University Press, 2005.

——. "The Decay of Lying" [1889]. In *Criticism: Historical Criticism, Intentions, The
Soul of Man*, edited by Josephine Guy. *The Complete Works of Oscar Wilde*, volume
4, 72–103. Oxford: Oxford University Press, 2007.

——. *An Ideal Husband* [1895]. In *The Importance of Being Earnest and Other Plays*,
edited by Peter Raby, 159–245. Oxford: Oxford University Press, 2008.

——. "Impression du Matin." In *Poems and Poems in Prose*, edited by Bobby Fong and
Karl Beckson. *The Complete Works of Oscar Wilde*, volume 1, 153. Oxford: Oxford
University Press, 2007.

——. "Letter to Robert Ross, 6 April [1897], H.M. Prison, Reading." The William
Andrews Clark Memorial Library, University of California, Los Angeles, MS. Wilde
box W6721L R825 [1897]. In *The Letters of Oscar Wilde*, edited by Rupert Hart-
Davis, 520. New York: Harcourt, Brace & World, 1962.

——. *The Letters of Oscar Wilde*. Edited by Rupert Hart-Davis. New York: Harcourt,
Brace & World, 1962.

——. *Miscellanies*. London: Methuen, 1908.

—. *The Picture of Dorian Gray* [1891]. Edited by Joseph Bristow. World's Classics Edition. Oxford: Oxford University Press, 2006.

—. *The Picture of Dorian Gray: The 1890 and the 1891 Texts*. Edited by Joseph Bristow. *The Complete Works of Oscar Wilde*, volume 3. Oxford: Oxford University Press, 2005.

—. *The Picture of Dorian Gray* [1890/1891]. Edited by Michael Patrick Gillespie. Norton Critical Edition, second edition. New York: Norton, 2007.

—. *The Picture of Dorian Gray*. Edited by Robert Mighall. London: Penguin, 2000.

—. *The Picture of Dorian Gray*. Manuscript. The Morgan Library, New York. MA 883, "Original manuscript."

—. *The Picture of Dorian Gray*. Typescript. The William Andrews Clark Memorial Library, University of California, Los Angeles, shelfmark W6721M3 P611.

—. "The Picture of Dorian Gray." *Lippincott's Monthly Magazine*, July 1890: 3–100.

—. *Poems and Poems in Prose*. Edited by Bobby Fong and Karl Beckson. *The Complete Works of Oscar Wilde*, volume 1. Oxford: Oxford University Press, 2007.

—. "The Portrait of Mr. W. H." [1889]. In *The Complete Works of Oscar Wilde*. Introduced by Merlin Holland, 302–50. London: Collins, 2003.

—. "Some Literary Ladies." *Woman's World*, January 1889.

—. "The Soul of Man" [1891]. In *Criticism: Historical Criticism, Intentions, The Soul of Man*, edited by Josephine Guy. *The Complete Works of Oscar Wilde*, volume 4, 229–68. Oxford: Oxford University Press, 2007.

—. *Teleny* [1893]. Edited by Winston Leyland. San Francisco: Gay Sunshine, 1984.

—. *A Woman of No Importance* [1893]. In *The Importance of Being Earnest and Other Plays*, edited by Peter Raby, 93–158. Oxford: Oxford University Press, 2008.

Wildman, Stephen, and John Christian. *Edward Burne-Jones: Victorian Artist-Dreamer*. New York: Metropolitan Museum of Art, 1998.

Wolf, Reva. *Goya and the Satirical Print in England and on the Continent, 1730 to 1850*. Chestnut Hill, MA: Boston College Museum of Art, 1991.

Wood, Christopher. *Burne-Jones: The Life and Works of Sir Edward Burne-Jones, 1833–1898*. New York: Stewart, Tabori & Chang, 1998.

Wright, Thomas. *Built of Books: How Reading Defined the Life of Oscar Wilde*. New York: Henry Holt, 2008.

Wyndham, Horace. *Speranza: A Biography of Lady Wilde*. New York: Philosophical Library, 1951.

INDEX

Page numbers in *italics* refer to figures and tables.

Adams, James Eli, 51–52
Aestheticism, 1, 8, 10–11, 33, 38, 75, 108
Albert Victor, Prince, 3
Amber Witch, The (Meinhold), 61, 66, 69
Anderson, Amanda, 120
"art for art's sake," idea of, 76, 145n40
Asís, Francisco de, 46

Balzac, Honoré de, 54
Barthes, Roland, 25, 26
Bartoszyńska, Katarzyna, 111, 119, 147n7
Bashford, Bruce, 44
Baudelaire, Charles, 54, 85, 89, 90
Bentley, Richard, 55
Bernhardt, Sarah, 129
Bildungsroman tradition, novel in relation to,
    7, , 17, 19, 21, 23, 27, 33, 102–3, 107
Bizzotto, Elisa, x
Black vision and knowledge, 134
Bork, Clara von, 70, *71*
Bork, Sidonia von: literary references to, 68–69;
    popularity of, 69–70, 72–73; portrait of, *62,*
    72, 73, 146n47; Pre-Raphaelite cult of, 77, 84;
    real life story of, 63
Boulton, Ernest, 137n8
Bridgwater, Patrick, 69, 77
Bristow, Joseph, xii, 4, 5–6, 7, 27, 49, 112
Brontë, Charlotte: *Villette*, 68, 145n33
Burne-Jones, Edward: *Clara von Bork*, 70, *71*;
    painting of Sidonia by, 9, *62*, 63, 69, 70, 72,
    73, 77

Burne-Jones, Philip, 69
byōbu, 16, 17, 24

Campbell, Alan (*Dorian Gray* character), 36
Carson, Edward, 25
censorship culture, 7, 9, 10, 30
Chatterjee, Ronjaunee, vii, viii, xiv, xv
Chatterton, Thomas, xii
Christian, John, 69
Clausson, Nils, 17
Cleveland Street scandal (1889), 3–4
Cohen, Ed, 18
comedy, 107, 109, 112, 117–18
Conan Doyle, Arthur, 2, 3
Constable, Archibald, 143n38
cosmopolitanism, 8
Criminal Law Amendment Act of 1855, 4
"Critic as Artist, The" (Wilde), 110, 117, 126
Crystal Palace Fire (1936), vii, *viii*

dandy, 120–21. *See also* female dandy
Decadence: archival practice of, 85; born in
    translation, 89; crisis of history of, 58;
    definition of, x; emergence of, 85; representa-
    tives of, 6; studies of, ix–x, 11, 135n6, 135n8,
    136n11; transnational, 64, 86, 89, 90, 106, 131;
    Wilde's engagement with, 2, 4, 8, 38, 75, 77,
    79, 84
"Decay of Lying, The" (Wilde), 109–10, 112, 113,
    117, 123, 126
d'Este, Isabella, 146n45

Devereux, Robert, 47
Devereux, Walter (Earl of Essex), 33, 47
Devereux family portraits, 51, 53
Devereux surname, 51
dialogue, 8, 11, 112, 113, 115–16, 117
Diana of the Crossways (Meredith), 113, 118, 120, 121
didacticism, 99–100
disnarration, 139n12
Disraeli, Benjamin: *Vivian Grey*, 148n11
Dobson, Austin: "To a Greek Girl," 79–80
Dollimore, Jonathan, 26
Dorian Gray (photographic prints), 131
Douce, Francis, 43
Douglas, Alfred, 65
Doyle, Arthur Conan, 2, 3

"Edward Randolph's Portrait" (Hawthorne), 10, 90, 94–95, 100
Egoist, The (Meredith), 108, 112–13, 118–19, 121
Eliot, T. S., xiii, 84–85, 86, 136n19
Ellmann, Richard, 4, 25, 64, 73
epicene style, 111, 118
epigram, 107–8, 120
epigrammatic speech, 118–19, 127, 149n32
erotic "stunner," cult of, 64, 66, 68, 69, 77–78, 84
Essex, Earl of (Walter Devereux), 33, 47
Este, Isabella d', 146n45
Euston, Earl of (Henry James Fitzroy), 3
Evangelista, Stefano, x, 85, 89

Fanger, Donald, 111
Fanny and Stella scandal (1870), 137n8
female dandy, 111, 118, 120, 127
femme fatale, 77, 83, 84
Fitzroy, Henry James (Earl of Euston), 3
Flying Dutchman fable, 76
forgetting the past, 47, 53, 59–60
Forster, E. M., 109
Frankel, Nicholas, 27, 140n26
free indirect discourse, 10, 34, 50, 58, 104–5
Friedman, Dustin, 6, 138n24; *Before Queer Theory*, 4

Gagnier, Regenia, ix, 26
George Meredith: Some Characteristics (Le Gallienne), 122
Gide, André, 25

Glorious Revolution in Spain (1868), 46
Goethe, Johann Wolfgang von, 61
Gonzaga, Federico (Duke of Mantua), 146n45
Gordon, Lucie Duff, 61, 66
Gosse, Edmund, 66, 67, 68
Gothic fiction, 43, 44, 54, 61, 89
Goya, Francisco de: Dorian's nickname and, 141n1; "El amor y la muerte (Love and death)," 41, *42*; *Los Caprichos* (*The Caprices*), 41, *42*; popularity of, 41, 43, 141n8
Gray, Dorian (character): aestheticism of, 51; background of, 33, 37, 41, 45–46, 48; Basil Hallward and, 21, 30–31, 79, 81, 82; beauty of, 78, 79–80, 81; character of, 23, 34, 78; at costume ball, appearance of, 48; degeneration of, 24; description of, 104–5; double life of, 21; erotic passions of, 52; family picture-gallery of, 52; Greek first name of, 80; impact of Lord Henry's yellow book on, 5, 23, 83, 104, 138n25; nighttime wanderings of, 146n55; in the opera, 130–31; parentage of, 46–50; in photography, 131–34; portrait of, 23–24, 57–58, 60, 78, 81; rejection of Sibyl Vane, 21; relations to the past, 59–60, 106; self-discovery of, 17, 19–20, 102; Spanish screen for, 21–22, 26; visit to opium den, 44
"gross indecency," x, 1, 4, 136n14
Gutkin, Len, 119

Hallam, Arthur, 140n24
Hallward, Basil (*Dorian Gray* character): decomposition of his body, 36, 37; depiction of, 30; encounters with Dorian, 21, 30–31, 79, 81, 82; murder of, 82; painting of, 20, 51, 78, 80; studio of, 15–16, 51
"Harlot's House, The" (Wilde), 90
Harris, Margaret, 111
Haslam, Richard, 44, 45
Hawthorne, Nathaniel: "Edward Randolph's Portrait," 10, 90, 94–95, 100; *Fanshawe*, 54; *The House of the Seven Gables*, 76; "The Prophetic Pictures," 10, 90, 93–94, 99–100; *Twice-Told Tales*, 76, 93, 95
Heaton, Ellen, 69
Heine, Heinrich: "From the Memoirs of Herr Schnabelewopski," 76
Hoffmann, E. T. A., 61
Hogarth, William, 41

Index   167

homo/heterosexuality, discourses of, 16, 22, 24
Huysmans, Joris-Karl: *Against Nature*, 43; *A Rebours*, 6–7, 53

Ideal Husband, An (Wilde), 120, 121
Irish Gothic, xi, 7, 44, 54, 58
Irish immigrants, 49
Isabella II (queen of Spain), 46

James, C. L. R., 135n5
James, Henry, 18, 44, 148n11; influence of, 75, 103, 147n10; "The Liar," 90, 97, 98–99, 101–2; "The Story of a Masterpiece," 10, 90, 97–98, 102; *The Turn of the Screw*, 91
Japanese screen metaphor, 22, 24, 26
Jenkinson, Mrs. Mountstuart (*The Egoist* character), 118–19
Jones, Gareth, 50
Joyce, James, 111; *Ulysses*, 76

Keats, John: "La Belle Dame sans Merci," 146n53
King, Mary, 44, 48

Lady Agatha (*Dorian Gray* character), 35–36
Lady Duff Gordon, 61, 66
Lady Narborough (*Dorian Gray* character), 36–37
Lawler, Donald, 27
Leathart, James, 72
Lee, Vernon, 89
Le Gallienne, Richard: *George Meredith: Some Characteristics*, 11, 122; photograph of, *125*; reading of Meredith, 112, 122–23; Wilde's letter to, 123
Lesjak, Carolyn, 120
Leverson, Ada, 129
Levine, Caroline, 26
Lewin, Alfred, 133
Lewis, Matthew, 54
"Liar, The" (James), 90, 101–2; motif of uncanny portrait, 97, 98–99
Lippincott's edition of *Dorian Gray*: library holding of, 30; novelization of, 37; public outrage to, 25, 27, 140n29; revisions of, 31–32, 37–38; Stoddart's possession of, 140n26
Lippincott's Monthly Magazine, 2, 3, 18; front cover, *28*

London's East End problem, 49, 50
Lord Fermor (*Dorian Gray* character), 35, 49, 50
Lord Henry Wotton (*Dorian Gray* character): aesthetic philosophy of, 20; Basil Hallward's encounters with, 30; conversations with Duchess of Monmouth, 37; Dorian and, 34, 51, 104–5, 107–8; gift of yellow book, 5, 23, 83, 104, 138n25; on London's East End problem, 49, 50; on mutilation of the savage, 130–31; panegyric on youth, 79, 80; personality of, 16; view of art, 83; wife of, 119
Love, Heather, 8

magic-portrait tradition: in American literature, 90–91, 93–98, 99; fascination with motif of, 75–76; Wilde's novel and, 92–93, 102, 143n39
male stunner, xii, 74, 84
Mallarmé, Stéphane, 89
Mann, Thomas, 25
Mantua, Duchess of (Margherita Paleologo): portrait of, 72, *74*, 146n45
Mantua, Duke of (Federico Gonzaga), 146n45
Maturin, Charles Robert: background of, 54; correspondence with Walter Scott, 61; death of, 54; influence on Wilde, 43, 44, 53; *Melmoth the Wanderer*, 7–8, 9, 43, 54
Medusa myth, 72, 78, 79, 81
Meinhold, Wilhelm: *The Amber Witch*, 61, 66, 69; description of Sidonia, 63, 73; life and career of, 66; novels of, 61; personality of, 66; Romanticism of, 78; *Sidonia the Sorceress*, 7, 9, 61. See also *Sidonia the Sorceress*
Melmoth the Wanderer (Maturin): comparison to Dorian's story, 43, 44, 54, 56–57; cover illustrations, 141n9; critical reading of, 59; influence of, 9, 54, 58, 141n10; Irish theme, 58, 59, 143n40; plot of, 55–56; reprints of, 54–55; structure of, 143n38; violence to portrait in, 57, 58, 60
Meredith, George: *The Amazing Marriage*, 117; critique of, 109–10; devotion to the epigram, 111; dialogues of, 113, 114–15; *Diana of the Crossways*, 113, 118, 120, 121; *The Egoist*, 108, 112–13, 118–19, 121; "Essay on Comedy," 107, 109, 117; family origins of, 111; female-dandy trope in works of, 120; imagination of reality, 112; influence of, 108, 109, 111–12, 126; Le Gallienne's reading of, 122–23; as novelist, 112;

Meredith, George (*cont.*)
  One of Our Conquerors, 111; *The Ordeal of Richard Feverel*, 112; reputation of, 108–9; style of, 111, 122–23; "Up to Midnight," 113–15; Wilde and, 111–12, 126–27; women and, 118
mimesis, 5. *See also* realism
Mireles Christoff, Alicia, vii, viii, xiv
Mitchell, Rebecca N., xii, xiii, 112, 113
Monçada, Alonzo (*Melmoth the Wanderer* character), 56
Morin, Christina, 58, 59
Morris, William, 63, 145n37
Mrs. Mountstuart Jenkinson (*The Egoist* character), 118–19
Mufti, Nasser, viii, ix
Murray, Isobel, 17
Mustafa, Jamil, 90

new Decadence, ix, x
New Gallery, 146n47
Nightmare Abbey (Peacock), 115–16
Nunokawa, Jeff, 52

Oates, Joyce Carol, 18
Ohi, Kevin, 110
O'Malley, Patrick, 9, 44, 59, 60
"Oval Portrait, The" (Poe), 95, 96, 101

Paleologo, Margherita (Duchess of Mantua): portrait of, 72, *74*, 146n45
Park, Frederick, 137n8
past: decay of, 84–85; as haunted problem, 44–45; imperial, 9, 47, 51, 59; remembering and forgetting of, 47; "that is not past," viii
Pater, Walter, 4, 5–6, 20, 69, 78, 147n57; *Appreciations*, 68; "Winckelmann," 6. See also *Studies in the History of the Renaissance*
Patterne, Willoughby, 113
Peacock, Thomas Love, 108, 113, 115; *Nightmare Abbey*, 115–16
performativity, 52–53
Picture of Dorian Gray, The (Wilde): 1891 version of, 32, 35, 36, 37, 38; adaptations of, 1; aesthetic philosophy of, 5, 19, 83; allusions to imperial history, 49, 53; American context of, 10, 36, 99, 105–6; anti-Englishness of, 43;

anti-Semitism of, 129; as archival record, xi; characters of, 5; colonial contexts, 44, 47, 59, 129–30; conclusion of, 80, 96; contemporary global resonance, xiv, 131, 134; criticism of, 3, 4–6, 16, 45; depiction of opium bar, 44; Devereux connection, 47–48, 49; direct borrowings in, 9; emphasis on sterility, 82–83; English literary context, 10–11, 108, 109; epigrammatic speech, 118–19, 127, 149n32; Faustian bargain in, 80–81; femme-fatale trope of, 77, 83; film adaptation of, 133; as formal achievement, 17, 27, 105; front covers of, *28, 29*; gender crossing in, 79–80; genre of, 1, 7, 9, 17, 23, 24–25, 33; Gothic elements, 9, 19, 21–22, 23, 25, 27, 58, 115; historical contexts, 45; homoeroticism of, 16, 22, 24, 25, 30, 139n11; hybrid form of, 9, 17, 18–19, 102, 103, 139n11; Irish theme, 43–44, 49–50, 58–59; irony of, 46; language of, 16, 21, 82; literary influence of, 4–5, 10, 131; magic-picture tradition and, 19, 92, 102; metaphor of Japanese screen, 22; moralism of, 103, 106; opening scene of, 15–16, 17, 19, 103; Orientalism of, 129; in photography, 131–34; plot of, 2, 6; postmodernism and, 25–26; preface, 8, 76, 82–83, 104, 131; publication history, 1, 18, 27; queer desire in, 20, 22, 26, 27, 77, 79; revisions of, 27, 29–30, 31–32, 34, 35–36, 37; scholarship about, xi–xiv; self-development narrative, 103, 104; sexual theme, 17–18, 38; significance of heredity in, 51–53; as social satire, 11, 35–37, 49, 127; sources of, 5, 6–7, 8, 9–10; structure of, 17, 23, 45; style of, 104, 105; textual versions, 29–30; third-person narrative, 104; trajectory of de-essentialism, 52; transgressive quality of, 16; translations of, 137n1; transnational contexts of, 8, 11; uncensored edition of, 27; use of focalization, 103. See also *Lippincott's* edition of *Dorian Gray*
Poe, Edgar Allan: Decadence and, 90; didacticism and, 100–101; echoic style of, 89–90; influence of, 75, 89–90; legacy of, 89; magic-picture stories of, 95; narrative method, 103; review of Hawthorne's tales, 95, 99; "The Oval Portrait," 10, 90; translations of, 89; Wilde's admiration of, 90, 91; "William Wilson," 10, 90, 95–96, 101

portrait, as repository of the true self, 93–94

"Portrait of Mr. W. H., The" (Wilde), 3, 59, 142n29

Potolsky, Matthew, ix

Powell, Kerry, 90, 92

Powell, York, 66

Praz, Mario, 69

Pre-Raphaelite painters, 67, 69, 70, 72, 146n53

Prim, Juan, 46

Pritchett, V. S., 108

"proper hatred," 135n5

"Prophetic Pictures, The" (Hawthorne), 10, 90, 93–94, 99–100

Protestant Ascendancy, 45, 60

publishing practices, 30

queer form, 18

queer formalism, 26, 27, 127, 139n12

queer sexual desire, 79

Rachilde (pseud. of Marguerite Eymery Vallette): *Monsieur Vénus*, 138n25

Radcliffe, Ann, 54

Rashkin, Esther, 47

realism, 111. *See also* mimesis

reasoning by analogy, 44

Richardson, Miranda, 72, *75*

Ricketts, Charles, 30

Riquelme, John Paul, 4, 5, 89

Robertson, Graham, 72

Roditi, Edouard: *Oscar Wilde*, 141n10

romance tradition, 75

Romano, Guilio: *Portrait of Margherita Paleologo*, 72, *74*

Ross, Alex, 31

Ross, Robert, 91, 117

Rossetti, Dante Gabriel, 9, 43, 63, 67, 68, 70, 85, 144n27

Rowlandson, Thomas, 43

Ruskin, John, 41, 69

Sammells, Neil, 44

Sarony, Napoleon, *124*

Savoy, Eric, 26

Schiller, Friedrich, 61, 143n1

Scott, Walter, 61

Sedgwick, Eve Kosofsky, 16, 46

Sharpe, Christina: *In the Wake: On Blackness and Being*, vii–viii

Shelley, Percy Bysshe, 115

Shonibare, Yinka, xiv; as Dorian Gray, 131, *132*, *133*, 133–34; photographic series, 131–34

Sidonia the Sorceress (Meinhold): Clark Library copy of, 63; description of Sidonia's portrait in, 76–77; emphasis on sterility, 82–83; English translation of, 65–66; eroticism of, 66; Gothic element of, 73, 76; haunted portrait in, 61–62, *62*; influence on Dorian's story, 61, 73, 74–75, 77, 78–79, 82, 84, 85–86; initial reviews of, 66; Kelmscott edition of, xi–xii, 63, 69; language of, 66; luxury edition of, 67–68; plot of, 63, 67; popularity of, 66, 69; Pre-Raphaelite enthusiasm for, 144n3; readers of, 67–68; structure of narrative, 67; style of, 76, 77; translation of, 9, 63; visual appeal of, 68

Sinfield, Alan, 1

Sleepy Hollow (film), 72, *75*

Small, Ian, 43

sodomy, prosecution of, 137n8

Somerset, Arthur, 3

Spanish screen, 24

Stilling, Robert, 133

Stoddart, J. M., 2, 30, 31–32, 90, 140n29

Stoker, Bram, 65

"Story of a Masterpiece, The" (James), 10, 90, 97–98, 102

Studies in the History of the Renaissance (Pater), 4, 6; famed conclusion to, 19–20, 112

stunner. *See* erotic "stunner"; male stunner

subaltern, 48, 142n26

Swinburne, Algernon Charles, 69, 81, 145n40

Symons, Arthur, x, 89

Tennyson, Alfred, 68, 69, 140n24

Thackeray, William Makepeace, vii

Tipper, Karen, 63

translation movement, 64, 85, 89

transnational archive, 1, 8, 11, 33

Travers, Mary, 64

Trollope, Anthony: *The Way We Live Now*, 54

Turn of the Screw, The (James), 91

Twice-Told Tales (Hawthorne), 76, 93, 95

Ulster, 47, 50
"Undisciplining Victorian Studies," vii, xiv
unnarration, 139n12
"Up to Midnight" (Meredith), 113–15

Vane, James (*Dorian Gray* character), 34–35,
37, 52, 131
Vane, Sibyl (*Dorian Gray* character), 19, 21, 34
Verdi, Giuseppe: *Don Carlos*, 143n1
Victorian Aestheticism. *See* Aestheticism
Vulpius, Christian August, 65

Wagner, Richard: *The Flying Dutchman*, 76;
Tannhäuser, 131
Walpole, Horace: *Castle of Otranto*, 48
Walshe, Éibhear, 44
Ward, Lock & Co., 4, 29
Whistler, James McNeil, xii
Whitford, Vernon, 108
Wilde, Jane Francesca (née Elgee): background
of, 54; children of, 65; death of husband, 65;
hospitality of, 65; house of, 64; influence on
Oscar, 75; "Jacta Alea Est," 64; journalistic
work of, 64; lawsuit against editor, 64; lit-
erary background of, 7; marriage of, 64; pen
name of, 64; personality of, 64–65; political
views of, 64; translation of *Sidonia the Sorceress*, xi, 61, 63, 65–66, 85
Wilde, Oscar: Aestheticism of, 1, 10, 63;
American sources of, 90–91; calling card
addressed to, 55; censorship culture and, 10;
colonial fantasies, 129; comparison with
Nietzsche, 25; Conan Doyle's account of,
2; conviction for "gross indecency," 136n14;
correspondence of, 2, 123; "The Critic as
Artist," 110, 117, 126; on critics, 131; death of,
122; Decadent archival practice of, 85; "The

Decay of Lying," 109–10, 112, 113, 117, 123, 126;
De Profundis, 41; dialogic essays of, 8, 113, 117;
early life of, 7–8; Eliot and, 136n19; engagement with Gothic, 5, 58; friends of, 118, 129;
Goya's influence on, 41; "The Harlot's House,"
90; *An Ideal Husband*, 120, 121; "Impression
du Matin," 117, 126; Irish dimensions of writing, 43–44; Le Gallienne and, 126; literary
experiments of, 7, 8, 26, 32–33; on Meinhold's
novels, 61; on Meredith, 107, 109–11, 113,
117–18, 123, 126–27; North American tour,
140n29; notebooks of, xii–xiii, 6; Orientalist
tropes, 139n2; Pater's influence on, 6; perception of von Bork paintings, 146n47;
photograph of, *124*; plagiarism of, xiii, 92;
"The Portrait of Mr. W. H.," 3, 59, 142n29;
queer formalism of, 127; *Salomé*, 77, 84; self-
censorings of, 30–32; society comedies of
1890s, 11, 26, 35, 118, 120; "The Soul of Man
under Socialism," 126; theory of "erotic negativity," 138n24; trials and imprisonment of, x,
1, 4, 118; use of epigram, 108, 111; Victorian
culture and, 2, 130; view of realism, 112, 113;
A Woman of No Importance, 2; women and,
118. See also *Picture of Dorian Gray, The*
Wilde, William, 64
"William Wilson" (Poe), 10, 90, 95–96, 101
witches, 69
Woman of No Importance, A (Wilde), 2
Wong, Amy R., vii, viii, xiv
Wotton, Henry (historical figure), 47
Wotton, Lord Henry (*Dorian Gray* character).
See Lord Henry Wotton
Wotton, Victoria (*Dorian Gray* character), 119,
127

Zola, Émile: and obscenity, 25

Ingram Content Group UK Ltd.
Milton Keynes UK
UKHW012303100723
424873UK00001B/25